BEYOND LANGUAGE

ALSO AVAILABLE FROM BLOOMSBURY

The Bloomsbury Italian Philosophy Reader, ed. Michael Lewis
and David Rose
The Withholding Power: An Essay on Political Theology, Massimo
Cacciari, trans. Edi Pucci
Introduction to New Realism, Maurizio Ferraris

BEYOND LANGUAGE

Emanuele Severino

Translated by Damiano Sacco

Edited by Giulio Goggi, Damiano Sacco, Ines Testoni

BLOOMSBURY ACADEMIC
LONDON • NEW YORK • OXFORD • NEW DELHI • SYDNEY

BLOOMSBURY ACADEMIC
Bloomsbury Publishing Plc
50 Bedford Square, London, WC1B 3DP, UK
1385 Broadway, New York, NY 10018, USA
29 Earlsfort Terrace, Dublin 2, Ireland

BLOOMSBURY, BLOOMSBURY ACADEMIC and the Diana logo are trademarks of Bloomsbury Publishing Plc

First published in 1992 in Italy as Oltre il Linguaggio by Emanuele Severino © Adelphi Edizioni

This book has been translated thanks to a translation grant awarded by the Italian Ministry of Foreign Affairs and International Cooperation.

Questo libro è stato tradotto grazie a un contributo alla traduzione assegnato dal Ministero degli Affari Esteri e della Cooperazione Internazionale italiano.

First published in Great Britain 2024

English language translation © Damiano Sacco 2024

Copyright © Giulio Goggi, Damiano Sacco and Ines Testoni, 2024

The translation of this book has been realised thanks to a grant awarded by SEPS – SEGRETARIATO EUROPEO PER LE PUBBLICAZIONI SCIENTIFICHE

Via Val d'Aposa 7 – 40123 Bologna
seps@seps.it – www.seps.it

Giulio Goggi, Damiano Sacco and Ines Testoni have asserted their right under the Copyright, Designs and Patents Act, 1988, to be identified as Editors of this work.

Series design: Ben Anslow
Cover image: Emanuele Severino (© Mondadori Portfolio / agefotostock)

All rights reserved. No part of this publication may be reproduced or transmitted in any form or by any means, electronic or mechanical, including photocopying, recording, or any information storage or retrieval system, without prior permission in writing from the publishers.

Bloomsbury Publishing Plc does not have any control over, or responsibility for, any third-party websites referred to or in this book. All internet addresses given in this book were correct at the time of going to press. The author and publisher regret any inconvenience caused if addresses have changed or sites have ceased to exist, but can accept no responsibility for any such changes.

A catalogue record for this book is available from the British Library.

A catalog record for this book is available from the Library of Congress.

ISBN: HB: 978-1-3502-8523-1
PB: 978-1-3502-8524-8
ePDF: 978-1-3502-8522-4
eBook: 978-1-3502-8525-5

Typeset by RefineCatch Limited, Bungay, Suffolk

To find out more about our authors and books visit www.bloomsbury.com and sign up for our newsletters.

CONTENTS

Being Beyond Language by Ines Testoni and Giulio Goggi vii
Beyond Translation by Damiano Sacco xxiii
Note xxxiii

PART ONE 1

1   Violence and Salvation 3

2   Anxiety and Will to Power 19

3   Scientific Specialization and Nothingness 37

PART TWO 51

1   Nietzsche and Gentile 53

2   Problematicism and Actual Idealism 73

3   Socrates, Silenus, and Virtue 91

PART THREE 103

1   On Identity and Difference 105

2   The Unfolding of Language and the Appearing
    of Destiny 125

3   Language and Destiny 163

Notes 193
Bibliographical Note 197
Index 199

BEING BEYOND LANGUAGE

Ines Testoni and Giulio Goggi

ontemporary philosophy and culture has generally become – and is still becoming – a complex scenario of post-structuralist approaches. The reflection on the meanings of things, as well as their definitions, mostly follows approaches that oppose modernity and, in particular, the subject developed from the Cartesian *cogito* deprived of any gnoseological or axiological privileges. These currents, which include post-modernist orientations, among which phenomenology, constructivism and deconstruction – or at least the approaches that pivot on the genealogical method – emerge in importance. Thus, on the one hand, rigorous neo-positivist analysis is criticized, and on the other, the symbolic and linguistic function upon which subjectivity is constituted is emphasized.

Contemporary Italian philosophy has recently gained wide recognition at an international level,[1] and many of its scholars have devoted their attention to the mainstream notion of Italian theory. According to the opinion of one of its most representative thinkers (Roberto Esposito[2]), their specificity pivots on some concepts, including the historicization of the nonhistorical (metaphysical concepts) and the disintegration and diffusion of individual subjectivity. These lines of thought primarily aim to avoid confronting universalism, epistemology and the transcendental challenge that somehow characterizes both so-called continental thought and analytic philosophy. The most significant problem with this theoretical attitude is the fact that these reflections, including the aforementioned part of Italian philosophy, do not specify the principles of truth that justify their descriptions of phenomena, regardless of the extent to which they clarify processes of analysis and criticism. This is because they specifically reject any structure that would ground the logic of their arguments. For this reason, the relationship between structuralism and post-structuralism has not been sufficiently clear.

It is certainly interesting to speak without questioning the truth and the meaning that permits reliable or even irrefutable discourse, and many of the descriptions produced as part of this philosophical posture are of extreme importance at pragmatic, social and psychological levels. Hence, these kinds of reflections fit well with political investigations, which functionally define what human beings desire and how power prevents them from fulfilling their needs of self-realization – or turns them into cannon fodder. In this regard, one should read the important works of Giorgio Agamben, who, in the wake of Michael Foucault's reflections, gained much deserved prominence by analysing the concept of *homo sacer*.[3]

However, the fact that a philosophical trend can achieve great success and interest at a social level inasmuch as it responds to important human and humanitarian needs in world-building processes does not detract from the fact that philosophy was born and developed first and foremost as a reflection on the meaning of truth. Moreover, the fact that the twentieth century has entirely exhausted every reflection on the meaning of truth that had been developed by metaphysics does not mean that further dialectical developments should not take place. Notably, the criticisms that have hammered down the epistemic edifices of entire centuries of the history of philosophy should be resolved.

Emanuele Severino represents the other side of Italian thought[4]. Indeed, he provides radically different perspectives from traditional or contemporary ones because his discourse offers one of the most significant reflections in the areas of phenomenology, hermeneutics and the philosophy of language, starting from an incontrovertible indication of truth. As a corollary to the necessity of truth, this clearly explains how contemporary philosophy unavoidably destroys traditional perspectives and specifically what he calls 'epistemic thinking', which establishes the immutable structure of universals. This argument is fully explored in the book, *Law and Chance*,[5] to which we refer here. The decline of traditional thought is inevitable because it illustrates the accomplishment of the basic error of all Western philosophy: the fundamental belief in the 'becoming of things' and the oscillation between being and not being. This accomplishment consists of irrevocably positing that if something oscillates between being and nothing, then everything may thus oscillate and no immutable universal being may exist or become necessary. If, in its initial configuration, traditional philosophy considers immutable being as the possibility of the existence of the becoming of the world (e.g. God versus contingent creatures), in its most consistent development, it has reached the conclusion that if becoming is possible (i.e. if things oscillate between being and non-being), then no immutable being can exist (Nietzsche's *Death of God*). *Law and Chance* perfectly explain the necessary mode of the decline of traditional thought, and it is possible to classify all critics of post-structuralism using this contemporary philosophical nomenclature.

Moreover, structuralism assumes that there are strong (non-accidental) relationships between events and that phenomena can be studied and interpreted, starting from the categories that describe systems and their relationships through language. In the first decades of the twentieth century, this perspective was characterized by the epistemologies of many scientific disciplines: psychology (e.g. *Gestalttheorie*), anthropology (e.g. Franz Boas, Ruth Benedict and Edward Sapir) and linguistics (Ferdinand de Saussure). Also belonging to structuralism is the origin of the philosophy of language, which finds in the diagramming of meaning the possibility of defining structural relationships that allow us to understand how we think and speak about the world. Although many different perspectives rise and triumph within post-modernism to question the relationships of meanings and words, they do not apply a stable model of interpretation because they consistently radicalize the demand for demolishing every immutable or necessary nexus within the interpretative process, regardless of any empirical or metaphysical grounding. Language is constantly changing based on its context and utility, and the relationships between words and things are regulated by changing conquests. Moreover, there are no specific rules establishing how words should be or have been constructed to indicate something.

The problem of the relationship between words and their meanings is considered by Plato in *The Cratylus*, in which Hermogenes presents the idea that names are arbitrarily decided by usage and convention. In contrast, Socrates refutes Hermogenes' thesis by showing how names represent something about the objects to which they refer. In this way, Plato sought an epistemic structuralism that would make it possible to recognize the true word form capable of indicating the presence (*parousia*) of an idea. Twentieth-century structuralism rejects this necessity, which had already been abandoned by Aristotle in his *Peri Hermeneias* (16a3–9). Thus, the fundamental constituent of a language (the word) establishes its non-self-evident nature, which results from more or less explicit agreements, while remaining free from any assumption of method or evaluation in terms of truth or falsehood. Language then expresses the concept of contingency in excellent ways because if there is no necessary link between a thing and its word, the words will change over time and in different places, as will the things themselves. If, for example, 'a' denotes 'X' at 'T1' in a country in the North, the same 'X' may be denoted by 'b' at 'T2' in the same place and by 'r' at 'T3' in a country in the South and so forth. Etymological research serves to trace the roots and evolution of the relationship between words and the objects they indicate. By recognizing the conventional value of language, the structuralism that characterizes logical empiricism and the linguistic turn of analytical philosophy maintain at its root the aim to limit the transformation of language – to force it to adhere to what is perceived as real instead of transforming reality. This is the essential characteristic that differentiates the knowledge of the hard sciences, which changes after long, complex and difficult confrontations, from narrative or post-modern types of knowledge that change quite rapidly.

Severino first and foremost considers things that cannot change throughout history and culture with regards to the indexing function of language. This begins with the notion that when something appears, language will indicate it. Hence, the change in language creates a cycle of meaning that frames the background against which events and things are indicated. Notably, a 'stable' language can be viewed as an event among many events and in contrast to any background. As discussed in *Beyond Language*, we can linguistically indicate this permanence, and with such permanence, logical rules are necessarily produced. In this way, structuralist linguistic currents can be used to radicalize certain logical issues, unravelling the knots maintained by realism throughout history and integrating aspects of phenomenology. Doing so underlies the continental perspectives of hermeneutic reflection. From philosophical and epistemological perspectives, the question concerns the need to determine whether there are structural constants, whereas the relationship between interpretation and reality is the fundamental aim of the philosophy of science. Severino's discourse radicalizes the indexing function of language with respect to its irreducibly ontological dimension of what words mean. This phenomenon provided the title, *Beyond Language*. Now, it is a question of understanding what it is about and, thus, what discourses fail to be meaningful and true with respect to their ontological dimensions.

Although post-modernists do not hesitate to question reality, the first problem of any structuralist theory hinges upon reality's definition. Severino was very aware of this substantial difficulty with any form of knowledge that seeks to affirm a meaning or deny a proposition, and he addressed the theme of the relationship between reality and thought by considering the position of Hegel's *Science of Logic*[6] on various occasions, particularly in *Istituzioni di Filosofia* (Institutions of Philosophy)[7] and in *La Filosofia Moderna* (Modern Philosophy).[8] In these monographs, which precede *Beyond Language*, Severino analysed the relationship between certainty and truth according to three historically recognizable philosophical phases: ancient and medieval (i.e. involving the affirmation of the identity of certainty and truth, the conviction that reality or truth is knowable as certain by thought and reality is external to and independent of thought), modern philosophy (i.e. up to and including Kant, holds the principle that reality exists externally and independently of thought, but Descartes emphasized that the content of mind and experience is always representative).

If the content of thought does not reflect external and independent reality, then beginning with Descartes, modern philosophy suggests that the basis of knowledge is the opposition of certainty and truth. Indeed, with Kant, scepticism concerning the knowledge of things as being external from thought is at its highest. However, Severino showed that, like Plato, Descartes and Kant assumed *a priori* that there exists a realm of things in themselves. Even if it is difficult or impossible to know reality, it exists externally and independently of human knowledge. Moreover, Kantian phenomenalism is a complex expression of realism. Hegel, whom Severino considered the grandmaster of the third phase, removed this opposition, including the contradictory concept of a 'thing in itself', which, insofar as it is conceived, is no longer 'in itself'. Idealism posits the unity of thought and being, thus re-proposing an identity between certainty and truth, which is no longer immediate but mediated by the negation of any external or independent self-contained reality.

Hegel performed the first step in solving the problem of the relationship between reality and thought. However, contemporary philosophy has introduced within the dialectic between Kantian criticism and idealism an additional gnoseological question relating to how this dialectic manifests itself linguistically, which relates to how concrete reality is interpreted by thought. Hence, the question turns to whether truth can linguistically be expressed and if the linguistic operation can reflect both thought and reality. Severino was very familiar with these arguments and the background of logical empiricism, within which the investigations of analytic philosophy and linguistics developed.

Essentially, *Beyond Language* fits this context of reflection. It was published in 1992, following the translation of Rudolf Carnap's *The*

Logical Structure of the World, and *Law and Chance*. Carnap,[9] like all logical empiricists, introduced the argument that most philosophical problems were nothing more than pseudo-problems: questions based on nonsensical propositions linked to a logical deficiency of language. Questions about the relationship between thought and reality surpass language and the possibility of logical reflection that would otherwise define the basic conditions of true or false assertions. This idea had already been developed by Hegel in his *Elements of the Philosophy of Right*, in which he affirmed that *'was vernünftig ist, das ist wirklich; und was wirklich ist, das ist vernünftig'* (the real is rational, and the rational is real).[10] This perspective assumes that reason manifests itself in reality.[11] Carnap replaced the term 'rational' with 'logic' and hence introduced the problem of logically founded assertions. We can therefore assert that logical empiricism introduces language and its rules into the thought/reality dialectic, which reintroduces modern scepticism by trying to overcome implicit Kantian realism by using the rules of logic. With Kant, Carnap assumed that there are individuals who believe, like Hegel, that reality is logical and therefore knowable. Hence, he asked the linguistic question of what resides between logical and illogical assertions; the latter is meaningless because illogical assertions cannot refer to reality.

In his introduction to the Italian translation of *The Logical Structure of the World*, which provides a redefinition of the meaning of reality, Severino questions the very concept of 'appearing'. Thus, he emphasized the problem of what can be said in a strictly logical manner as an assertion of truth. The philosophy of language originates from the assumption of neo-positivism and of the *Tractatus Logico-Philosophicus*,[12] which provides a logical foundation for the definition of what is real. It is mostly concerned with the relationships between language, thinking and reality so that the nature of meaning, reference, mind and intentionality can be investigated. Carnap adopted the realistic perspectives of the logician and mathematician, Gottlob Frege – one of the most significant founders of analytic philosophy owing to his valorization by Bertrand Russell. Aligning with Frege's logic, Charles Kay Odgen and Ivor Armstrong Richards developed the semantic triangle theory (STT),[13] which describes the elements involved in the meaning that language carries. Gaining considerable interest throughout the twentieth century, STT defines the processes of reality interpretation based on linguistics. This structural model postulates that meaning can be construed as a mental reference (i.e. subjective thought or representation) at the vertex of a triangular diagram. The symbol (sign or word) is positioned at the lower-left corner, and its referent (thing) is positioned at the lower-right.

Strongly influenced by the logical atomism of Bertrand Russell, STT claims that during interpretation, the actor conceptualizes the referent and uses the sign or word to refer to the objects instead of the real ones. The relationship between symbols and referents is indirect, whereas symbol – reference and reference – referent relationships are direct. SST remains an excellent expression of the structuralist perspective, with which Ferdinand de Saussure viewed language as a system of signs based on the relationships between a signifier (referent) and the signified (reference), which are connected by interpretation.[14] De Saussure agreed with the Hermogenes' position from *The Cratylus* that words are conventional signs consisting of two faces: signifier and signified. Thus, from this perspective, the nexus of the sign with the thing is the fruit of convention. Similarly, as inspired by Saussure's structural perspective, the pragmatist Charles Sander Peirce conceived a triadic model composed of signs (symbols), interpretations (references) and referents (objects), whereas the assignment of meaning substantially relies on the construction of the reference.

The simple structure of these models responds to the original need for logical empiricism and analysis to detect errors in language and to assess the relationship between logically definable reality and the non-meaning that characterizes the beliefs intrinsic to common, everyday life. Based on the sign-signified relationship alone, as conceived by de Saussure, Frege considered the binary view of signs insufficient, arguing for the need to refer to reality (i.e. denotation). This perspective is based on the structural idea that reality is logical and that language can respect this logic, even when challenged by reality itself. Thus, as Hegel indicated, there is no logic without reality. As considered in the famous argument of the 'morning star versus the evening star', according to Frege, the identity principle is essential to the truth value as long as it refers to something. For example, the statement 'a = a' has a different meaning from 'a = b'. That is, 'Tom is Tom' does not equal 'Tom is Bob'; however, if, in reality, Tom is also named 'Bob', an identity is maintained. The investigation of reality permits us to learn the truth values of identity claims. With the use of a binary conception of a sign, an utterance expressing an identity can represent either the identity of the meaning of the different signs or their equivalence. In neither case does the utterance provide information about the reality indicated by the utterance because, in the former case, the utterance merely represents the identity of a thing with itself (i.e. identity principle). In the latter case, the only information conveyed concerns the use of words. To understand the meaning of 'Tom is Bob', one must empirically investigate the principle of identity linguistically. Thus, the meaning of 'a = a' clearly differs from the meaning of 'a = b', but if Tom is identical to both 'Tom' and 'Bob', then the two cases represent the same identity. However, we can assert this only if Tom appears in the circle of appearing; the principle of verification consists precisely of this effort.[15]

Despite its reductionist successes via the languages of physics and of the hard sciences, this perspective seems to be philosophically unable to overcome the relativism of post-modernism, in which reality ultimately corresponds to language itself. That is, language definitively loses its referent, and the scientific popularization of Heisenberg's uncertainty principle plays an important role. Since the Würzburg physicist demonstrated quantum mechanically that a fundamental limit exists in the ability to interpret the values of dyadic physical quantities (e.g. position and momentum) of a particle, a significant amount of non-scientific literature has used similar principles to debate whether matter can be considered real, questioning whether physics can say anything about the reality of the universe.[16] If this is true, then owing to post-structuralist approaches, all knowledge appears to be exposed to processes of construction and representation that do not hold anything of permanence (i.e. they lack sufficiently strong support from the realism of structuralism). Another directional impetus is provided by dialetheism, of which Graham Priest is a leading proponent.[17] Dialetheism is not a formal logic structure, but it provides a simple thesis about truth that influences the construction of logical constructs based on pre-existing logical systems, and it permits philosophers to assert things that can be both true and false. On the other hand, this philosophical position consists of affirming a true statement whose negation is also true. From this perspective, true contradictions exist in which logic as a whole can be held illogical, betraying its original intentions.

This apparent dialethic paradox was resolved by Severino's indication, which uses language according to the dynamic of the *élenchos*, which consists of showing the incontrovertibility of a true statement. In the works preceding *Beyond Language*, Severino developed a structurally coherent system that radically redefined the meaning of truth and its radical logical coherence, referring to the incontrovertibility of the self-contradictory and self-negating nature of what intends to deny true assertion. Thus, a sidereal distance was established that distinguishes Severino from any traditional and contemporary philosopher.

In his discourse, the concept of identity is crucial for logical empiricism and analytic philosophy. However, with logical empiricism, truth must indicate reality, which is material; hence, the language of physics is the most suitable, according to different degrees of truth[18]. From this reduction, it is assumed *a priori* that only what appears is. On the contrary, Severino considered that not all that is appears, and that everything that is – appearing or not appearing – has something fundamentally identical: its 'being' a being. Reductionism fails in this case because it does not consider the fact that any specific observation should consider the fact that not all that is appears. Moreover, science is significant in this case because its process discovers precisely what does not appear, while stating that the totality of being is that which appears. However, this apparent paradox implies radical elements that must be further considered. Being is the totality of what is; some beings appear, and some beings do not and will not. Thus, what we can truthfully say is exclusively inherent to being. The meaning of truth indicated by Severino is 'the originary structure of truth', given that it is possible to say something that makes sense in a true and incontrovertible way only with respect to what is inherent to the being of every being.

To simplify Severino's indication of what can be truly said of the being of all beings, we quote the pentapartite structure summarized by Ines Testoni[19] from *La Struttura Originaria* (The Originary Structure)[20] and 'The Essence of Nihilism'.[21] The five co-originary axes that permit one to understand the difference between error and truth are as follows:

1   In the first axis, the foundation of the originary structure of truth occurs through the *élenchos* – an argumentative dynamic that illuminates the self-negation of the erroneous content of the arguments that seek to negate truth. The *élenchos* is based on the undeniable fundamental opposition of the positive (affirmation) and negative (negation), such that the affirmation does not correspond to and is opposed to the negation.

2   The second axis leverages the principle of non-contradiction (PNC), or the law of contradiction (Aristotle). Hence, for all propositions, p, it is impossible for both p and not-p to be true (i.e. $(p \cdot \sim p)$ is not possible). In the 'Returning to Parmenides' chapter of *The Essence of Nihilism*, Severino reiterated the incontrovertible assertion that

being is and cannot be nothingness and that nothingness is not and cannot be being. When discussing Aristotle's *Metaphysics IV*, Gamma 3–6, he affirmed that, without the PNC, we cannot know anything that we do know. In other words, if I affirm that being is being, I am not affirming that being is not being or that being is nothing.

3 The third axis leverages the principle of identity: A = A, in which every being is identical to itself, or ($\forall$x, x = x). Another formulation of the principle derived from the basic form asserts that if a propositional function, F, is true of an individual variable x, then F is indeed true of x (F(x) $\supset$ F(x)). In summary, being is being and is not nothing.

4 The fourth axis leverages the principle of the excluded middle (or third): p or ~p must be true, with no third or middle true proposition between them (p $\vee$ ~p). This implies that between affirmation and negation, there is no third proposition. Because being is being and nothing is nothing, whereas nothing is non-being, these axes simply confirm that being is necessarily eternal, as is everything that respects the identity principle; hence, each being is and is as it is (A = A). If it is impossible for any being not to be (~[p $\cdot$ ~p]), then annihilation is impossible. Because the world of beings appears, everything that appears is not nothing but each is a being and thus is eternally itself. Beggining to 'appear' means entering into the horizon of experience (the circle of appearing). Everything that appears is and is forever, as whatever is cannot come into being from nothingness, nor can it cease to be by falling into nothingness. Every discourse that attempts to negate this basic structure is nihilistic in nature and identifies being with its negation to nothingness. What is incontrovertible is the appearing of a self-identical being, beings or non-contradictory being/beings. Hence, being identical implies the eternity of every being as being.

5 The fifth axis exclusively involves the scientific observation of phenomena, which is crucial to the way we observe facts and interpret them. The interest of Severino in Carnap's philosophy is inherent to the concept of appearing, which is radical but also cogent, such that it can be assumed by even the most rigorous neo-positivist thinkers. Actually, the rigorous observation of what appears (the mediated concept of reality) permits us to assert that

it is impossible to affirm that we can observe an act of creation and an act of annihilation. It is thus impossible for nothingness to appear. Severino shows that, contrary to Western philosophical assumptions, becoming does not appear in the sense of the appearing of annihilation or *ex nihilo* beings.

In *Beyond Language*, the problem of a linguistic sense of being is resolved. The aporia generated by the fact that being can assume infinite forms – similar to Frege's problem of the morning and evening star – from which we obtain the conviction that being cannot be defined is resolved by indicating that if something is, concretely appears and is identical to itself, then it cannot be said to be other than itself. Therefore, whatever word is used to indicate the being or the totality of everything that is, despite whether it concretely appears, can only be identical to itself. The basic formula with which to indicate this identity principle is $[(A = A) = (A = A)]$. However, this is only the most general problem logically solved in the book, in order to define the relationships between what appears and what does not appear and their logical and theoretical implications.

Below is a guide to reading the most relevant themes dealt with by Severino in *Beyond Language* about the relationship between language and truth.

* * *

'If any language refutes the irrefutable, that language negates its own negation of the irrefutable' (Part III, ch. I, art. 6). The negation of the being-self of the being, regardless of how this negation is concretely configured, implies the appearance of the difference of beings:

> If the negation does not remain distinct from its other, there is no longer negation; if each term of the negation is not distinct from every other term [...], again there is no negation [...] In order for there to be negation, the negation must be determinate, both with respect to its other, and in the terms that constitute it; and therefore it presupposes and is grounded upon that which it denies.[22]

By negating its own foundation, a thought that negates the self-being of being, and thus its being other than what is other than itself, negates itself. There is therefore a *linguistic core* capable of resisting any attempt at negating it: the word that has as its object the incontrovertible self-being of beings. By developing this proposition, it should be noted that the syntax of the originart structure, which Severino also calls the 'destiny of truth', is composed of complex meanings that must appear for any being to appear. Indeed, nothing could appear, if what appears did not appear in the form of its self-being and its being other than its own other, that is in the form of the *opposition of the positive and the negative*.

Additionally, this structure implies a series of determinations without whose appearance the self-being of being would lack incontrovertibility. The most relevant of these determinations is what Severino called the 'golden implication',[23] which refers to the relationship between the self-being of being and its eternity. This is the implication between the self-being of being and its eternity, which we have already mentioned and which we can recall as follows: to think that things come out of nothingness and return to it – and that in this process beings have been nothing and will return being nothing – is to think that beings (any non-being) is nothing, i.e. it is to negate the self-being of being (which is that whose negation is self-negation). The relationship that exists between the originary structure of the truth and the eternity of a being also exists in relation to all determinations based on this structure. If they did not appear, the incontrovertible would be refutable.

Severino calls *persyntactic field* the appearing of this synthesis between the essence of the originary structure (i.e. the appearing of the irrefutable self-being of being and of the determinations from which this structure is constituted, namely, being, self-being, appearing, negation, self-negation, etc.) and the totality of its implications. It is a semantic – syntactic plexus that appears eternally from ever and forever, which cannot enter appearing. Hence, the absence of the persyntactic determinations (e.g. the self-being of being, its being other than its own other, its being other than nothing, its eternal being) would imply the impossible annihilation of that being that is the appearing of that being.

Given this construction, we can dwell on the first aspect of the contradiction of language that speaks of truth. It is said that the appearing of the synthesis between the originary structure and what is necessarily implied by it is incontrovertible. However, the persyntactic determinations constituting the everlasting and not supervening background of every appearing are indicated *processually* by language:

> In other words, the determinations of the originary structure may not arise as part of appearing, since, insofar as they are separated from one

another (and if they arise – that is, if some of them appear without the others – they must be thus separated) they are controvertible: and, in fact, they are negations of the originary structure. And yet, they appear as part of an arising and an unfolding that is therefore not *their* unfolding but the unfolding *of language*. If that unfolding were their own unfolding, the incontrovertible would not be able to exist; the incontrovertible, however, *qua* destiny of truth, does exist (for, indeed, the negation of the appearing of the self-being of beings is self-negating), and therefore, it is necessary that the unfolding as part of which they appear should be the unfolding of language.

Part III, ch. II, art. 7

Qua will to speak truth itself, language that intends to testify to the originary meaning *isolates* the parts of the originary structure by enclosing them in the form of the word, thus turning persyntactic determinations into something that, in supervening, begins to be indicated by the word. However, something supervening cannot belong to the timeless background of truth, which is a transcendental predicate without which nothing can appear. Moreover, in the processual development of language, it happens that the part, insofar as it is isolated from the concrete totality of the originary structure, cannot be what it is in truth (i.e. it is other than what it is insofar as it is concretely united to that totality). Hence, we locate the contradiction of the language that intends to speak truth. In the proceeding of the word, it happens that a trait of the originary structure is separated from another trait that supervenes in the linguistic exposition at a second moment. Isolated in this way, the first persyntactic trait is non-truth; this is the contradiction in which a trait of fate consists insofar as it is separated from the totality of the originary syntax.

When considering the persyntactic determination that is the self-being of being, after expressing the identity according to $A = A$, one observes that the self-identity with A implies a certain difference between the first and second A. It thus appears that the identity of a being is a non-identity, and that the non-identity is the foundation of the position of identity. This seeming contradiction – a contradiction of the originary can only be a seeming one – is overcome in the linguistic exposition of the originary structure by noting that to be identical with itself, A cannot be separate from itself. Being 'A' is predicated of 'A'-that-is-'A', and the being 'A' that is predicated is, precisely, the being 'A' of 'A'. The concrete formula of identity expresses the originary *identity of identity with itself*: $(A = A) = (A = A)$. Thus, in its processual development, the contradiction of language that argues that $A = A$ is thus overcome by the enlargement of the circle of language, and it comes to include the formula $(A = A) = (A = A)$.

However, isolated from the further persyntactic determinations that supervene one after the other in language – isolated, for example, from that implication of the identity of every being that is the affirmation of the eternity of the being as being –, the very concrete formulation of identity is a refutable content. Overcoming a contradiction *specific* to language thus opens a new one, given the absence of another specific persyntactic designation.

There is then a second aspect of the contradiction of language that speaks of truth, which is also mentioned in *Beyond Language*, that such language is also an expression of the will:

> The interpreting will and the will for something to be a sign of something else are part of the will that separates the earth [By the word 'earth' Severino means everything that begins to appear and ceases to appear] from the irrefutability of destiny [...]. A *will* to assign words to things, however, is also present in the language that testifies to destiny. The will to speak of truth does not belong to truth itself.
>
> Part III, ch. I, art. 7

Certain events are considered 'language' on the basis of a decision that creates a designating sign and its designated and corresponding meaning. And the language that bears witness to the truth of being is a contradiction because it is, itself, a form of will to power that separates beings from the originary structure of truth. Hence, by deluding itself that it can dispose of things, language isolates a being from its relationship to the totality of beings, making something that as such is not a sign become a sign and making something that as such is not a designated become a designated.

It would seem, then, that truth is not 'sayable', not only because language constrains it in the form of a word – thus constrained, truth is separate from itself; that is, it is not truth – but also because language is the expression of the will that persuades itself that it can dispose of events by making them signs, coordinating them with certain meanings and not with others. Under what conditions is testifying to truth possible? The following is Severino's answer.

The coming into linguistic expression of the originary determinations cannot be the supervening of those determinations as such because they appear *simul*. However, it is their beginning to appear in the synthesis of the word. It follows that everything indicated by language that speaks of truth is a contradiction, not insofar as it is such, but as it is enclosed in the form of the word. In what sense then do we say that the linguistic essence of the originary structure (i.e. the definition that encloses the originary in the form of the word) is incontrovertible? Severino writes:

> That essence is not the incontrovertible by virtue of its explicit meaning, but by virtue of its *implicit* one: namely, by virtue of the totality of determinations of the originary structure that, while being originarily and necessarily implied by that explicit meaning, originarily appear already prior to their appearing as part of the unfolding of language (i.e. of the unfolding of the explicit meaning) – that is to say, already prior to their coming and going in and out of language. The 'implicit' element of the language that speaks of the originary is the *appearing* of the totality of the originary. This totality is the element that *underlies* the definition: i.e. the linguistic essence of the originary.
>
> Part III, ch. II, art. 11

The underlying meaning, i.e. the 'implicit one' linked to what is said, is the totality of the persyntaxis without which destiny would not be destiny. Thus, what the language that testifies to the originary structure says is the incontrovertible self-being of being, and this testimony is itself incontrovertible insofar as what it says is united to the *unsaid* which is the eternal appearing of the totality of persyntactic determinations that necessarily appear where any being appears.

Insofar as they are separated from the totality to which they belong, persyntactic determinations are other than what they are in truth. However, unlike a contradiction whose content is null (e.g. the contradiction that affirms the being of non-being), the contradiction of language that testifies to destiny, and thus the appearing of the self-being of being, is that form of contradiction – which Severino called 'Contradiction C' – that besets the finite to the extent that the concrete configuration of the whole to which the finite necessarily belongs does not appear. Truth-telling language is therefore a negation of destiny because it does not show the totality of the implications to which the meaning it affirms is necessarily united. However, since what that language indicates is a trait of the originary essence of truth, or an implication of it, the negation of its non-truth cannot be the negation of its content, but it is the appearing of the *concreteness* of that content, a concreteness that must necessarily appear and that language attempts to indicate.

Furthermore, it is true that language that speaks of the originary meaning of being is an alteration because language, as an expression of the separating/isolating will, renders it designated. However, this is only one aspect of language that testifies to truth. If, on the one hand, such language is a negation of truth, on the other hand, it is truth: it is a negation of truth because it is the will to place destiny as a designated; it is truth because that which is signified is that whose negation is self-negating.

Ultimately, if it is true that the originary meaning currently appears in language 'in those linguistic forms that may be interpreted as the historical forms of language'; however, 'it is by appearing *within* language that the originary manifests its very transcendence of language [...]. It is as part of a circumstance in which the word is inevitable that there appears the necessity for the thing (i.e. for destiny) to transcend and enclose the word itself' (Part III, ch. II, art. 20). *Beyond Language* provides a glimpse of the themes that Severino developed in his later works: the concrete meaning of self-being can only appear with the decline of designating, that is, with the decline of language, on the understanding that: 1) the decline of language does not indicate overcoming Contradiction C, which necessarily envelops the finite, and 2) the contradiction of the finite appearing of the whole, determined by the non-appearing of all that is necessarily implied by the finite, has always been completely overcome in the infinite appearing of the totality *simpliciter* of the being.

Hence, 'contrary to the finite form of destiny – which surpasses the word, but which is also reached by it – the infinite form of destiny, as the pure light of meaning, eternally leaves the word behind' (Part III, ch. III, art. 13).

BEYOND TRANSLATION

Damiano Sacco

As Emanuele Severino's works are gradually translated into English, new elements appear that contribute to an understanding of Severino's theoretical apparatus. The preface to Severino's *Law and Chance* (London: Bloomsbury, 2023) already contains some of the key elements concerning the connection that indissociably links an understanding of 'the language that testifies to destiny' to the question of translation.[1] This connection obtains insofar as:

(i) Severino testifies to the impossible translation that determines the identification of the history of the West with the history of nihilism. This is the translation that abstracts ('isolates') every meaning (every being) from the concrete totality to which it belongs. Thus abstracted, every meaning is first of all abstracted from its own being, and it is therefore nothing (equivalently: every meaning, abstractly conceived as to its abstraction from the concrete totality, is a self-contradictory meaning – the meaning of nothingness). The history of the West, *qua* history of nihilism, coincides with (the belief in) the translation of every meaning into the meaning of nothingness.

(ii) Severino testifies to the faith in the existence of the impossible transition (i.e. translation) between being and nothingness constituted by the becoming of abstract beings. Insofar as a being becomes, something of that being must turn into nothing: that is to say, according to the notion of becoming of the tradition of the West, something-that-is must become – i.e. must be translated into – something-that-is-not.

(iii) Severino testifies to the untranslatability of the originary concreteness of being (the 'destiny of necessity') – an untranslatability that pertains not only to the totality of being, but to every meaning and to every being. The untranslatability of every being coincides with its eternity: namely, with the impossibility for any being to be translated as part of time and becoming.

(iv) Severino testifies to the concrete notion of the becoming of untranslatable beings: a becoming that consists in the appearing and disappearing of the eternals – a becoming through which their being (including the very being of their appearing) is preserved and saved from an impossible translation into nothingness.

(v) Severino testifies to the very alienated nature of his own testimony, according to which the very language that testifies to destiny believes to be a translation that abstracts what it testifies to (i.e. the 'destiny of necessity') from its own concreteness. The language that testifies to destiny is thus the one language that testifies to its own impossible abstraction or translation (and, in fact, to the *belief* in the existence of that translation, for that existence is in truth impossible, and constitutes the originary meaning of impossibility).

The testimony of the language that testifies to the destiny of necessity is thus indissociable from the question of translation. The question of translation is, in turn, the question of language. Every translation results in a 'language', and, conversely, every 'language' constitutes a form of translation – or, in fact, an attempt at one: for, insofar as every translation attempts to translate the untranslatable, it necessarily fails; every translation is a failing *will* that believes to translate the untranslatable. A 'language' consists precisely in the will for a certain appearing content (a 'sign' or a 'signifier' – a sound, an image, a gesture, etc.) to signify (i.e. to refer to) a certain other appearing content. This word or this written mark signifies a concept; that facial expression signifies a feeling; those clouds signify a coming storm. Every 'sign' thus refers to and signifies a 'meaning' or 'signified'. Every language thus consists in the abstraction of a certain appearing content: that is to say, in the extraction (*ab-trahere, ex-trahere*) of a certain quantum of appearing from the totality of what is immediately present ('the name', Plato writes, 'is an instrument for dividing being' [*órganon diakritikòn tês ousías*], *Cratylus* 388b–c). Thus abstracted and extracted, this content may constitute an ideal and reproducible unity: a sign. In turn, what is referred to or signified by a sign, too, is abstracted from the concrete totality of what presently appears. Even in the case of the signs 'being', 'totality', 'God', etc., what is signified is the abstract notion

xxiv   BEYOND TRANSLATION

of totality, and not *this*, concretely present content that manifestly appears (and even the complex sign '*this*, concretely present content that manifestly appears' only refers to an abstract notion of what presently, manifestly and concretely appears). As soon as a certain content is abstracted from the totality of appearing, there a 'language' appears. The appearing of a 'language' is thus the appearing of a translation of the concrete totality into an abstract system of signs; conversely, every abstraction of the concrete totality of appearing constitutes a 'language'.

As a result, however, the appearing of language (the appearing of *every* language) is the appearing of a contradiction (and, in fact, of a system or structure of contradictions) – precisely insofar as the meaning of every translation (i.e. the meaning of every abstract meaning) coincides with the originary meaning of impossibility: the meaning of nothingness (the self-contradictory meaning). For, indeed, every abstract meaning – as abstracted from the concrete totality in which it appears – is first of all abstracted from its own being: that is to say, from its own self-identity (for, if it did include its self-identity, it would nevertheless not include the self-identity of the complex meaning formed by its abstract meaning and its self-identity, thus giving rise to a *regressus in indefinitum* that mirrors the seminal aporia of passage 142b–143a of Plato's *Parmenides*, discussed in Chapter 2 of Part Three of *Beyond Language*). Thus abstracted from its self-identity, every abstract meaning is therefore self-different. It is a self-identical meaning that is self-different: a self-contradictory meaning – the meaning of nothingness. As abstracted from the concrete totality of being, every abstract meaning *differs* from itself as included in that concrete totality; the concrete totality of being, however, is precisely what may *not* differ from itself – it is the immediate self-being of being itself; that whose negation is self-negating. What differs from (and thus negates) the concrete self-identity of concrete being is therefore *nothing*: the self-contradictory and self-negating meaning. The appearing of every language, *qua* abstract appearing of a system of abstract signs, thus coincides with the appearing of a contradiction, and the history of the West coincides with the history of nihilism: that is to say, with the appearing of the meaning of nothingness.[2]

Beyond language

'Beyond language' thus means: 'beyond translation' – that is to say, beyond the abstraction and translation of language. This 'beyond' points to the site that always and forever abides in its untranslatability 'beyond' the domain of abstractions, translations and isolations. That site, however – 'the destiny of necessity' – is *not* the 'original text' (the text in-itself) that precedes and gives rise to all translations. It is on the contrary every language, every translation or abstraction that is always 'beyond' that site: in that this site is that *beyond* which there is – nothing. In other words, what is 'beyond language' is not what is 'real' beyond language; what is 'beyond language' is the originary site in which there appears *the belief* that the abstraction of language is successful and that what is 'real' stands opposed to, or beyond, language. Equivalently, what is 'beyond translation' is not the original text that precedes the translation of language; what is 'beyond translation' is, precisely, what is beyond the possibility of being translated. 'Beyond language' indicates the site as part of which every abstraction, isolation or translation (i.e. every language) is impossible:

> It is necessary that this syntactical concreteness of destiny should always already appear beyond the isolation of the earth – beyond language, beyond the language that testifies to destiny, and, therefore, beyond the very language that here, now, is asserting the necessity that the totality of the syntax of destiny should appear beyond language.
>
> This 'yonder', however, is the absolute 'hither': the absolutely 'right here', the originarily manifest place as part of which alone the earth and its isolation from that place may begin to appear.
>
> La Gloria, Milan: Adelphi, 2001, p. 476

What is 'beyond language' or 'beyond translation' constitutes the concrete ground for the appearing of the belief in the existence of the contradiction of every language, translation and abstraction. According to Severino, the contradiction of language may appear only insofar as it is negated by what is 'beyond language': the destiny of necessity.

What is 'beyond language' is therefore the *concrete* identity that underlies the system of abstract differences of language – that is to say, the concrete identity that underlies language as conceived of by the 'philosophies of the linguistic turn' (i.e. by all those philosophies that, in one way or another, may be traced to a conception of language as a system of pure differences). In Part Three of *Beyond Language*, Severino indicates the necessity of the appearing of a concrete identity underlying the differential system of (any) language (i.e. the necessity of the appearing of a concrete meaning or signified underlying every system of signifiers).

For, indeed, even if the meaning or signified of every sign does always appear, once again, in the form of a sign – that is, even if the meaning or signified of the expression 'the night comes' is this coming night, which, in turn, appears in and through the expression 'this coming night' – these two 'differences', precisely insofar as they are two 'signs' of the same meaning, must share an identical meaning. (And any two differences must always share an identical meaning, since, even if they are 'altogether' unrelated to one another, they always share *at least* the identical meaning of 'being a difference'.) What is therefore identical, and thus 'beyond' language regarded as a system of differences, is the identical meaning that is shared by two differences *insofar as they are differences (or signs) of the same meaning*. Their being signs of the same meaning, however, does *not* itself appear as a sign (that is, as a difference), but it is the identical meaning by virtue of which two differences (e.g. 'the night comes' and 'this coming night') *appear as* signs of the same meaning. This identical meaning is 'beyond language' in that it coincides neither with the 'sign' nor with its 'meaning' (a meaning that, in turn, appears in the form of a sign).

According to Severino, this identical meaning is 'beyond language' in that it consists in 'this' or 'that' sign's being *any sign whichever* of a certain meaning ('The identity that is present in a set of differences is a difference that, in its being *any* difference *whichever* [*in quanto differenza qualsiasi*] – and not in its being the specific difference that it is – constitutes what is identical in the totality of differences of a certain kind'). 'The night comes' and 'the coming night' are certainly two different signs (i.e. two different differences), but *they are identical as to their being signs of the same meaning* – that is to say, they are not identical insofar as they are *this* sign ('the night comes') or *that* sign ('the coming night') of the same meaning, but insofar as they are *a (any, whichever) sign* of that meaning. 'Being sign of the same meaning' is an identical meaning that is shared both by 'the night comes' and by 'the coming night' – once again, *not* insofar as it is a meaning that appears in the form of *this* difference or sign (i.e. 'being sign of the same meaning'), but insofar as 'the night comes' and 'the coming night' *appear together*, and in their appearing together, their shared segment of identity (their being signs of the same meaning) concretely appears 'beyond language' (see the next section: The aporia of translation).

Equivalently, insofar as the word 'originary' is a translation of the word '*originario*', these two words must share an identical meaning by virtue of which their appearing together appears as the appearing of two words signifying (at least partially) the same meaning, albeit in two different natural languages; this identical meaning, however, consists neither in the difference 'originary' nor in the difference '*originario*', but in each of their concrete being a (or any) sign of the same meaning (a concrete being that does not itself appear in the form of an abstract difference, but that is the identical meaning concretely shared by the differences 'originary' and '*originario*').[3] Analogously, for instance, insofar as the script of a play is the script of *that* play, and not of another one, that script and that play must share a concretely identical meaning: this meaning, however, is neither expressed (or express-able) in the semiotic system of the script (words, signs, written marks, etc.) nor in that of the play (acts, gestures, utterances, etc.). 'Inter-semiotic' translations, too, must thus share a segment of identity that coincides neither with the 'original' text nor with its translation, but with their respective being different semiotic translations *of the same* concrete 'meaning' or 'text'.

The aporia of translation

The essential aporia of every abstract notion of translation (that is to say, of every abstract notion of abstraction; see *La struttura originaria*) consists in the appearing of a translation that is regarded in its being abstracted ('isolated') from its original 'text'. As a result of this abstract configuration, the meaning of the original text appears to be modified by the appearing of its translation: that is to say, the original text that appears with (i.e. in relation to) its translation is not identical to the original text that appears in its being unrelated to that translation (for instance, before the appearing of that translation). In turn, however, the translation itself comes to appears as a translation of this latter 'original' text, which consists in the original text in its being related to its translation. Except that this 'original' text is now modified by this second 'translation' (i.e. by the translation of the original *qua* modified by its relation to its translation). And so on, on *ad infinitum*.

This aporia characterizes the abstract appearing together of every 'original' and of every 'translation' (and, in fact, the abstract appearing together of any two beings). For, indeed, the same aporetic situation is generated by the abstract notions of being and appearing, noumenon and phenomenon, thing and sign, signified and signifier, etc. Abstract signs signify things, and language signifies reality, by disregarding (i.e. precisely by *abstracting* from) the fact that those signs and that language, abstractly conceived, modify the very things and realities that they attempt to signify (which in turn modify their signs, thus giving rise to a *regressus in infinitum*). Contemporary thinking is either unaware of this aporia or believes to be able to dwell in this very aporetic situation: in the first case, contemporary thinking coincides with a form of realism (in that a certain dimension is, precisely, believed to be 'real' in its abstract immediacy – i.e. disregarding its translation by thought, language, experience, etc.); in the second case, contemporary thinking believes to be able to posit the aporetic character of the real, and dwell, through an infinite 'play' and 'deferral', in the very dimension of meaning opened by that infinite *regressus* (Jacques Derrida being one of the crucial interlocutors of Part Three of *Beyond Language*). Contemporary thinking thus oscillates between the contradiction of realism – according to which what is 'real' is both unrelated to language (respectively: thought, consciousness, intentionality, etc.) and, at the same time, appears in and through the latter – and the contradiction of that infinite *regressus*: an infinite *regressus* that believes to avoid the contradiction of realism by deferring its outcome *ad infinitum*. On the contrary, this latter perspective must instead surreptitiously re-introduce that contradiction as the very 'principle' that gives rise to the *regressus* itself (in the form of an Other, absolutely other, trace, a-dialectical absolute, etc.: i.e. as a 'principle' believed to lie beyond the opposition of being and nothingness).

According to Severino, even a philosophical system like Hegel's – 'the most radical attempt in the history of Western thought at grounding the inseparability of the opposites', (*La struttura originaria*, p. 47) – does not succeed in thinking the *originary* unity of the original and of its translation (be that the unity of meaning and sign, reality and language, thought and being, etc.). For indeed, according to Severino, Hegel's dialectics thinks that unity *as a result* – a result of a becoming that, however, is impossible from the very standpoint of the *originary* unity of the original and of its translation. ('Of the Absolute it must be said that it is essentially a *result*, that only in the end is it what it truly is', *Phenomenology of Spirit*, Oxford: Oxford University Press, 1977, p. 11; 'Within the Science this standpoint, which in this first act appears as *immediate*, must make itself into the *result*, and (what is more) into its last result, in which it reaches its beginning again and returns into itself', *Encyclopaedia Logic*, Hackett: Indianapolis, 1991, § 17; for a discussion of Hegel's dialectics, see *Tautótes*, Milan: Adelphi, 1995; *La struttura originaria*, 'Introduction' and Chap. IX).[4]

The aporia of translation – that is, the aporia of language and abstraction – is superseded by the concreteness of the *originary* appearing together of the original and of its translation. That the original and its translation originarily appear together means that the original is not abstracted from, and presupposed to, its appearing together with its translation, but *immediately* coincides with that very appearing together. Insofar as the concrete original (i.e. the originary) is not the original *qua* abstracted from its translation, but the original-that-appears-with-its-translation, there arises no *regressus in infinitum*: for, indeed, the originary or concrete original, which appears together with its translation, is not modified by its appearing together with its translation, because it immediately coincides with that appearing together; and, conversely, the concrete translation of the original coincides with the very appearing together of this translation with the original, which thus makes it immediately a 'translation-of-the-original' – a translation whose meaning is not modified by its appearing together with the original. It is not the original, as abstracted from its translation, that appears with its translation, but it is the original-that-appears-with-its-translation that appears with the translation-of-the-original. The originary structure is the structure of this concrete immediacy. (It is thus explained why a translation of the term '*originario*' into 'original' would have lost precisely the difference between abstract and originary appearing of every original.)

The concrete appearing together of a sign and its meaning (i.e. the concrete appearing of language) is thus the originary and immediate appearing together of an original and of its translation. Insofar as 'the night comes' immediately appears together with 'the coming night', these two meanings share a concretely identical meaning: the meaning of their immediate and originary appearing together as signs of the same meaning. Insofar as the language that testifies to destiny immediately appears together with the destiny of necessity (a meaning that, once again, appears in and through a word), these two meanings share a concretely identical meaning (a 'segment' of identity) – which differs from the one shared by the incontrovertible and any other (controvertible) language.

La Gloria, la Gioia

'Beyond language' indicates, on the one hand, the site that is always sheltered from the abstraction and translation of language. 'Beyond language' may, on the other hand, also indicate the end of the appearing *of the belief* in the abstraction and contradiction of language: namely, it may also indicate what lies beyond the history of the appearing of this belief. When *Beyond Language* (*Oltre il linguaggio*) is first published in 1992, the question of the end of the history of the essential alienation of the West still remained a problem (or, in fact, *the* problem) for the language that testifies to destiny. That is to say that, while it incontrovertibly appeared that all languages and all translations appear (or, rather, are believed to appear) by virtue of the untranslatable background of the destiny of necessity, it still remained a problem whether the history of this *belief* (the history of the fundamental alienation of the West: the history of nihilism) should come to an end (according to the meaning of becoming a 'past' or a '*perfectum*' indicated in Chapter VI of *Destino della necessità*: namely, as the completion of the series of eternals that form that history). That this question remained an open problem means that it was non-contradictory to postulate either that that history would come to an end or that it would not. It does *not* mean that the answer to that question was not yet part of the eternal determinations of the truth of the destiny of necessity; it rather means that language had not yet testified to that (so-called 'syntactic') determination of the originary structure (i.e. to those eternal beings that are always part of the appearing of the originary structure): that is to say, the relation between that always-already appearing determination and language had not yet entered the circle of appearing (as outlined in Chapter 2 of Part Three of *Beyond Language*). That problem is posited at the end of *Destino della necessità* (Milan: Adelphi, 1980; Chap. XVI), and finds a solution in *La Gloria*, whose subtitle reads: 'Resolution of *Destino della necessità*' (in the same way in which *Destino della necessità* answers the essential question, formulated at the end of *The Essence of Nihilism*, concerning the freedom or necessity of the appearing of the eternals). *La Gloria* concretely indicates the necessity of the coming to pass of the end of the essential alienation of nihilism – i.e. the necessary coming to pass of that 'beyond language' that follows the end of the abstraction and alienation of language: 'With the twilight of the isolating will and of language, there remains, beyond language, the infinity of the infinite and infinitely many paths of the Glory [*la Gloria*] as well as the infinity of the infinite appearing of the Joy [*la Gioia*]' (*La Gloria*, p. 481; cf. *La morte e la terra*, Milan: Adelphi, 2011, pp. 144–5). As part of the language that testifies to destiny, 'beyond language' thus indicates, on the one hand, the infinite path (*la Gloria*) that has always awaited the earth after the end of the history of the belief in the alienation and abstraction of language – and, on the other hand, the site (*la Gioia*) that, in its eternity and untranslatability, is always sheltered from every translation and every violence that language, *qua* abstraction, believes to be able to accomplish.

NOTE

These pages take a few steps forth in the clarification of the meaning of the originary (Part One, Chapter 1), and of the connection that links the originary to language. These pages also extensively develop (Parts One and Two) different aspects of the relationship between the originary and the different forms of civilization of the West. The connection between language and the originary is here considered (Part Three) as part of a deeper confrontation with *La struttura originaria* (Milan: Adelphi, 1981), *The Essence of Nihilism* (London: Verso, 2016; *Essenza del Nichilismo*, Milan: Adelphi, 1982) and *Destino della necessità* (Milan: Adelphi, 1980). The originary – the destiny of every being – constitutes the clearing as part of which everything comes to light. The second chapter in Part Three indicates what it means to take a step forth in the clarification of the originary (this question is addressed at the beginning of the '*Avvertenza*' of *La struttura originaria*).

E. S.

PART ONE

1 VIOLENCE AND SALVATION

1

Only a God may save us? The God to which the Greek-Judeo-Christian tradition turns? Today, there exists an ever more dominant conviction that salvation may only come from Technics, as guided by modern science. The remedy to the harms caused by Technics lies – so it is believed – with Technics itself. In any case, salvation is first of all salvation from violence, and from the destruction that originates from violence. The 'categorical imperative' to treat humans as ends and not as means prohibits precisely violence – which, in having its own exertion as an end, destroys humans themselves.

Violence crosses the limits that ought not to be crossed. These limits *ought not to* be crossed – and yet, they *can* be crossed. Humans struggle to understand that if a limit *can* 'truly and really' be crossed, then, any ground as to why it *ought not to* be crossed comes to disappear.

And yet, when the Greek-Judeo-Christian tradition states that, sooner or later, a divine punishment catches up with the evil-doer, that tradition holds that the evil-doer does not 'truly and really' cross the limit of the divine law: rather, the evil-doer crosses this limit provisionally, and, therefore, seemingly – for, in the end, the evil-doer meets precisely the punishment that expresses the inviolability of that limit. Men 'ought not' to violate the divine law because, in the last instance, they 'cannot' do so: it is impossible that they should succeed in 'truly and really' violating it.

Kant, too – who, incidentally, fully belongs to that tradition – certainly aims to radically distinguish ought or duty (*Sollen*) from necessity (*Müssen*); however, when he states that virtue renders humans worthy of happiness, he in turn believes that a happy life is precluded to those who transgress the moral duty. As a result, according to Kant, too, every transgression of the law ends up proving to be illusory and provisional, and every 'duty' appears, in the last instance, in the form of a necessity. In spite of the intentions of the Kantian argument, humans 'ought' because they 'cannot' have a happy life without virtue. Since 'happiness is the state of a rational being in the world in the whole of whose existence everything goes according to his wish and will' (*Critique of Practical Reason*, Book II, Chap. II, V), were it possible to be happy without being virtuous, there would be no reason why men ought to follow the moral law.

2

If everything that is willed may be obtained, why should there be any limits that the will ought not to cross? If it is possible to destroy the voice of conscience and the kingdom of God, why should they not be destroyed? Why should a God, who may be violated, not be violated?

This violation and this destruction do not constitute a form of violence, for if violence crosses the limits that *ought not* to be crossed, then, when those limits *are* 'truly and really' crossed, they are not something that '*ought not to have been*' crossed – in such a way that their being crossed lacks precisely the character of violence. If what the will wills is *possible* – that is, if it is possible for the will to obtain what it wills – then the will that obtains what it wills, no matter what that is, does not constitute a form of violence.

3

In order to determine whether what is willed is 'truly and really' possible, the philosophical tradition of the West adopts the *epistéme* as a measure of the consequences that originate in a necessary way from what the will obtains without any mediation. What is 'truly and really' possible is not what is obtained in an immediate way, but that in which what is immediately obtained is not negated and nullified by the consequences that necessarily originate from it, and that are measured by the *epistéme*. The *measuring epistéme* (*metretikè epistéme*), mentioned by Plato in his *Protagoras* (357b), is entrusted precisely with the task of establishing whether what the will obtains is 'truly and really' possible. (A pleasure that is inevitably followed by a great sorrow is not something 'truly and really' possible.)

In our times, however, the twilight of the *epistéme* coincides with the twilight of the epistemic measure of the consequences that originate from what is immediately obtained. The twilight of the *epistéme* consists in the refutation of the existence of every necessary connection between different states of the world – and, therefore, of any connection that should necessarily link what is immediately obtained with its consequences.

That is to say, what is obtained in an immediate way appears as what is 'truly and really' obtained, and, therefore, as what is 'truly and really' possible. No future judgement is any longer awaited, which would compel to give back more than has been obtained. Since there exists no necessary connection between the states of the world, the meaning of a state no longer refers to any other state; as a result, the way in which a state immediately appears constitutes its 'true and real' meaning. It thus may not happen that what at first appeared as something obtained by the will should, at a later point, come to manifest an unavoidable consequence that puts it at risk and nullifies it – a consequence, that is, that would be able to show that, from the standpoint of the total and immutable Order of reality, what was seemingly obtained by the will had in fact not 'truly and really' been obtained.

It is certainly the case that, following the twilight of the *epistéme*, every state of the world issues from nothingness and returns to it, and therefore that everything that is obtained by the will is destined to nothingness – in such a way that the inevitable consequence of everything that issues from nothingness is its own annihilation. (To this extent, there is nothing that is 'really and truly' obtained.) Nothingness, however, constitutes precisely the destiny of all things – and, by avoiding to annihilate other people, it does not follow that one is in some way saved from nothingness; in fact, for the most part, it happens that one may survive and delay one's own annihilation only by annihilating other people.

4

Regardless of how one may solve the problem of establishing whether what is obtained is 'truly', rather than seemingly, obtained, if the will *does* obtain what it wills, any law (any restriction to the will), which forbids the will to will what it wills, merely constitutes a rival and losing will – regardless of what is being willed and obtained. A winning will constitutes a form of violence only from the standpoint of a losing will.

If it is *possible* for the will to obtain what it wills, the violation of the law that forbids this possibility does *not* constitute a form of violence: that is, it does not constitute the crossing of a limit that ought not to be crossed. It is only from the standpoint of the losing will that this limit ought not to be crossed. If the devastation carried out by humans throughout world history *has taken place*, and if it has succeeded – if the annihilating will has *obtained* what it willed – then the laws that have been violated possessed a merely apparent sanctity and inviolability; they constituted a form of will that turned out to be a mere desire, utopia, aspiration or hope. If it was possible to cross the limits that those laws presented as impossible to cross, then, the will that crossed them did not constitute a form of violence.

Crossing what can be crossed does not constitute a form of violence, but an abiding by the nature of what can be crossed. If human beings *can* be killed, killing them does not do them violence, but rather abides by their 'nature': their 'nature' being precisely their being able to be annihilated – according to what, by now, the West thinks of all things.

5

It thus appears that, if violence exists, it may not consist of a will that wills what is possible, but it must rather consist of a will that wills the *impossible*. Violence wishes to cross the limits that are *impossible* to cross, and it wishes to violate the laws that are *impossible* to violate. This means that, if what is necessary is what is impossible to sway, violence wishes to sway *necessity* itself.

Violence does not know necessity *as* necessity: namely, violence does not know that it wills the impossible – for, otherwise, it would not will what it wills. Violence stands in front of necessity, but sees contingency; it stands in front of the impossible, but sees the possible. And yet, violence is such only insofar as what it sees as being contingent and possible (as the possibility of transforming what is contingent) *is* necessary and impossible (namely, *is* the impossibility of transforming what is necessary).

6

The will that wills the impossible does not obtain anything of what it wills. However 'self-evident' may the success of violence be, it is necessary to state that this is an illusory self-evidence. *It is therefore necessary* that

 BEYOND LANGUAGE

what appears should have a different meaning from the one ascribed to it when believing that violence succeeds in obtaining what it wills. The will – which, in willing the impossible, believes to obtain what it wills, and, thus, to be a winning will – deludes itself; but so does the will that believes to have been defeated. *It is necessary* that the world should have a meaning that *differs* from the one that appears in the glorification of victory and in the agony of death and defeat.

If violence exists, it consists of a will that wills the impossible; that is, of a will that wishes to sway what is necessary. Impossibility and necessity, however, are fundamental categories of the *epistéme*; the twilight of the *epistéme* thus also constitutes their twilight. In fact, the twilight of the *epistéme* has a character that is essentially more inevitable and definitive than the one that appears in the forms of contemporary culture that drive the *epistéme* to its twilight. The faith in the existence of becoming – the faith that believes that all things oscillate between being and nothingness – grounds the entirety of the history of the West, and entails the necessity of the destruction of every immutable being: and, thus, of every necessity and impossibility. Only a thinking that does not dwell within the confines of the fundamental faith of the West may think the authentic meanings of 'necessity' and 'impossibility' (and of the *necessity* with which the faith in the existence of becoming entails the destruction of every 'necessity').

7

The essence of the will is to will that something should become something other than itself. That is to say, the will joins the forces that it, itself, regards as being able to make things become other than what they are. Insofar as one conceives of the world as something that can be transformed by a force (and, therefore, also by that force – the will – that consciousness believes it controls), or as something that can transform itself independently of the presence of any external forces, one thinks that all things (bodies, states of mind, relations, thoughts, etc.) can become – and, as a matter of fact, do become – other than what they are. Willing the construction of a house entails willing those forms of becoming-other constituted by, among others, the fact that a construction project becomes real, that the available construction material becomes a determinate material unity, that a land becomes a construction area, and that certain human individuals, according to specific ways and times, become workers.

VIOLENCE AND SALVATION   **7**

Every transformation of the world entails that something should *become other than itself*. Becoming consists precisely of a process through which something becomes other than itself. The accomplishment of that process consists in a situation in which something has become other than itself – and, having become other than itself, is other than itself. Becoming is realized when a thing, having become other than itself, is other than itself.

When becoming is realized – so it is believed – there remains only the other of what, as part of the process of becoming, has been lost. Becoming, however, is not simply a being-other: it consists, precisely, in the becoming-other of a thing. If, once becoming is accomplished, there is only the other, becoming is nevertheless a process in which *a thing* becomes other than itself. When becoming is realized, there can be the other only insofar as *a thing* has become other than itself.

What becomes other than itself comes to coincide with this other. If something, in becoming something other, did not become identical with this other, it would remain self-identical: it would remain different from what is other than itself, and it would thus not become other – there would be no becoming. The fact that something, when it is no longer itself, should have become other than itself (and, therefore, that it should be something other than itself) cannot therefore be thought: it cannot be thought because this something, in order to no longer be itself, has had *itself* to become other than itself. It has had to become identical with what is other than itself; and an identification is a process in which *something* comes to coincide with what is *other than itself*.

Nor, however, may one argue that something becomes other insofar as it *is* other; for, in that case, there would be no becoming-other of that something, but the being-other of the other. Insofar as becoming precisely constitutes the differentiation of a thing, it constitutes an identification of the different. If there were no differentiation, the thing would eternally remain self-identical; if there were no identification of the different, the differents would eternally remain different from one another. Becoming is a differentiation of the identical (namely, of the identical being that becomes other than itself) and an identification of the different (namely, of what differs from its other and becomes identical with this other).

8

However, that something (namely, a being, a determinacy, a meaning) should be other than itself is impossible: it is the very originary meaning of impossibility. That is to say, to be self-identical – to be oneself – is the very originary meaning of necessity. Every thing – every determinacy, every meaning – is itself, and it is not other than itself; it is what it is and it is not other than what it is.

The West is a failed attempt at thinking the self-identity of what is. Indeed, becoming constitutes the realization of an impossibility: the impossible as a result. What is impossible, however, is precisely what cannot be, and, thus, what may not be produced or be a result. Becoming is thus impossible (contradictory, absurd).

Precisely insofar as becoming is impossible, it does not and cannot appear: the variations of the appearing content do not constitute a differentiation of the identical or an identification of the different, but the appearing and disappearing of the identical beings: that is, of the eternals.

That the firewood turns into the ashes does not appear, and nor does the being-ashes of the firewood. Rather, in the circle of appearing, there appears first the identical (that is, the eternal) being of the firewood, then that other identical being that is the burning firewood, and, lastly, that yet other identical being that are the ashes.

The identity of the firewood with the ashes (their being the same) does not and may not appear – it does not and it may not appear that the firewood coincides with the ashes. Therefore, this identity may not appear as the result of a process in which the firewood would turn into the ashes; and, therefore, nor may this process – i.e. becoming itself – appear: for becoming precisely constitutes a resulting identity of the different; namely, that identity as a result. Not only does the being-ashes of the firewood not appear as a matter of fact, but neither *can* it appear, for it constitutes an impossibility: it is impossible that it may be or that it may appear.

9

Starting with Greek thought, the becoming-other of a thing consists both in the annihilation of that thing insofar as it is a self-identical thing, as well as in the issuing from nothingness of that other of the thing with which the thing becomes identical. Indeed, if the thing from which becoming begins, and which is swept over by becoming, did not turn into nothing, that thing would remain self-identical, and there would be no becoming-other. (Precisely for this reason, in certain forms of mythical thought, in which nothingness has not yet been thought, a thing may explicitly persist as part of its other.) And if the other of the thing, with which the thing becomes identical, did not issue from nothingness, that very other would already be together with the thing – and, once again, there would be no becoming-other of the thing. The becoming-other of a thing is conceived of as an issuing from nothingness and a returning to it (the other issues from nothingness and the thing returns to it; the thing turns into nothing in that it becomes identical to what is other than itself). Conversely, issuing from nothingness and returning to it are regarded as the becoming-other of a thing.

However, the contradiction of becoming is not in this way eliminated, but rather driven to its extreme form. Indeed, if a thing, insofar as it is self-identical, were not annihilated, it would not be able to become what is other than itself – and if this other of the thing did not issue from nothingness, this other would already exist, rather than being the result of becoming. We are claiming, however, that the contradiction is thus only seemingly eliminated – and it is, in fact, reinforced.

Indeed, on the one hand, by being annihilated, the thing becomes that other of itself that is nothingness; on the other hand, the other of the thing coincides with the nothingness into which the thing turns in order to become that other of itself (namely, that other of nothingness), which is the other of the thing. By turning into a nothingness, the thing (a non-nothingness) becomes identical with nothingness; it is nothing. And nothingness, insofar as it is what the other of the thing issues from, becomes identical to this other, which is in turn another thing (another non-nothingness).

Or, equivalently: when it is believed that, in order for the firewood to turn into the ashes, it is necessary that the firewood itself, *qua* firewood (*qua* that specific and determinate firewood), should turn into nothing – and that nothingness should turn into the ashes (insofar as the ashes did not yet exist) – first, the firewood comes to coincide with nothingness, and, then, nothingness comes to coincide with the ashes.

And yet, these identifications are precisely what is implicitly thought when it is asserted that becoming constitutes an issuing from nothingness and a returning to it.

10

In the Aristotelian theory of becoming, for instance, becoming consists in the transition of a substrate (*hypokeímenon*) from the privation of a certain form to its possession: through this transition, the substrate comes to acquire that form. A body (the substrate), which warms up, comes to possess the form determined by the heat – namely, it transitions from a privation (insofar as being cold coincides with being deprived of heat) to the possession of that form. This privation (*stéresis*) 'is, in itself, a non-being' (*ésti kath'autò mè ón, Physics* 191b, 15–16). That is to say, the privation of a form in a substrate coincides with the being-nothing of that form – of that form insofar as it belongs to the substrate. In a cold body, the heat is a 'non-being' – namely, it is nothing – and so is the synthesis of the body with the heat: even though this body, as well as the heat *qua* form possessed by a substrate other than the cold body, are not nothing. The cold body is 'potentially' warm precisely because its synthesis with the heat is nothing. However, 'nothing comes out of non-being as such' (*gígnesthai mèn oudèn aplôs ek mè óntos*, ibid., 13–14) – even if it is possible for something to become out of non-being *per accidens* (*katà sumbebekós*, ibid., 15): in the sense that something becomes *per se* out of the substrate, and *per accidens* out of the privation that pertains to the substrate.

Thus, also in the Aristotelian doctrine, while a substrate persists through becoming, becoming itself constitutes a process in which something – namely, the synthesis between the substrate and the privation – becomes something else: namely, it becomes the synthesis between the substrate and a form (and vice-versa). A cold body becomes a warm body: the body persists, but its relation (synthesis) with its being-cold becomes its relation with its being-warm – namely, it becomes something other. This other is something that has been nothing (a 'non-being'): the privation of heat is, in the substrate, a 'non-being' – namely, it is the non-being of the synthesis between the substrate and the heat.

Indeed, had this synthesis not been nothing, the cold body would not have been 'potentially' warm, but 'actually' so. In turn, the synthesis between the substrate and the privation, insofar as it becomes the synthesis between the substrate and the form, must turn into nothing: for, otherwise, when the synthesis between the substrate and the form becomes actual, the synthesis between the substrate and the privation would remain actual, and the substrate would *sub eodem* (namely, actually) lack and possess this form.

Thus, for Aristotle, as well as for the entirety of Western thought, becoming constitutes a process in which a thing may become its other insofar as this very other issues from nothingness and insofar as that thing comes to be annihilated.

11

If violence consists of a will that wills the impossible, and if every form of will essentially consists in willing that something be other than itself, then – since every becoming-other is something impossible (for to be 'impossible' means first of all for something to be other than itself) – every will, *as such*, wills the impossible: and, therefore, every will constitutes, *as such*, a form of violence. The devastation of the planet and of human beings is the visible form of violence; charity, love, and tolerance are its hidden forms.

Thus, even every salvational will – and every 'creational' one – constitutes a hidden form of violence. No creator and no saviour may save us – but not because salvation should be sought elsewhere, but because the notion of salvation itself, as it appears throughout the history of the West, coincides in its essence with that of violence: namely, with a will to transform the world – and, therefore, with a will that wills the impossible.

If, instead, 'salvation' indicates the appearing of a freedom from the will – and this freedom may appear only if the eternity of all things appears (including, therefore, the eternity of this freedom) – then 'salvation' 'saves' from saviours and creators: that is, it saves from God, who is the first Technician, and from Technics, which is the last God. All saviours who save from violence, as well as all creators, share the same soul with violence; and so does every other form of will. The commandment not to kill shares the same soul with murder.

Stating that the world cannot be transformed, however, entails stating that no being may be other than itself; it does *not* entail that we are necessarily bound to what presently appears: that is, it does not entail that experience preserves the order of things that currently appears. The eternals enter the circle of appearing one after the other, and one after the other they leave it. Only the sequence of the appearing and disappearing of the eternals makes the constant change and the unremitting succession of what appears possible and conceivable – that is, makes possible and conceivable 'becoming' itself, according to the authentic meaning that pertains to it, and that remains alien to the West (and all the more so to the East). Becoming is not impossible only if it consists of the appearing and disappearing of the eternals. What renders it impossible is the way in which it is conceived by the West: namely, as an oscillation of beings between being and nothingness.

12

In the Judeo-Christian tradition, as well as in every form of Western culture, being is either a form of will or an object of the will: it is either God's creational will, which confers being to all creatures, or the will of human beings. Since God is an immutable being, he wills himself eternally, and he thus does not want to be other than himself. However, since he 'freely' creates the world, God is (and has always been) different from what he could have been: for, insofar as he creates, he is (and has always been) different from the non-creating God that he could have been. As such, he has always willed for himself to be other than himself, and he has always become something other than himself. Had it been impossible for this 'self', from which God has always already differed, to be – and had it been a nothingness, and always destined to remain such – God would not be a creator out of freedom, but out of necessity.

The faith in the existence of becoming – regarded as the becoming-nothing of being and as the becoming-being of nothingness – constitutes the origin of the West, which thus represents the culmination of the dimension of faith itself; accordingly, everything that comes to manifest itself out of this origin constitutes a form of faith. However, what constitutes a form of will, and, thus, of violence, is not only the *content* of the Christian faith (and of every faith of the West) – the *fides quae creditur* – but faith itself in its being faith – the *fides qua creditur* (and, therefore, not only the essence of Christian faith, but of every faith).

The Christian faith reaches deep in its own essence, and, thus, in the essence of faith as such. According to this essence, faith is 'an argument concerning things that do not appear' (*argumentum non apparentium, élenchos ou blepoménon, Hebrews*, 11, 1). Faith is an 'argument' because it consists of a 'will' to regard the non-appearing things announced by the Revelation as actually existing (cf. Thomas Aquinas, *Quaestiones disputatae*, XIV, *De fide*, art. 1, *responsio*). This 'will' constitutes the 'argument' according to which faith asserts the existence of what does not appear as part of experience or human reason.

This assertion constitutes a 'most certain', 'firmest' and doubtless 'acceptance' (*adhaesio*) (ibid.). These attributes, however, which are ascribed to the 'acceptance' of the content of faith, are attributes that pertain to the knowledge of what appears: namely, of what is visible and self-evident (*apparentia* – the things that appear – have, in the patristic-scholastic interpretation, the stronger meaning of 'self-evident things':

that is, things that are visible to the eye of *scientia*; namely, of the *epistéme*). Faiths do not claim to see what is not visible, or to have access to the appearing of things that do not appear; and yet, they confer to the knowledge of things that do not appear the essential attributes (certitude, firmness, lack of doubt) that pertain to the knowledge of things that do appear. They confer to what does not appear – to what is obscure, not visible and not self-evident – the attributes of what appears: of what is clear, visible and self-evident. Even though faiths do not claim to be able to see the things that lie in the shadows, they ascribe to them the attributes of light: they posit shadows as light, and, thus, they posit light as other than itself; they identify light with the negation of light itself.

Every identification of the different, however, is impossible. Thus, every faith, too, insofar as it is a (having) faith (*fides qua creditur*) – regardless of the configuration of its content – consists of a will that wills the impossible. This will wills, precisely, the achievement of a certainty that would be free of any doubts concerning things that are not visible. Thus, faiths, too – *qua* faiths – constitute a form of violence. (The *epistéme* is a form of violence, too, but not in itself – *scientia qua scitur* – but insofar as it aims to make the becoming of the world conform to its own incontrovertibility; namely, insofar as it aims to control and determine the very becoming that it, itself, as *scientia quae scitur*, aims to posit and incontrovertibly coordinate with an immutable being.)

13

Thus, the form that the faith in the existence of becoming – the dimension within which the entire 'history' of the West appears – takes within Greek thought coincides with the most extreme form that violence can take. Not only does this faith, in its being a faith (*fides qua creditur*), regard what is not self-evident and undoubtable as being self-evident and undoubtable – namely, not only does it will the identification of the different (of what is self-evident and of what is not); and not only does it constitute, in its being a faith in the existence of becoming (*fides quae creditur*), a faith in the identification of the different contents that appear as part of becoming – but it also drives this identification to its extreme form: that is to say, it makes it *infinite*.

The faith in the existence of becoming believes that, when a thing becomes its own other, that thing turns into nothing (since it becomes something other than itself), and nothingness becomes the other of that thing (since this other does not already exist before the result of becoming). To this extent, the faith in the existence of becoming identifies a thing with nothingness, *as well as* that thing with that other thing which is the other of the first thing, *as well as* nothingness with that other thing. (Indeed, if a thing, in order to become another thing, must first of all turn into nothing, and nothingness must first of all become that other thing, it is nevertheless *that first thing* that becomes other than itself; as a result, not only does that thing become that other of itself that is nothingness, but it also becomes that other of itself that is the other thing.)

When a thing turns into nothing, however, the identification of that thing with its other becomes *infinite*, for there is nothing in common between a thing (any thing) and nothingness; on the contrary, a thing and that other of that thing that is the other thing have in common their being a thing – namely, their being a being: something that is not a nothingness.

Insofar as A and B are both beings, the becoming-B of A does not constitute an identification of the different – precisely because A and B, *insofar as they are both beings*, are not different, but the same. When A becomes B, the identification of the different is therefore *finite*: that is to say, it is limited to the dimension relative to which A is not B – the dimension constituted by the *different way* in which A and B are beings.

The difference between A and nothingness, however, does not constitute a finite dimension, for, between A and nothingness (and between any being and nothingness), there is nothing in common and nothing identical. The difference between a being and nothingness is infinite, and infinite is therefore their identification: infinite identification of the different and identification of the infinitely different; and infinite violence that aims to realize that identification.

14

All my writings, from *La struttura originaria* to *The Essence of Nihilism* and *Destino della necessità*, consider this infinite identification of the different, and identification of the infinitely different, which constitutes the content of the faith in the existence of becoming. The way in which this identification is indicated in these texts is fundamentally connected to the one presented in the previous pages. In detail:

Stating that a being issues from its own nothingness, and there it returns, entails stating that there exists a time – when that being is still a nothingness, as well as when that being is once again a nothingness – in which a being (namely, something that is not a nothingness) is nothing. This is a time in which the impossible exists (or, rather, wishes to exist). This is an impossible time: a time that may not exist.

The original identity between a being and nothingness – namely, that being's having been (or still being) a nothingness, from which that being itself issues – is already something impossible. However, it is also something impossible that nothingness (with which that being originally coincides) should become a being – and that this nothingness, having become a being, should *be* a being (namely, that it should be what is infinitely different from itself). That first impossibility is the starting point of becoming; this second one (as considered in the previous pages) is its end point. One entails the other.

In stating that a being returns to nothingness, one states, once again, that there exists an impossible time in which that being, having turned into nothing, is nothing. Remarking this entails remarking that this being-nothing of a being is the result of a process through which a being becomes identical – and, by becoming identical, is identical – with its infinitely other: nothingness. And, conversely, it means remarking that nothingness (with which that being, in turning into nothing, becomes identical) has been a being. In the same way in which it is necessary that a being should have been nothing in order for that being to arise, so is it necessary that nothingness, before arising, should have been a being in order for the nothingness of that being to arise. Thus, the fact that nothingness has been a being is already something impossible, in the same way in which it is impossible that a being, having turned into nothing, should be nothing. Once again, these two impossibilities imply each other, for, when a being is, the fact that nothingness is a being constitutes the starting point of the process through which that being becomes identical, and *is* identical, with nothingness; and this being-nothing of that being presupposes the existence of a time in which nothingness was a being.

At the same time, the infinite identification of the different (all the same, the identification of the infinitely different: a being and nothingness) takes the contradictory character of the identification of the different *as such* to an extreme (infinite) form. Precisely for this reason, the claim developed in the previous pages, according to which every becoming-other is in itself something impossible, has a wider scope compared to the claim developed in my other writings, according to which the specific – ontological – way in which the West understands every becoming-other entails the identification of a being with nothingness. This is the case despite the fact that, as has been said, Greek thought has introduced that specific way in order to attempt to avoid the contradiction that haunts the generic – not yet explicitly ontological – concept of the becoming-other of a thing; and despite the fact that this specific way has become the dominant form of the entirety of Western civilization.

15

All the great forms of Western civilization come to appear as part of the faith in the infinite identification of the different (a faith that, however, is not aware of being a faith in that identification): that is, within the domain of infinite violence. As such, all those forms are forms of infinite violence. The Judeo-Christian tradition, too, is one of these forms: it is futile to think that its God could represent salvation; it is futile to think this of any God, if in 'God' one sees a will and a power that are able to make things become other than themselves. Every salvational will, insofar as it is a will to transform the world, is a form of the will to power: namely, infinite violence. In the civilization of the West, every will is, *qua* will, a will to power and a form of infinite violence.

Nor may it be claimed that the will of the East is free from violence: it is simply violence in its finite and implicit form (in as much as the East and the pre-history of the West do not indicate the infinite opposition of beings and nothingness; in this respect, nor may they express becoming as the identification of beings and nothingness *qua* infinitely different).

The will that appears in the forms of love and tolerance does not constitute less of an infinite violence than the will that appears in the forms of hate and intolerance. Certainly, we all prefer to live surrounded by love and tolerance, rather than hate and intolerance; this preference, however, does not entail that love and tolerance should constitute a way out of violence. Despite their profound difference, love and hate, tolerance and intolerance, share the same soul – that of infinite violence. And violence, regardless of how far removed it is from its manifest forms, may not serve as a way out of violence; and nor may the way that leads outside of violence be a form of becoming – of becoming-other – brought about by human or divine forces: it may not be a will to salvation.

16

Since every becoming-other is impossible, every being is eternal – including the faith in the existence of becoming, and including every form of will. What that faith believes in, and what this will wills, is the impossible; faiths and wills, however, are not impossible: that is to say, they *are*; they are beings.

As the eternal being of the will appears, the eternal spectacles of violence appear (which also include the failures of the will). Not in the sense that the will obtains the impossible, and that the impossible not only is, but is even eternal (the failure of the will, too, is an impossibility, for it presupposes the possibility of the success of the will) – but in the sense that the totality of being responds to the will in such a way that the will believes to have (or to have not) obtained what it willed. The totality of being responds by showing that part of itself (those eternal beings) that the will interprets as being what it has obtained, or failed to obtain. The eternal spectacles of violence appear together with the eternal being of the interpretation of those spectacles given by the will of those who believe either to have succeeded or to have failed.

That the will appears, however, or that it wills this thing rather than that thing, is not something obtained by the will itself: the appearing of the eternal constellations of being belongs to destiny. Destiny sends the eternal being of the will (namely, the will that wills the impossible: the folly), and destiny sends the eternals that respond and correspond to the violence of the will – a correspondence that appears in the twofold form of believing to have and to have not obtained.

But in order for the eternals that are free from the dialogue with violence and the will to appear – is it not perhaps necessary that this dialogue itself should first of all appear? Is it not perhaps necessary that there should come to appear the folly of violence, and the folly of the faith that makes this violence possible?

2 ANXIETY AND WILL TO POWER

1

Western humans, too, seek salvation. First, they believe to find it in God; then, in Technics: in the God of the Greek-Christian tradition, and in Technics as guided by modern science.

Humans feel safe when they succeed in avoiding their destruction; they feel anxious when they cannot find shelter from it. The specific form of anxiety is determined by the specific form of destruction: it depends on the meaning that destruction acquires through the history of humans. What it means 'to destroy' is not an immutable datum of experience. In the civilization of the West, destruction acquires a meaning that had never appeared before. That is to say, destruction is conceived of as a form of annihilation.

In the civilization of the West, anxiety, too, thus acquires an unheard-of meaning: humans feel anxious when confronted with *nothingness*. By thinking for the first time *nothingness* as infinitely opposed to *being* – and thus thinking, for the first time, destruction as annihilation – Greek philosophy brings to light the characteristic form of anxiety of the West: the anxiety over one's own annihilation. In the civilization of the West, every salvation is a salvation from nothingness. This is the constant background as part of which the immense volume of differences and variations that constitute the history of the West has progressively appeared. (Thus, the distinction between industrial and post-industrial society, too, takes place as part of the age of Technics.)

Western society has invoked nothingness – *it consists* of the invocation of nothingness. God and Technics are the two fundamental ways in which the West believes to save itself from nothingness. The anxiety and the apprehension of the age of Technics reveal their authentic meaning only if they are traced back to the originary invocation of nothingness, from which the history of our civilization begins.

2

Technics consists in a coordination of means and ends according to the predictions devised by modern science. By now, it is not only the operations of the industrial world – regulated and driven for two centuries by physical-mathematical (and, later, chemical-biological) knowledge – that have a technological character, but also the systems that in advanced societies render those operations possible: that is to say, the juridical, financial, economic, bureaucratic, military, scholastic and health systems, which tend, ever more decisively, to be organized according to procedures that are characteristic of the application of modern science to industry. 'Technics' consists in the integration of this plurality of systems in a single world Apparatus that tends to overstep State borders and ideological boundaries – despite the fact that the administration of this Apparatus is, to this day, still split across a few large centres of power (the USA, the former Soviet Union, Japan, Europe). The scientific-technological Apparatus consists of the set of most effective means that are today available to humans for saving themselves from destruction and from nothingness. Human beings of advanced societies no longer turn to God in order to obtain salvation, but to Technics. Technics displays a power that is greater than God's (and greater than that of the Gods of the East).

3

That God has been substituted by Technics does not constitute an arbitrary decision: it is not the simple expression of a *fact*, and of a de facto transformation of human minds and customs. God constitutes the unity and culmination of the Apparatus: namely, of the Instrument prepared (*ad-paratum*) by the tradition of the West for finding a shelter from nothingness. The theological Apparatus, however, has proved to be more destructive than the very destruction from which it was supposed to protect. Today, there is a widespread belief that this is also the destiny of the scientific-technological Apparatus. This belief lies at the foundation of the repudiation of the different forms of Western tradition. This repudiation can take root insofar as contemporary culture fails to discern the unavoidability of the process that leads from the theological form of the Apparatus to the scientific-technological one (cf. *La tendenza fondamentale del nostro tempo*, Milan: Adelphi, 1988, and *La filosofia futura*, Milan: Rizzoli, 1989).

The scientific-technological Apparatus constitutes the current form of salvation from annihilation; and yet, the possibility of the most radical annihilation of humans, and of the Earth, lies with this very Apparatus. The enduring possibility of nuclear conflicts (increased by a trend towards the proliferation of nuclear weapons), the pollution of the biosphere and the irreversible depletion of energy resources, the unequal distribution of wealth, the stifling of individual freedoms, and the reduction of the world to scientific parameters constitute the principal aspects of the annihilation of existence. Large sectors of contemporary culture believe the scientific-technological form of the Apparatus to be responsible for this annihilation. It is believed that, by oppressing human beings, Technics, like God, will end up suppressing them. In defending humans from Technics, it is not even suspected that Technics itself is the most accomplished realization of what being human means for the entirety of Western thought – that is to say: being a conscious force that is able to arrange means with the aim of bringing about certain ends.

4

Destruction is feared because the world is believed to change: destruction arises together with the transformation of the world. On the one hand, what is feared is destruction; on the other hand, what is feared is the unpredictability of change: namely, the unpredictability of the events that lead to destruction.

When Greek thought brings to light the meaning of 'being' and 'nothingness', it interprets the change of the world as a process in which things and events issue from their having been nothing and return to it. Due to this interpretation of change, the unpredictability of events becomes extreme. Nothing is more unpredictable than what irrupts and originates from its own nothingness: and, therefore – since what induces anxiety is what is unpredictable – nothing generates more anxiety than the meaning that the change of the world acquires with Greek thought. The anxiety induced by the change of the world becomes extreme: on the one hand because the events that lead to destruction are events that lead to annihilation – that is, they render that destruction extreme; on the other hand, because the annihilating events issue from nothingness, and their unpredictability is therefore extreme.

In the civilization of the West, this extreme character of anxiety originates from the extreme character of destruction – and of creation. As long as destruction is not conceived of as annihilation, things that have been destroyed may come back. Indeed, prior to and outside Greek thought, the birth and death of human beings have a cyclic character. What turns into nothing, instead, is definitively destroyed, and may not come back. In Attic tragedies, Greek thought stares at the annihilation of things, and at the extreme anxiety generated by this annihilation.

5

It is however within these same Attic tragedies – and later in the entirety of Greek thought, as well as in the entirety of the Western philosophical tradition – that it is believed that there may exist a 'remedy' to the anxiety induced by the becoming of the world. 'Predictions' constitutes this remedy. Contemporary culture is still far from understanding that the philosophical contemplation of *truth*, as conceived of by the Greeks, forms the model of scientific predictions – even though science has had to reconfigure its own structure in order to free itself from anxiety.

For the first time, the Greeks think truth as an incontrovertible manifestation of the Meaning of the totality of being. Truth may not be confuted, modified or altered by any change in the world. On the contrary, every change – regardless of how radical it may be – cannot but conform to truth. Truth is what asserts itself over every change and innovation. It may not be overthrown by the annihilation or creation of anything; it *stands*: that is, it does not let itself be confuted. This *standing* of truth is named by the Greeks *epistéme* – a word that is normally translated as 'science', but that in a literal sense indicates a 'standing' (*-stéme*) 'over' (*epí*) what successively irrupts as part of the becoming of the world: a standing that stands over every irruption and dominates it. This means that truth *anticipates* the essence of every future. What appears within truth is the essence of the Whole – which is, therefore, also the essence of any most distant future. The contemplation of this essence constitutes the essential prediction of any possible change of the world, as well as of the most distant future.

Starting with the Greeks, and throughout the entire philosophical tradition of the West, the Meaning of the totality of being – which manifests itself within the dimension of truth – is indicated by the principle according to which God's absolute and immutable power dominates the becoming of the world. 'God' constitutes the essence of being; it constitutes the totality of what, within being, is essential. The essence of human beings is always safe in God's eternity. The positing of the existence of God constitutes the fundamental form of the positing of human immortality: it is the original way in which, in the West, humans have sought salvation from annihilation and from anxiety.

The anxiety of the West is extreme because it points to the extreme destructiveness of the annihilating events: these are events whose unpredictability is extreme insofar as they irrupt and issue from nothingness. Truth constitutes the first grand form of remedy developed by the West for its anxiety. Truth frees from anxiety because, on the one hand, it incontrovertibly predicts the essence of every change, event and future – that is, it frees from the anxiety towards the unpredictable; on the other hand, it frees from anxiety because that essence, which contains everything and which anticipates and predicts every future, coincides with the immutable divine power that dominates the becoming of the world.

The *epistéme* of truth therefore constitutes a standing that dominates the becoming of the world in a twofold sense: becoming is dominated by the incontrovertibility of the *epistéme* – that is, by its incontrovertible *form* – as well as by the divine and immutable *content* that the *epistéme* posits as the foundation of becoming. The Greeks – and, after them, the whole Western tradition – invoke the extreme meaning of destruction, but find salvation in the incontrovertible appearing of the eternity of the essence of every being – and, thus, also of human beings.

6

All the forms of *stability* that have been thought and constructed by the tradition of the West within any religious, economic, juridical, moral, political or aesthetic sphere are thought and constructed in accordance with the stability of the *epistéme*. The Christian faith, for instance, conceives of itself as an absolute certitude of truth; however, it is from the *epistéme* that the Christian faith draws the meaning of 'certitude', of its 'absoluteness', of 'truth' and of God's 'eternity' (as opposed to the 'contingency' of the world). Greek thought constitutes the fundamental structure of what Christianity has been throughout the history of the West; and Christianity has passed on to the masses the salvation that Greek philosophy would set aside for the *élite* of the sages.

For it is indeed true that, for Christianity, humankind has been saved because God became man and died on the cross in order to atone for all sins; but the salvation brought about by God's incarnation is a *consequence* of the originary – that is, epistemic – meaning of salvation. This consists in an unwavering faith in the existence of an eternal God (and this unwavering character corresponds to the incontrovertibility of the *epistéme*), by means of which that faith predicts every essential thing that may occur to humans. Through an alliance with God, humans join the ground of their own salvation from nothingness, and find shelter from any surprise and threat caused by becoming. This alliance is mirrored in all the alliances that, in the West, humans establish with the different forms taken by the notion of stability within culture and social institutions.

7

And yet, the theological-epistemic Apparatus – namely, the instrument and prediction available to Western humans for freeing themselves from the anxiety over their annihilation – fails. The theological-epistemic prediction anticipates the *essence* of events, but not what, of these events, is *accidental*. It is, however, precisely the accidental element that constitutes the fabric of human life; it is with the so-called accidental element that, day after day, humans have to reckon. What, at first, appeared to be irrelevant in terms of essence is that with which humans come to increasingly identify themselves. Humans know that their own essence is safe from nothingness (and they can also believe in the immortality of their individual souls), but they nevertheless keep being confronted with the spectacle of their own births and deaths, of their own issuing from nothingness and returning to it, and of the unceasing annihilation of everything they hold dear in life. They know that God is their ally, and that a divine Providence shelters them from nothingness; but, in the meantime, they *witness* the annihilation of everything they love and that they wish would continue to exist. Life itself, in its immediacy – the collection of the immediate problems of life – consists in this so-called accidental element. Relative to the immediacy of life, this so-called accidental element is what is integral and essential – it is what matters the most. However, precisely insofar as it is regarded as what is accidental relative to a transcendent essence, it remains altogether unpredictable; and the anxiety induced by the unpredictable endures – unhealed. The epistemic-theological remedy appears to modern human beings as an illusion. A new shelter from pain, death and anxiety is required: a new form of domination, a new prediction. Scientific predictions step forth – on their way to the age of Technics.

8

The theological-epistemic Apparatus annihilates what it was supposed to save: human life. Fear, apprehension, anxiety, concern, pain and despair constitute the different ways in which human beings perceive their own destruction – that is, the limit of their own power. They are the forms of unhappiness. On the one hand, unhappiness presupposes the will to live (if there is no will to live, nor is there any anxiety over one's own impotence and destruction); on the other hand, it presupposes the conviction that what is being willed is not being obtained: that is, it presupposes the feeling of one's own impotence in avoiding one's destruction, as well as the destruction of what is loved.

The will to live is a form of the will to power: namely, a will to dominate what threatens life. It is, therefore, a will to salvation. In order to dominate what threatens life, it is necessary to be safe from the destructive force of this threat; in order to be safe, it is necessary to dominate that force. Power and domination are also required in order to save one's soul; what is required in this instance, however, is not only the power and domination exerted by humans, but God's power. In the civilization that today dominates the earth, the salvation of human beings is no longer entrusted to God's power, but to the power of Technics; and yet, the meaning of power is essentially identical for the self-understanding of the epistemic-theological-religious age and for the self-understanding of the age of Technics. To have power is to be safe from nothingness: that is, to dominate the forces that wrest things from nothingness (and drive them back into it).

9

However, the will to power – namely, the will to life, salvation, and domination – may begin to arise only if it is accompanied by a faith that believes that what is to be dominated exists. The faith in the existence of what can be dominated is the faith in the existence of life: for to live is to dominate what constitutes a threat, and be saved from it. It is possible to will to live and dominate only by having faith in the existence of what is to be dominated. If one were convinced that there exists nothing that can be dominated, the will to live and dominate would appear as an absurdity. What can be dominated is available to the forces that want to modify its state: what can be dominated is the becoming of things. There can be a will to power only if there exists the belief that things change, are born, perish, begin and end, are altered, differentiated, corrupted, flow, and become. The faith in the existence of becoming constitutes the originary form of the will to power.

In order to dominate – in order to pick up a stone, to conquer a kingdom, to establish the dominion of Technics over the universe – it is necessary to believe that things are not linked to each other by inseparable connections, and that they are not inseparably connected to an all-uniting ground. In the civilization of the West, the possibility of dissolving the connections that link things together, as well as the possibility of separating things from each other and from any ground, becomes extreme. Becoming achieves an extreme intensity insofar as things may be separated from their own being (when they are annihilated) and from their own nothingness (when they are created). In the civilization of the West, the will to power achieves its culmination insofar as the originary form of the will to power (namely, the faith in the existence of what can be dominated – a faith that lies at the foundation of the will to dominate things) consists of a faith that believes that things (objects, functions, substances, events) issue from nothingness and return to it. The extreme form of the will to power presupposes the extreme form of the faith in the existence of becoming.

10

The extreme form of this faith, however, induces an extreme form of anxiety: that is, the anxiety induced by a destruction that coincides with the annihilation of things. In order to dominate, the will to power frees things and releases them from their connections: that is to say, it frees an extreme danger and threat for existence. The theological-epistemic Apparatus constitutes, indeed, a remedy against the danger, threat and anxiety of becoming, but it also suppresses this very becoming: by anticipating and predicting the essence of everything that is yet to begin and be born, it reduces becoming to something accidental, marginal and apparent. By filling the void of the future and of the past, it erases the nothingness from which things are nevertheless believed to originate and into which they are believed to return.

In order to be powerful, the will to power invokes becoming, and in order to have power over becoming and over its annihilating forces – and thus be saved from them – the will to power of the West first erects the theological-epistemic Apparatus; this Apparatus, however, suppresses becoming, and thus suppresses that very will to power which, in that Apparatus, should have fully accomplished itself. That is to say: in the theological-epistemic Apparatus, the will to power suppresses itself. When the will to power realizes this, it inevitably seeks a different form of remedy against – and shelter from – the anxiety induced by becoming (a becoming that the very will to power needs to invoke in order to have power over things). The will to power heads in this way towards the age of science and technics. It embarks on this path in order to free itself from the contradiction within which it negates and suppresses itself.

11

In the West, human anxiety exhibits, beneath its various forms, a unitary feature that corresponds to the trait that unifies the history of the West: the Greek meaning of becoming. The two different primary forms taken by the anxiety of the West are the anxiety whose remedy is the theological-epistemic Apparatus and the anxiety whose remedy is the scientific-technological Apparatus. The configuration of anxiety is indeed determined not only by what causes it (the unitary trait of Western anxiety arises relative to this determination), but also by the way in which humans find shelter from it. One thing is the anxiety that is driven away by asking for help to God, another is the anxiety that is driven away by asking for help to the instruments of modern scientific technology.

These two forms of the unitary trait of Western anxiety are still intertwined, but God's twilight also constitutes the twilight of the first of these two forms. In modern Europe, the ever more unbearable anxiety induced by God, and by the forms of stability and immutability that in the world mirror the stability of God, comes to be added to the anxiety from which God frees. Afflicted by this additional anxiety, the will to power feels anxious because it feels annihilated by the theological-epistemic Apparatus. Life feels annihilated by what was supposed to defend it and has invoked for this reason. Thus, the will to power feels anxious because the forces that annihilate it are no longer only outside of it, but rather, through their invocation, act in its interior: the will to power becomes in this way a self-annihilating force. The will to power finds a way out of this contradiction by abandoning the theological-epistemic form of the Apparatus.

12

According to the entirety of Western civilization, the Greek meaning of becoming constitutes the ultimate *self-evidence*. The faith in the existence of becoming – considered as an oscillation of things between being and nothingness – conceives of itself as an undoubtable and absolute form of self-evidence; that is to say, it refuses to be considered as a simple faith. According to this faith, it is manifest that things provisionally stretch out of nothingness and return to it. The faith in the existence of becoming is not aware of being the originary form of the will to power. When this will looks at itself, it sees both a force that is able to dominate becoming and a force that is split into human and divine forces. The self-annihilation of the will to power appears to this very will in the form of God's annihilation of human beings. In the eye of the will to power, the self-evidence of becoming is also the self-evidence of that prominent and specific form of becoming that consists in the will with which humans will the domination of becoming.

The theological-epistemic form of the Apparatus must be destroyed because it renders the absolute self-evidence of becoming inconceivable. By rendering this self-evidence inconceivable, this form of the Apparatus annihilates the forces of becoming; by annihilating these forces, it renders the self-evidence of becoming inconceivable. In order to survive, humans (namely, the will to power that, looking at itself, sees itself as 'human') need to destroy God; and, in order to be saved from the annihilation and from the anxiety from which God was supposed to save them, it is inevitable that humans should turn to Technics – as guided by science – and that Technics itself should develop into the civilization of Technics: namely, into the civilization of the scientific-technological form of the Apparatus.

13

Contemporary philosophy is in profound agreement with this form of the Apparatus – even when it presents itself as a critique of the civilization of technics. It is indeed within contemporary philosophy that the awareness emerges that truth (the *epistéme* of truth) does not free from anxiety, but intensifies it. It becomes clear that becoming does not let itself be dominated by the theological-epistemic Apparatus – namely, that becoming remains unpredictable and anxiety-inducing – and that a subjection to this Apparatus erases becoming, the will, freedom, and human life. The becoming of life, which is in fact regarded by traditional thinking as a radical innovation (the innovation produced by what issues from nothingness), is reduced within that thinking to a repetition and imitation of the eternal model that constitutes the essence of the Whole. By anticipating the essence of life, the epistemic prediction not only destroys the anxiety that is intrinsic to life, but also life itself. God (the theological-epistemic Apparatus: the epistemic prediction) constitutes an illusory remedy against the anxiety and annihilation of life; the subjection to this illusory remedy, however, constitutes a real annihilation of life.

14

And yet, the anxiety induced by the unpredictability of the annihilating events may be overcome only through a prediction; predicting what will arise still remains the fundamental condition for the possibility of a defence from the danger of annihilation (an annihilation that destroys life in its entirety as well as its particular aspects).

However, in order for predictions not to annihilate the becoming of life – by anticipating the future – it is necessary that they should *not* be epistemic. That is to say, it is necessary that they should not constitute incontrovertible, definitive, and absolute truths, but *hypothetical* predictions; and it is necessary that the content of these predictions should be amenable to be modified in case it should no longer agree with the changes that *experience* attests in the world.

Not only: in order to be able to free from anxiety, predictions must also *work* – that is to say, they must be able to effectively predict events. Predictions can work precisely because, in being hypothetical, they are not bound to the contents on the basis of which, at each turn, they predict the events of the world: they can thus do away with the contents that turn out to be ineffective for predicting, and include those that afford more extensive and more certain predictions. Predictions that work are quantitative ones (and are therefore finite – that is, they give up the qualitative infinity of epistemic truth) precisely because of their ability to become 'more' extensive and 'more' certain. If a prediction works, insofar as it indefinitely extends the domain of what may be predicted, it also indefinitely extends the domain of the means through which humans realize the ends that they set for themselves – and that they set for themselves in relation to what they are able to predict. This entails that an indefinite increase in the power of the means affords a containment and a gradual reduction of the annihilation of life.

What is required in order to be freed from anxiety is thus a *hypothetical prediction*: namely, one that is open to the rule of *experience* – one which *works*, which has *no* (epistemic) truth, and which does not save from annihilation in an immediate way (that is, through the knowledge that humans are, as to their essence, *already* safe from nothingness), but through a *gradual reduction* of the annihilation – a reduction that tends towards a liberation of humans from death.

This form of prediction constitutes the very soul of modern science, and of the way in which modern science has both taken control of Technics and taken the form of the scientific-technological Apparatus.

The faith in the existence of becoming and the anxiety that originate from this faith – this is the dimension opened up by Greek thought – lie at the foundation of the scientific-technological Apparatus; which, in turn – despite not being aware of it yet – is the most coherent and rigorous expression of that dimension precisely because it provides a shelter from the anxiety of becoming without annihilating the becoming of life.

15

However, in many areas of contemporary culture, the scientific-technological form of the Apparatus is precisely deemed responsible for this annihilation, and it is thus identified with the theological-epistemic form of the Apparatus. It is indeed a matter, for both forms, of an *apparatus*: namely, of a means or instrument prepared (*ad-paratum*) for saving from the anxiety induced by the annihilation of life. In this sense, the first form constitutes a model for the second one. However, the culture that critiques the civilization of Technics, with the aim of saving humans and their individuality, forgets the difference between epistemic and hypothetical predictions: that is to say, it forgets that the latter, contrary to the former, does not erase the nothingness from which things originate – namely, it does not erase the becoming of life (cf. *Law and Chance*, First Part, London: Bloomsbury, 2023). As such, it does not erase the will to power that constitutes life.

In certain parts of the world, individuals undoubtedly tend to shut themselves away and withdraw from the series of arrangements that constitute the expression of the scientific-technological Apparatus. Through this phenomenon, it is possible to witness one of the characteristic features of the so-called 'post-industrial society'. Individuals, and, in particular, the culture that stands up for them, tend to discern in those arrangements the greatest threat to life. 'Humans' and 'individuals' are thus stood up for, without even suspecting the profound *consonance* that exists between Technics and the way in which, from the outset, Western culture has understood 'humans' and 'individuals'.

According to Greek thought, Christianity, and every form of humanism and spiritualism, as well as according to the materialist and sensualist interpretations of human reality, human beings are indeed centres of force that are able to coordinate means in order to realize certain ends. This definition of the human, however, also defines the essence of Technics. Within Western thought, the human has an essentially technical character. It has this character also within the cultural forms that aim to defend the human from Technics, and which, by now, see in the scientific-technological form of the Apparatus the true and fundamental origin of anxiety. The advocates of the human look away from the technical soul of the human as such, and interpret human activities as something that is autonomous, and, thus, irreducible to the essence of Technics and of the Apparatus that expresses it.

Humans and Technics are consonant with one another because the will to power can dominate becoming, after having invoked it, only insofar as it conceives of itself as a centre of force that is able to coordinate means in order to realize certain ends. The process, as part of which the will to power sees itself as 'human', is the very same process within which it sees itself as 'God' and as 'Technics' – that is, as the theological-epistemic Apparatus and as the scientific-technological one.

16

Humans (as individuals, social groups, institutions), God, and Technics share the same soul. Relative to this shared soul, humans do not feel anxious over God and Technics, but rejoice. The anxiety of modern humans over their annihilation by God does not refer to God's technical soul, but to what in God hinders that very soul, and renders any claim to absolute power impotent and unreliable.

Within the civilization of Technics, the will to power achieves its most radical expression. As part of the interpretation given by the cultural tradition of the West (grounded in the theological-epistemic form of the Apparatus), God and humans are inadequate forms of their own technical soul – that is, inadequate forms of the will to power (and so is the notion of the human that certain areas of contemporary culture aim to save from Technics). Insofar as they are interpreted in this way, they are certainly irreducible to Technics, and are annihilated by it.

God and the human of the Western tradition aim, whether united or separated, to *take advantage* of the scientific-technological Apparatus in order to realize the kingdom of God, of the human, or of their alliance. It is thus overlooked that this Apparatus has *in and of itself* a purpose: that is, the indefinite increase of its own power; namely, of the capacity to generally achieve ends. It is thus overlooked that it is inevitable that the will to realize the kingdom of God or the kingdom of the human ends up – by fragmenting itself into a multiplicity of incompatible and conflicting paths (a plurality of conflicting ways of understanding the human and the divine) – subordinating its own purpose to the indefinite increase of the power of the Apparatus (cf. *La tendenza fondamentale del nostro tempo*).

The human, conceived of by tradition and certain aspects of contemporary culture as being irreducible to Technics, is certainly annihilated through this subordination – and so is God (or what remains of God: less and less) insofar as God is forced to speak with a human voice. In this situation – that is, through the forgetting of the shared technical soul of the human, God and Technics – the scientific-technological Apparatus induces anxiety in humans (or in the God that is forced to speak with a human voice); it induces anxiety in humans insofar as they believe to be irreducible to the Apparatus itself. This anxiety, however, is destined to its twilight insofar as it comes to appear that the soul of God and of humans coincides with the very essence of Technics: that is to say, it coincides with the will to power that achieves its most radical expression in the scientific-technological form of the Apparatus.

This form satisfies the most profound need of human beings – for their most profound need is to indefinitely increase their own power. The scientific-technological Apparatus constitutes the most profound fulfilment of the desires of what the West names 'human', 'individual', 'subject', 'person', 'spirit', 'consciousness', or 'soul'. The Apparatus coincides with the meanings of joy and happiness: even though, in order to appear in this form, it is necessary for the 'scientific' culture to become aware of its own historical origins, and leave behind everything that today places it in opposition to the culture of the 'humanities' due to a delay that cannot be ascribed to the soul of science and Technics, but to their contingent configurations.

17

Is this the last word? Far from it. We add here a few remarks, which hint at what is decisive for what has been said so far, and at the distance in which it lies.

The paradise of the civilization of technics is not a utopia. The divide in wealth between North and South of the planet, environmental pollution, the irreversible depletion of resources, and the persistent danger of nuclear conflicts are not due to the scientific-technological Apparatus as such, but to its 'ideological' fragmentation into different centres of power. That is to say, they are due to the 'ideological' organization of the fragments of the Apparatus that are available to those centres of power. The word 'ideology' indicates here the way in which contemporary culture inherits the forms of the cultural tradition of the West, divests them of their epistemic foundation, but does not rethink them according to the procedures of scientific rationality (in such a way that, in the present world, 'ideologies' constitute an echo of the theological-epistemic form of the Apparatus). Technics is in itself already able to solve the fundamental problems connected to the survival of the human race.

Precisely because the purpose of the scientific-technological Apparatus is the indefinite increase of its own power – this is the purpose to which it is inevitable that any other purpose should be subordinated – the Apparatus itself moves towards the overcoming of its own ideological fragmentation (a fragmentation that limits the increase of the power of the Apparatus).

The paradise of technics is the situation in which all human needs may be satisfied: including the need to always have new needs – namely, the need to always transcend every situation and to not withdraw in any 'one-dimensional' world. The will to infinitely increase power satisfies every need for 'transcendence' of any humanism of the West; the infinite increase of power also transcends every physicalist or sensualist configuration of the scientific-technological Apparatus; it promotes the creation of beauty, of feelings, of love, of historical consciousness, and of the philosophical reflection on the essential meaning of the West. It indefinitely amplifies not only every form of human 'having', but also every form of human 'being'. As a matter of principle, there exists no absolute limit that would hinder the development of the Apparatus in this direction. The Apparatus may even transform the human biological structure and thus erase not only the later stages of ageing, but even death.

18

And yet, there does exist an absolute limit that the paradise of technics may not overstep. It belongs to the very essence of the scientific-technological form of the Apparatus. Through this form, humans in the West find happiness and the fulfilment of their desires (and of the desire to indefinitely expand the very dimension of their desiring). However, precisely when, in the paradise of Technics, Western humans become aware of their happiness, it is inevitable that they should encounter that limit.

Scientific-technological predictions succeed in saving humans from the anxiety over their own annihilation because, contrary to theological-epistemic predictions, *they have no truth*. They save precisely because they are hypotheses that work without having the truth of the *epistéme* (namely, a truth that aims to be absolutely undoubtable and irrefutable, and that while aiming, in the tradition of the West, to save from annihilation, annihilates the very will to power that constitutes life). This means that, within the civilization and paradise of Technics, this indefinitely self-increasing power works without having any truth. It means that it cannot be excluded that the happiness that has been obtained should suddenly be lost.

If truth does not exist, every state of the world constitutes an instance of *chance*. Therefore, the fact that scientific-technological predictions work also constitutes an instance of chance (cf. *Law and Chance*, First Part; *La tendenza fondamentale del nostro tempo*, Chapter II, par. 11) – and so does the existence of the lowest level of power, as well as the increase of power, the fact that this increase finds no obstacles, and the existence of the paradise of Technics (should it come to be realized). The very salvation from annihilation constitutes an instance of chance.

When, in the West, humans become aware that this is the meaning of their happiness, each form of happiness – thus also including that of the paradise of Technics – is transformed into the peak of the anxiety that may be experienced by the inhabitants of the West. The peak: for, the greater the happiness, the greater the will to preserve it – namely, to save it from nothingness; but if there exists no truth, the claim that happiness should be safe from nothingness cannot, precisely, constitute a truth. Thus, the will to preserve happiness turns into the fear of losing it – a fear that is all the greater the greater that happiness. This fear reaches a maximum – a peak – if what is at stake is the happiness of the paradise of Technics. Technics may free humans from death, but the immortality that is obtained in this way is threatened by the possibility of its own annihilation. The paradise of Technics constitutes the point at which anxiety becomes extreme. In the interval that separates the present time from the paradise of Technics, every increase in happiness constitutes, at the same time, an incubation of this extreme form of anxiety.

19

Anxiety thus constitutes the destiny of the will to power. The originary form of the will to power is the faith in the existence of the becoming of things: a faith that in the civilization of the West, beginning with Greek thought, believes in the issuing of things from nothingness and in their returning to it. By invoking the creation and annihilation of things, the originary form of the will to power induces an anxiety over nothingness itself, and pre-arranges the remedies that free from it. The two great forms of remedy prepared by the will to power in the history of the West, however, fail: the theological-epistemic form of the Apparatus fails, and so does the scientific one.

The very notion of a 'remedy', and of an 'instrument prepared (*ad-paratum*) for healing', fails. These two forms of the Apparatus exhaust the possibilities of a remedy, for any possible remedy cannot but be an apparatus of truth or an apparatus of untruth. Those who, while remaining within the originary form of the will to power – namely, within the faith in the existence of an annihilating becoming – are under the illusion of saving the human, build nests suspended over the abyss.

Shall we persist, however, in not looking into the abyss of that faith? Shall we continue to believe that the only meaning of truth is the one instituted within the will to power, as part of which truth constitutes a remedy, an apparatus, and a power that grounds and dominates the becoming of things?

3 SCIENTIFIC SPECIALIZATION AND NOTHINGNESS

1

By now, the specialized character of science belongs to the essence of scientific research and scientific practice. There may be no science without specialization: that is, without the application of the experimental method to a specific domain of objects. This is a rather recent occurrence in the history of our civilization. The way in which the specialization of science accounts for the world, however, is much older. It traces back to a time in which humans begin to perceive themselves as autonomous centres of action: that is, ones that are able to *decide*. Decisions render actions autonomous: by acting without deciding, one relies on something else. We are claiming that the meaning of the specialization of science is essentially connected to the meaning of decisions. But what is the meaning of this assertion, and what are its conditions of possibility?

Specializing means turning to a *species*.[1] According to its original meaning, a *species* is an aspect, appearance or figure – something that lets itself be seen. The old Latin verb *specere* means, precisely, 'to see', in the strong sense of 'looking towards an object, an aim or a goal'. In Greek, *sképt-ein* corresponds to *spec-ere*; from an etymological perspective, the Greek word corresponding to *spec-ies* is *skop-ós*, which means precisely 'aim', 'goal', or 'what is observed and looked at'. The visibility of a *species* is what makes it possible to observe that very *species*: to analyse it, control it, measure it, desire it, fear it, reject it or abandon it.

A *species* is all the more visible the less it blends in with what surrounds it; that is, the more it is distinct and separated from its surroundings. A *species* is all the more visible the less what surrounds it overlaps with it by covering and altering it; that is, the more it is kept away and separated from its surroundings. This frame constitutes one of the decisive factors that lead humans out of the existence governed by myths – as part of which, on the contrary, the context infiltrates what it surrounds, overlapping and mixing with it, and as part of which a thing may thus simultaneously be many other things: a tree or an animal, and at the same time a demon; the wind and the voice of the gods; nourishment and the vital force of the ancestors; a cleft in the earth and a maternal womb.

The force with which humans have freed themselves of this mode of feeling has driven them towards the opposite end. The conviction gradually arises that the necessity of keeping the context separated from the thing (so that the latter may be visible, and constitute precisely a *species* or a *skopós*) is equivalent to the independence of the visibility of the *species* from the visibility of the context. The belief in the existence of a *difference* between things (for instance, between a cleft in the earth and a maternal womb) becomes the belief that the visibility of a thing is independent of the visibility of its context, and, more generally, of the visibility of other things. In the meantime, the scope of the physical meaning of 'visibility' widens, and what is visible comes to be identified with what is observable, knowable and experienceable. The visibility of a *species* is regarded as being independent of the visibility of other *species*; when modern science rigorously understands this independence, scientific specialization comes to light – precisely in *isolating* a part (*species*) of reality, and separating it from the other ones with the aim of observing its configuration and its behaviour without any limitations. The absence of limitations in the observation is proportional to the degree of separation and isolation of what is observed.

The criterion for the demarcation of a part – insofar as this part is considered by the specialization of science – is given by the principle according to which a demarcation has a scientific value only if disregarding the context entails neither altering the knowledge of the part nor preventing that part from being used towards the goals that research has set for itself. While this principle is clear for what concerns its abstract formulation, certain difficulties arise in trying to apply it. As a matter of principle, science does not exclude the possibility that a specific portion of the context, which was at first regarded as being inessential for the isolated part, should later come to appear as being essential, and that it should therefore not be possible to disregard it; the general direction of the development of science, however, consists in a gradual expansion of the contexts that may be disregarded by specialized research.

2

Humans no longer let themselves be guided by myths as soon as they begin to perceive themselves as centres of action that are able to *decide*. Even when they structure their existence according to a mythical meaning of the world, humans undoubtedly still decide and act: they reap the fruits of the earth, they hunt and tame animals, they build shelters, they mate, they fight enemies. Within the sphere of their actions and decisions, however, humans perceive the presence of the divine Forces that sustain the universe. Humans do not perceive their actions as being *their own*, but as the very acting of the Whole. Precisely for this reason, humans, in acting and deciding, do not feel separated and isolated from the Whole; in this sense, strictly speaking, they do not 'decide'. Once again, language reveals the meaning that humans ascribe to the world. The Latin word *decido* signifies first of all – that is, even before 'taking a decision' – 'I cut' or 'I cut away from'. *Decido* is indeed equivalent to *de-caedo*, which means 'I strike, in order to *separate* what is struck *from* what it was linked to'. Precisely for this reason, *caedo* also means 'I kill' [*uccido*], which in turns originates from the Latin word *oc-cido*, once again meaning *ob-caedo* (where the *ob-* indicates *against* what the *caedere* is performed).

This proximity of deciding and killing may seem contrived. It is commonly held that decisions and deciding humans perform a separating act, and that it is this act that separates the choice that has been taken from the other alternatives, thus freeing from indecision. When humans are undecided, the alternative choices are equipotent, and, therefore, they stand united before the will: thus united, they preclude any action. Decisions separate the unity formed by the equipotent alternatives that render acting impossible. One may say – by means of a metaphor that, however, seems too forceful to be instructive – that decisions 'kill' one of the alternative choices.

And yet, this way of accounting for decisions remains at a superficial level. Every decision precludes a mode of life – both for those who decide and for those who are affected by the decision. The set of decisions that determine our lives preclude the life or the lives that we could have lived or let others live, and to which we often look with a regret and a grief that, however different, often have the same intensity of the regret and the grief that we feel towards the lives that have actually been destroyed (by others or by nature). Stating that the act of deciding kills a life that could have been lived is not an overstatement.

We have, moreover, begun to shed light on a meaning that is even more profound than the disquieting proximity between deciding and killing – a meaning that dictates that what is separated is not only the unity of the equipotent choices that keep humans undecided, and that what is killed is not only a life that *could* have been lived, but the life that is *actually* being lived. Language expresses this profound correspondence between deciding and killing insofar as the latent knowledge of the language that forms these words is still directed at the Whole that appears within myths, which is a *living* Whole; within this Whole, every part is essential for the other ones, and the separation and isolation of two or more parts coincides with their being killed – namely, with their no longer being what they were when they were united (i.e., alive). When, as part of the existence governed by myths, humans perceive in their acting and in their willing the action and the will of the Whole, their actions do not turn to the world by separating and isolating its parts: their actions do not separate *from* the Whole because their actions constitute an action *of* the Whole. In this case, the alternative choices constitute the pure negativity of a life separated from the Whole: acting does not preclude anything, but prevents from sinking into the darkness. It is not a matter of preventing potential lights from shining, but of keeping close to the light.

Afterwards, there come the epochs in which humans no longer perceive the Whole in their actions, but begin to perceive themselves as autonomous centres of acting and willing. This is a process that begins from within the very existence governed by myths, as soon as it appears impossible that *every* action, even the most irrelevant and trivial one, should constitute an instance of the acting of the Whole – and, in particular, as soon as humans come to reflect on *transgressions*. These are kinds of actions that diverge from those in which the social group perceives the totality of Forces that govern the world as playing the most prominent role. In this way, myths create a form of antagonism in the very interior of the divine Forces, and begin to distinguish between a 'sacred time' and a 'profane' one. In the former, humans perceive, as part of their actions, the acting of the Whole and of the divine Forces that support it; in the second one, as part of their acting, humans only perceive their own initiative. By starting to see in themselves a principle of action, humans take the first step on the path that leads them to regard themselves as being the *only* principle of action. The scientific-technological Apparatus that today dominates the earth constitutes the way in which humans, by overcoming even modern 'individualism', come to objectivise and posit themselves as the ultimate principle of acting and deciding.

Along the path that leads to the dominion of Technics, the more humans perceive themselves to be autonomous, the more they perceive the Whole to be outside of them; and the more they perceive themselves as doers and masters of their actions (and, thus, the more they perceive themselves as being responsible for these actions), the more their acting becomes a form of deciding. If the Whole is perceived as a living unity, the conviction of being a – however limited – autonomous principle of acting is perceived and expressed precisely as a *de-cision*: namely, as an isolation or separation that *kills* [*uc-cide*] this living unity. The proximity between deciding and killing is a generalized phenomenon in Indo-European languages. The Greek verb *kríno* means, at the same time, 'I separate' and 'I decide'; the German verb *entscheiden* ('to decide', where the prefix *ent-* corresponds to the Latin *de-*) is formed by the verb *scheiden*, which means 'to separate'.

3

That deciding is a form of separating, however, is not only to be learned from language. In our civilization, deciding the simplest or most complex thing entails being convinced of having and being *everything* that is required for the realization of what has been decided, and being convinced that nothing else is required. I decide to pick up an object (I decide: namely, I do not find myself unknowingly picking it up). As part of this decision, the existence of the object is not decided (I do not decide that the object exists), and nor is the existence of the hand with which I pick up the object (I do not decide to have that hand): I decide that the object should come to be found in my hand. However, if I were convinced that the object is indissolubly connected to its current place, I would not decide to pick it up. Indeed, insofar as we are convinced that the sun cannot be reached by extending an arm or by standing on our tiptoes, we never decide to grab the sun. (Even madmen, if they decide to grab the sun, they do so because they believe to be able to reach it by extending their arm, and not because, in spite of being convinced that the sun is unreachable, they nevertheless try to get ahold of it.) If I were convinced that the object that I want to pick up is under the sway of some (natural, human or divine) force that is not in my control, and which is able to prevent me from interacting in any way with the object, I would not decide to pick it up. I may certainly try to overcome that force; but, then, what I decide is not to pick up an object, but to try to overcome the force that prevents me from doing so.

Thus, I decide to pick up an object *only* if I am convinced that its current state (for instance, its being placed on a table) is not linked to the rest of the world by means of an indissoluble connection; and, therefore, *only* if I am convinced that this state is separated and isolated (or can be separated and isolated) from its current context. Regardless of how many connections may link the object on the table to the rest of the world, I decide to get ahold of this object only *if I am convinced* that those connections may *all* be dissolved by means of the gesture with which I grab the object with my hand. I decide to grab the object because I am convinced that, *insofar as it lies in my hand*, it is separated and isolated from the rest of the world, and it is entirely determined by me.

In feeling autonomous and free, modern humans do not perceive the presence of the Whole in their decisions; their acting is neither the acting of a divine Whole nor its reflection; and, thus, the act of deciding coincides with that of separating a part from the Whole. Before building a hydroelectric power plant, which separates the water of a river or a lake from its original state (linked with the rest of the world), the very *decision* to build a power plant *assumes* that the water is originally separated from its context. That is to say, that decision assumes that the water is something that can be known and used independently of all the infinite domains of the universe that do not feature in the *finite* set of factors that the available scientific knowledge regards as being connected with the construction of a hydroelectric power plant. Deciding means being convinced of constituting an autonomous centre of action – one on which what is decided, as well as the thing that is affected by the decision, uniquely depends. In the same way in which the specialization of science isolates a *species* from its context, and posits the knowledge of this *species* as being independent of the knowledge of its context, so decisions consider the parts they act upon as being isolated from, and independent of, their own contexts. That is to say, decisions believe to be able to dissolve all the connections that, as a matter of fact, link a part with its context. As such, decisions regard the knowledge of the context as being irrelevant for the knowledge of what they aim to transform. The specialization of science constitutes the most radical form of deciding.

4

In remarking that the specialization of modern science realizes in itself – and in a radical way – the very isolating attitude that determines how human deciding and human acting are constituted in the forms of existence no longer guided by myths, we have not yet addressed the essential aspect of the matter at hand. If every decision assumes that the things of which, and about which, it decides are separated from the rest of the world, *how are things in the world?* Are things in the world connected or separated? The question may not be avoided.

There is no doubt that humans decide – and that by now they decide about everything – only insofar as they regard the world as an assemblage of parts that are not linked with each other by means of indissoluble connections. If the world appeared as an infinite net, whose nodes are things and whose threads may not in any way be torn apart, humans would not be able to take even the most irrelevant of decisions – for even in that decision, in trying to take possession of the smallest node of the net, they would be forced to seize all the infinitely many other nodes: that is to say, they would have to transform the infinite Whole. We may decide to pick up an object only if we are convinced that the node to which it corresponds is linked to the other nodes of the net by threads that can be torn apart. But if it were truly impossible to corrupt and violate these threads, the act of deciding would, on the contrary, constitute the illusion of tearing them and violating them; the world obtained by means of decisions would be illusory, and so would the world obtained through that act of deciding constituted by the specialization of modern science.

Scientific specializations and scientific decisions are possible only if there exists *no necessary* connection between the things that they are aimed at. A reflection on the meaning of 'necessity' begins with philosophy – that is, with the originary form of Western rationality. Myths effectively conceive of the Whole as a living being – namely, as a domain whose parts are indissolubly linked with each other. Myths, however, do not state what the 'indissolubility' of that link consists in; they do not state it because they first of all do not state what constitutes the indissolubility of the links that connect the words of their own speech. Since they do not indicate the meaning of the necessity of their own speech, neither can they indicate the meaning of the necessity of the connections that link parts of the Whole to the Whole itself. It is precisely for this reason that the birth of philosophy coincides with a refutation of the reason and of the universe of myths, and with a pursuit of the authentic *necessity* of reason and of the world. (This is also the necessity according to which it is possible to determinately chart the limits of the Whole.)

From the Greeks to Hegel, philosophical thought is convinced of having uncovered the authentic meaning of necessity. And yet, it is precisely as part of philosophical thought that, for the first time – and in the most definitive and self-conscious way – human acting is conceived of as a form of deciding. It may be stated that what still today is asserted concerning human actions lies, in its essence, within the confines of what Plato and Aristotle have first thought of it. As part of the philosophical tradition of the West, necessity and decisions may coexist because philosophy, with its own birth, has brought to life the radical meaning of necessity as well as the radical meaning of *becoming*. In fact, it is precisely because philosophy thinks becoming in a radical way that it comes to think necessity in the same radical way. It is then necessary to understand that philosophical thinking, in bringing to light the radical meaning of becoming, has opened up a dimension that renders possible decisions, the separation of things, and, therefore, the very specialization of modern science.

5

Specializations, as we have said, have a scientific value only if the separation of a *species* from its context does not alter the *species* itself, and does not compromise the aims that are to be achieved by means of its transformation. This is possible only if there exists no necessary connection between the *species* and its context. Decisions, in turn, are possible only if the *species* – of which and about which one decides – is not linked in a necessary way to the world. What is required, however, in order for this necessary connection *not* to exist?

If the things of the world had always existed, and if they were to forever remain in the state in which they are found at a certain time, it would not be possible to separate them from that state (that is, it would not be possible to transform them). Nor would it therefore be possible to think of them as *separable*: that immutable persistence would constitute the connection that links them in a necessary way. In order for necessary connections *not* to exist, it is necessary that the world should change and transform itself. This is necessary, but not sufficient; for it is conceivable that a necessary connection could link the starting and end points of a transformation. One speaks, indeed, of necessary transformations. In a transformation in which the starting point is connected in a necessary way to the end point, however, the state that constitutes this end point *is already in some way present* in the state that constitutes the starting point. A necessary connection between two points entails, indeed, that one may not be thought without the other, and that, therefore, one should in some way be present in the other one. In a transformation in which the starting and end points are connected in a necessary way, the state that constitutes the starting point *already* contains in some way the end point, and the state that constitutes this end point *still* contains in some way the starting point. 'In some way': for if the starting point already contained the end point 'in every way' (that is: plainly, absolutely) – and if the latter still contained the starting point 'in every way' – there would be no transformation. In order for a transformation *not* to constitute a necessary connection, it is therefore necessary that the starting point should not already contain the end point *in any way*, and that the latter should no longer contain *in any way* the starting point. However, stating that something *is not present in any way* in the starting and end points of a transformation means that *there is nothing* of that something at the starting and end points – that is to say, it means that, at the starting and end points, *this something is nothing*. This means neither that at the beginning of the transformation there is nothing nor that at the end of the transformation nothing is left of the world. A transformation, however, does *not* constitute a necessary connection only if what ends at the end point is nothing at the starting point, and if what starts at the starting point is nothing at the end point. Strictly speaking, therefore, there are no starting and end 'points', but starting and end *planes*.

In a transformation, a point in the starting plane is set into a motion that leads it to be *nothing* at the end point, and a point of the end plane is the result of a motion that originates from a starting plane in which that point is *nothing* (granting that not every point of the starting and end planes are nothing).

The word 'nothingness', however, may not be understood indeterminately, or according to the relative and vague meaning that is used in everyday language. 'Nothingness' means: absolute absence of everything; absolute negativity; negation of everything that one way or another *is*. Everything that one way or another *is* has been named by Greek philosophy *tò ón*, a *being*; nothingness has been understood as a non-being, *tò mè ón*. Greek philosophy has once and for all understood transformations as transitions from a non-being to a being, and from a being to a non-being – or: from nothingness to being, and from being to nothingness.

Let us review what has been said. There can be decisions and scientific specializations only if the parts upon which these are exerted are separated from the Whole. However, they may be separated only if they are not linked by means of a necessary connection. But, for there to be no necessary connection, it is necessary that the state of the world should not be immutable; that is to say, that it should change and transform itself. A transformation, however, may constitute a non-necessary connection only if the end point is not in any way already present in the starting point, and only if the latter is not in any way still present in the end point. But the starting and end points are not present in any way in each other only if the end point is still nothing at the starting point, and only if, at the end point, the starting point no longer is – that is, it has turned into nothing. In order for decisions and scientific specializations to be possible, it is therefore necessary to think the becoming of the parts of the world as a transition from nothingness to being and from being to nothingness. If the meaning of nothingness is not thought in a radical way, not only is it not possible to understand the essence of the specialization of science, but neither is it possible *to put it into practice*. If one ignores the radical meaning of nothingness, one simply *attempts* to put this specialization into practice.

This series of concepts may also be expressed by stating that, for there to be no necessary connection between two things, it is necessary that they should be 'contingent': that is to say that, while being, they may not be (namely, they may turn into nothing), and, while not being (namely, while being nothing), they may be; or that, while being, they could have instead not been (namely, they could have remained nothing), and, while not being (namely, while remaining nothing), they could have instead been. The contingency of things is the condition of possibility of their oscillation between being and nothingness – that is, of their becoming. There may be no necessary connection that links what exists with something that exists insofar as it has been a nothingness, will again be a nothingness, or could have remained one.

6

The radical meaning of nothingness is not something that we have devised here in order to make it possible to conceive the specialized character of modern science. The radical meaning of nothingness has been brought to light for the first time by Greek philosophy. Precisely for this reason, at the end of Paragraph 4, we have stated that Greek philosophy, by bringing to light the radical meaning of becoming, has opened up a dimension that makes possible decisions, the separation of things, and the specialization of modern science. If the world constitutes a domain in which its parts arise from their own having been nothing, and return to this nothingness, there can be no necessary connection between the parts that already exist and those that arise from nothingness, as well as between the parts that still exist and those that return (or may return) to nothingness. A profound consonance links philosophical and scientific thinking in the West.

Certainly, humans decided and regarded partial areas of reality as being isolated from the Whole even before Greek philosophy had brought to light the radical meaning of *nothingness* – and of *being*. Leaving aside the fact that this is a marginal stance in relation to the centrality of the mythical one, which points in the opposite direction, if humans do not have the radical meaning of nothingness before them, they are not able to radically separate things; therefore, on the one hand, they are not able to decide in a radical way, and, on the other hand, they are not able to establish the conditions required for the specialization of modern science. The power of scientific specialization results from the radical way in which humans decide and act within it. The West acts and decides in relation to the nothingness that belongs to the essence of things, and which makes things mutually indifferent and isolated. By now, according to Western culture, nothingness belongs to the essence of all things: for all things are regarded as being subject to becoming – as being temporal, historical, contingent, and transient. This is the unavoidable consequence and result of the way in which Greek philosophy has paved the way to the West.

Nevertheless, Greek philosophy, followed by the entirety of the Western philosophical tradition, invokes not only the radical meaning of *becoming*, but also that of the *immutable beings* – and, thus, of necessary connections. It posits the immutable – the divine – *beyond* becoming, as the very ground for the possibility of thinking becoming: that is to say, it thinks that if the world of becoming is the world of separateness, it is nevertheless, as a whole, connected in a necessary way to the world of the immutable – insofar as it may exist only if the immutable exists.

Contemporary thought, on the other hand, has come to refute the existence of *every* necessary connection, and, therefore – and first and foremost – also of the one that, in the philosophical tradition, links becoming to the immutable. As such, the world of becoming constitutes the totality of what exists; *all* things are separated from one another, and *all* things are mutually accidental and indifferent. As such, this separation fragments both the macro-physical world and the micro-physical one, both the parts of reality that are infinitely large and those that are infinitely small. There exists no necessary connection not only between galaxies and dimensions that are infinitely distant in time, but also between the elements that constitute the infinitesimal particles of matter, or between an instant in time and the one that immediately follows it. The statistical-probabilistic character that, by now, *all* scientific laws are coming to acquire constitutes precisely a rigorous expression of the absence of any necessary connection between the entities governed by these laws. Heisenberg's 'indeterminacy principle' excludes, in its essence, the possibility of any necessary connection between any state of the world and the state that immediately follows it. Once again, the rejection of the absolute character of the 'principle of causality' – and the reduction of this principle to a record of empirical regularities – excludes that there may exist a necessary connection between coexisting parts of the world. The world is an assemblage of juxtaposed parts that are, originarily, mutually independent and mutually indifferent.

7

All of this means that decisions, actions, and scientific specializations are forms of separation that, in spite of reaching in Western civilization as radical a character as had ever appeared in human history, *do not perform any violence* in the world that this civilization brings to light. The specialization of science does not only constitute a form of *thought*, but also a separating *decision* and *action*. If there exists no necessary link between things, it follows that *no* separating thought, *no* decision, and *no* action alters or attempts to alter the order of things: no actual separation of connections constitutes a violence on the order of the world as such – for that order does not exist, since it would be one of the names used to indicate the necessary link between the parts of the world. If there exists no necessary connection, the authentic ground on the basis of which the moral and religious traditions of the West condemn the destructiveness of certain actions comes to disappear. *Every* destruction, regardless of how heinous it may be from the standpoint of the tradition of the West, is a form of *de-struere* (where *struere* means 'to lay in strata', like '*sternere*', whose supine form is precisely *stratum*): that is to say, a form of separation of the *strata* – which, through their *stru-cture*, constitute a thing (be that alive or not) – from (*de*) each other. This extreme separation of the strata separates them either by annihilating them or by annihilating their structure (namely, the contingent unity in which they are found). *Every* separation is innocent – that is to say, it does not undermine any connection that would claim to link the strata of a thing to one another in a necessary way. It does not undermine them because, according to the dominant mode of thinking of the West, no such connection may exist. At this point, the act of recalling the disquieting proximity between *de-ciding* and *killing* [*uc-cidere*] – as well as the immanent presence of that proximity in the radical and extreme form of deciding constituted by scientific specialization – may no longer appear as a more or less disguised condemnation of modern science (in relation to the fundamentally specialist character of its procedures). Every form of killing is innocent, and so is every transformation of human beings that aims to transform their structure in order to eliminate certain strata or in order to create new ones. Once the existence of any necessary connection has been refuted – namely, once nothingness has been posited as being part of the essence and being of all things – science (*qua* apparatus concerned with its own specializations, and with the technical aspects through which these specializations come to operate on things) may no longer have any qualms about destroying the old world and creating a new one (or, in fact, infinitely many new ones).

These are the unavoidable consequences of the thinking that dominates Western civilization and that makes the specialization of science possible: the thinking of *nothingness*. Certainly, we are dismayed before these consequences. Dismay, however, may constitute the way in which the mode of feeling the world that is specific to the Western tradition comes to be expressed, but to which contemporary culture has refused any value by rejecting its ground: by rejecting the existence of any necessary connection between the parts of the world. Our moral demands may not constitute a criterion for judging things – because the dominant thinking of Western civilization conceives of things in a way that divests these demands from any force. If nothingness belongs to the essence of things, every set of morals is destined to its twilight: morals are founded on the notion of a necessary connection, which is eliminated by the presence of nothingness in the world.

Precisely at this point, however, there arises the authentic task of the thinking that addresses the question of the essence of modern science. It is not possible to think this essence while disregarding the very *nothingness* that comes to light at the origin of our civilization – and whose coming to light constitutes, in fact, that very origin. We are asserting this in a sense that is profoundly different from the one considered by one of the most prominent contemporary thinkers – Martin Heidegger. Heidegger does not take into account the absolute negativity of nothingness, which has been thought for the first time by the Greeks. He is thus not able to discern the path that leads from that absolute negativity to the extreme radical character of the decisions that are peculiar to scientific specializations and to humans in the West. Even Heidegger's thinking operates entirely *within* the framework as part of which the West understands the relationship between things and nothingness. For fundamentally different reasons, however, and in fundamentally different ways – which we have attempted to indicate – the problem that Heidegger had caught a glimpse of comes here in full light. Science may not comprehend its own essence independently of the nothingness that philosophical thought has invoked since its own origin. Not only is science unable to comprehend its own essence: in being unable to comprehend it, science may not even unfold from it all the practical possibilities that determine its own dominion over the world.

Over and above this problem, an even more radical one comes to light: the problem of the *truth* of the way in which the West has understood the relationship between nothingness and things. What, in the last instance, we can think of the truth of science depends on the solution of this problem.

PART TWO

1 NIETZSCHE AND GENTILE

1

Philosophical thinking inaugurates and protects the dimension of becoming. The entire civilization of the West – including the specialization of science, which forms the soul of the civilization of technics – is grounded in that dimension.

From the standpoint of Greek thought – and of the whole metaphysical tradition up to Hegel – the becoming of beings, which is regarded as an irrefutable self-evidence, would be an absurd (or contradictory) concept if there existed no immutable dimension of being. After Hegel, philosophical thinking has instead ever more radically refuted every immutable structure – be that structure transcendent or immanent relative to becoming itself. This destruction of the immutables – which is the trait shared by the entirety of contemporary philosophy – does not consist in a mere will to refute: that is, in an abstract and arbitrary scepticism. The immutables include the God of the philosophical-theological tradition of the West, natural and social-economic laws, the laws of morals and art regarded as natural laws, every ultimate truth, every absolute knowledge and incontrovertible principle of reason, as well as every essence, ground, and centre of reality. The refutation of the immutables carried out by contemporary culture does not constitute an abstract and arbitrary form of scepticism, insofar as contemporary philosophy perceives – in many different but complementary ways – that becoming itself would be inconceivable if an immutable being were to exist. The meaning of this 'inconceivability' certainly still tends to remain implicit in contemporary thinking. What is completely explicit, however, is the following: that the refutation of every immutable being is carried out because it is believed that the existence of an immutable being would render the existence of becoming impossible – that is to say, it would render impossible the existence of what contemporary philosophy, *too*, regards as the irrefutable and ultimate form of self-evidence.

2

The becoming of beings has been regarded as an irrefutable and ultimate self-evidence since its invocation by Greek ontology. Before the Greeks, becoming does not appear: that is to say, the becoming to which the entirety of Western civilization turns, and as part of which it dwells, does not appear. According to the Greeks, becoming is the 'unity of being and non-being'. This unity may come to light only if the notions of 'being' and 'non-being' have first come to light – that is to say, only if the radical and unheard-of meaning that Greek thought attributes to these words has appeared (without this meaning the very civilization of technics, as culmination of the civilization of the West, is inconceivable). According to Plato, what becomes is *háma ón te kaì mè ón* (*Republic*, 478 d), 'a being and, at the same time, a non-being'. This unity of being and non-being *anánke phanênai* (ibid., 479 b), 'necessarily appears': in the sense that 'it is necessary to *acknowledge* that it appears'; that is to say, its appearing, visibility and self-evidence may not in any way be confuted. According to the West, the ultimate form of self-evidence coincides with what the Greeks begin to see (or, rather, begin to believe to see).

The Greek meaning of becoming persists throughout the history of the West; what changes is the dimension as part of which that meaning comes to be instantiated. Becoming is first conceived of as a reality that is external to thought, and independent of it, and it is then identified with the becoming of thought itself – the becoming of the subject, of the will, and of experience – to then, lastly, be traced back to the becoming of language. Nevertheless, what is in each case located and displaced across such different sites is still the Greek meaning of becoming: the unity of being and non-being – being that coincides with an issuing from nothingness, and a returning to nothingness that coincides with an issuing from being; *hústeron gígnesthai próteron ouk ónta* (*Sophist*, 265 c), and, therefore, *hústeron apóllusthai próteron ónta*.[1]

3

According to the dual conviction that becoming, thus understood, constitutes the originary form of self-evidence, and that the existence of any immutable structure is incompatible with the existence of becoming, contemporary philosophy has come to a most uncompromising destruction of every immutable being. The faith in the existence of becoming is the fundamental faith of the West; the assertion of the impossibility of reconciling the existence of becoming with the existence of any immutable being is the distinctive feature of contemporary thinking – a feature that is shared by the (seemingly) most diverse philosophical positions. A reflection on Friedrich Nietzsche and Giovanni Gentile's thinking may indeed exhibit the presence of that essential feature – shared by all the different forms of contemporary thinking – through a discussion of two thinkers who are seemingly far removed from one another, and who instead singularly converge as to the logic that underlies their enquiries.

4

In the essay 'On Truth and Lie in a Nonmoral Sense' (1873), Nietzsche writes:

> Only oblivion of that primitive world of metaphors, only the congealment and solidification of that original mass of images pouring forth as a fiery liquid out of the primal force of human imagination, only the invincible faith that *this* sun, *this* window, *this* table is a truth in itself – in short, only forgetting that they are themselves subjects, and *artistically creative* subjects at that, enables humans to live with a degree of peace, certainty and consistency.

The 'subject' mentioned here is not the subject *qua* metaphysical and moral unity against which Nietzsche addresses his critique. As such a metaphysical and moral unity, the subject is itself one of those 'truths in themselves' that come to be constituted through the self-forgetting of the 'artistically creative subject'. The passage that we have quoted states:

1 That the 'artistically creative subject' is the primordial creative act that produces the world, as a world of images and metaphors.

2 That this production of the world – its 'pouring fourth as a fiery liquid' – coincides with the becoming of the world.

3 That this creative act may forget itself, and that, therefore, it may equally stand before itself outside of this forgetfulness – as it is the case for the act of thinking, through which Nietzsche recalls and indicates that primordial creative act and the process through which that act comes to forget itself.

4 That, when this creative activity forgets itself, the images and the metaphors that it produces appear, as part of an 'invincible faith', as 'truths in themselves' – that is to say, as realities that are independent of (and unconditioned by) both that primordial creative activity and the faith that believes in them.

5 That the self-forgetting of this 'artistically creative subject' coincides with the very believing, with an 'invincible faith', that the objects of the world in which we live are 'truths in themselves'; this faith constitutes the positive aspect of the negativity of that forgetting.

6 That, as part of this self-forgetting of the creative activity, the becoming of the world (its 'fiery fluidity') 'congeals and solidifies': namely, it takes the form of a reality that does not and has not become. It takes the form of a multiplicity of stable and permanent objects (this sun, this window, this table) that are believed, 'with an invincible faith', to be 'truths in themselves'. Relative to that originally creative activity, these 'truths in themselves' appear as immutable realities.

7 That the originally creative activity constitutes a form of 'imagination' and 'art', precisely because it is creative: that is to say, precisely because it does not have to conform to any pre-existing model; for something like a pre-existing model appears only insofar as the original creativity forgets itself, and believes that the things of the world exist, and constitute truths in themselves – that is, models that pre-exist everything that must conform to them.

8 That when the original creativity forgets itself and manifests the stable and self-identical world of those truths in themselves, 'humans' can live with 'a degree of peace, certainty and consistency'; that is to say, life becomes bearable for 'humans' if they believe with an invincible faith in the existence of a stable and permanent world.

9 That 'humans' coincide with these 'artistically creative subjects' insofar as they forget themselves, believe with an invincible faith in those immutable truths in themselves, and, as part of this faith, manage to bear life – achieving peace, security and consistency from the invocation of these truths in themselves.

5

According to Nietzsche, the ultimate 'truth in itself', which gathers together all the other ones – namely, the ultimate immutable being that grants stability to all worldly things – is God. By stating that 'God is dead', Nietzsche asserts the death of the very dimension of the immutable: that is, he asserts the death of the self-forgetting of the originally creative activity. Stating that God is dead means stating that the original creativity of the subject recalls itself, places itself before its own eye, and sees that the dimension of the immutable, and of any 'truth in itself', only exists as part of an illusory faith. It sees that this dimension only exists as part of a faith that arises in looking away from the original becoming of the world – namely, only insofar as becoming looks away from itself.

Furthermore: stating that God is dead means stating that the 'human' is dead – precisely insofar as this 'human' arises through the self-forgetting of that original becoming, and through the latter's belief (with an invincible faith) in those 'truths in themselves' in an attempt to make life bearable. Life, however, coincides with becoming, and 'humans' themselves coincide with that original becoming in its looking away from itself – and in its doing so in order to be able to bear itself through a faith in an immutable truth: that is, through the 'yes' that humans address to the immutable being. If the death of God is the death of the self-forgetting of the original creativity of becoming – if the death of God coincides with the self-recollection of becoming, and, therefore, with the death of the 'human' – this self-recollection of becoming is a step that leads beyond the human itself.

The '*Übermensch*' consists precisely in a recognition of the original creativity of becoming: namely, in a 'saying yes to life', as Nietzsche writes in the last paragraph of *Twilight of the Idols*, 'even in its strangest and harshest problems' – and in its most distressing and dreadful ones – renouncing the calm, security and consistency of life. 'Saying yes to life' means saying yes to the becoming that constitutes the 'Dionysian'. In the

'*Übermensch*', 'over and above all horror and pity, *we ourselves* are the eternal joy of becoming – that joy that also includes in itself *the joy of annihilation*'. This 'saying yes to life', in which '*we ourselves*' are that 'eternal joy of becoming', coincides with becoming itself – with the very 'artistically creative subject' that says yes to itself, thus not only recognizing, but willing, obtaining and relishing itself (*Twilight of the Idols*, 'What I Owe the Ancients', 5).

6

According to Nietzsche, Hegel's merit consists in having brought to light the notion of 'development', and in having attributed 'a deeper meaning and a greater value to becoming and development than to what "is"' (*The Gay Science*, 357). However, the fundamental structure of the passage that we have quoted from 'On Truth and Lies in a Nonmoral Sense' is, in fact, Hegelian.

Through the conceptual structure discussed above, Nietzsche asserts that the 'artistically creative subject', through its own self-forgetting, finds before itself a 'congealed' and 'solidified' world, and believes that the things that make up this world are truths in themselves. We are claiming that this structure explicitly and directly reiterates the motif of a Hegelian 'alienation', as it appears (for instance) in the last chapter of the *Phenomenology*, where it is shown that the Subject alienates itself – i.e. forgets itself – insofar as it 'posits itself as object'. That is to say, the Subject alienates itself insofar as it regards the determinacies that it produces as being autonomous, and independent of itself: that is, as being 'truths in themselves'.

According to Hegel (*Encyclopaedia of the Philosophical Sciences*, § 80), the creative Subject looks, through its own alienation and self-forgetting, at its own product with the eye of the 'understanding' (*Verstand*), which 'stops short at the fixed determinacy and at its distinctness vis-à-vis other determinacies; such a restricted abstraction counts for the understanding as one that subsists on its own account, and [simply] is' ('*bleibt bei der festen Bestimmtheit und der Unterschiedenheit derselben gegen andere stehen; ein solches beschränktes Abstraktes gilt him als für sich bestehend und seiend*'). Hegel's 'understanding' corresponds to Nietzsche's 'believing', 'with an invincible faith', that the images – which 'congeal' and 'solidify' when the creative subject forgets both itself and the fluidity of its own producing – are 'truths in themselves'.

The faith in the 'truth in itself' of things believes that these things are self-identical, mutually different, separated, stable, substantial, autonomous, and enduring above the becoming of the world. This faith – which lies at the heart of Nietzsche's critique of metaphysical thinking – reproduces the essential traits of the Hegelian *Verstand*, in spite of the fact that Nietzsche excludes that a 'system' of the Idea may originate from the contradiction of the finite and abstract determinations of the *Verstand*.

7

That system constitutes precisely the way in which epistemic-metaphysical thinking aims, for the last time, to posit an immutable being above becoming. The self-identity of beings, as well as their difference from other beings, constitutes for epistemic-metaphysical thinking an immutable being that persists in spite of the becoming of all beings. For, indeed, the Aristotelian principle of non-contradiction is a principle of all beings, and, therefore, also of those beings that are immediately manifest: i.e. of beings that become. As a result, the non-contradictory character of beings (their self-identical being, and their being other than their own other) has the nature of an immutable being that dominates and sustains becoming.

An abyss separates this meaning of the identity of beings from the identity – and eternity – of beings that appears *outside* of the faith in the existence of becoming: that is, outside of the faith that dominates the entirety of the civilization of the West.

While remaining grounded in the faith in the existence of becoming, it is *inevitable* that the identity of beings, as well as their immutability and their being other than their own other, should end up appearing, to the self-understanding of contemporary philosophy, as what it effectively is for epistemic-metaphysical thinking: namely, as the content of a mere 'faith', which has the illusion of being able to posit something stable above becoming.

However, the meaning that beings exhibit *outside* the faith in the existence of becoming affirms that what constitutes a faith is precisely the assertion of the existence of becoming: this is the faith (the content of which constitutes the extreme form of error) as part of which today the entirety of the Planet proceeds. This is also the faith that grounds the 'faith' refuted by Nietzsche – and, more generally, by contemporary thinking – which, by positing the *acknowledgment* of the existence of becoming as its own foundation, believes to be able to assert something stable above becoming (a 'truth in itself'), and to thus constitutes a form of 'meta-physics' – namely, a going 'beyond' (*metá*) the becoming of *phúsis*.

Therefore, there exists an abyssal difference between the form of *standing*, which takes place *outside* of the faith in the existence of becoming – this is the *standing* that constitutes the *destiny* of every being (cf. *The Essence of Nihilism, Destino della necessità*) – and 'metaphysics': namely, that going above and 'beyond' becoming, which, however, remains *within* the faith in the existence of becoming.

8

What should be remarked here, however, is that, according to Nietzsche, the faith in the truth in itself of things is only a faith – something that is not 'original', but a 'result of becoming' (*Human, All Too Human*, vol. I, 18). This faith is in fact a 'lie' and an 'error', because the ultimately irrefutable and originary self-evidence is – according to Nietzsche, too – given by *becoming* itself: namely, by the creative and annihilating activity of the 'subject' (which, in Nietzsche's jargon, also appears as 'will to power' and 'interpretation'). According to Nietzsche, the entirety of philosophical thinking is held captive to the Eleatic mind-set (*Twilight of the Idols*, '"Reason" in Philosophy', 1): namely, it is characterized by a 'lack of historical sense', a 'hatred of the very idea of becoming' and of 'sensory perception' (which lies at the heart of that idea), and a conviction that becoming is a 'deception' and that 'the senses are deceiving us about the true world'.

Nietzsche is in this respect uncompromising: 'The senses are not lying when they show becoming, passing away, and change… Heraclitus will always be right in thinking that being is an empty fiction' (ibid., 2). The senses 'are not lying' – it is 'reason' that introduces a 'lie' in their non-deceiving 'testimony': 'For instance, the lie of unity, the lie of objectification, of substance, of permanence. 'Reason' makes us falsify the testimony of the senses' (ibid.). What, in this text, is named 'reason' is precisely the 'invincible faith' in the 'truth in itself' of the things that appear as soon as the creative act of becoming forgets itself. This 'reason' thus coincides with the Hegelian *Verstand*. 'Reason', Nietzsche writes (ibid., 5), is a 'fetishism' that 'creates the concept of "thing"'. (Becoming is 'creative' even when it produces what suppresses becoming.) According to Marx, Hegel's mistake consists in regarding 'things' as products of alienation: namely, of the 'fetishism' through which the subject sees what it has produced as being independent of itself. And yet, in Marx's thinking, the 'fetishism of commodities' presents the same conceptual structure of Nietzsche's 'fetishism' of things: the structure of a subjectivity that, through its self-forgetting, loses itself in the object.

9

According to Nietzsche's thought, it is therefore the very self-evidence of the world of becoming (namely, of what he, together with the entirety of Western thought, *believes* to be a self-evidence) that requires us both to refute every 'true world' that would lie beyond the present one, and to regard the faith in the 'truth in itself' of the things of the world as a lie and an error. Indeed, if there existed a 'true' – and immutable – 'world' beyond the world of becoming, the world of becoming would itself become 'illusory'. However, 'change, alteration, and becoming' (ibid.) 'attest to the reality' of this world (ibid., 6); that is, 'the reasons for which this world has been called illusory' (the reasons consisting precisely in its change, alteration, and becoming) 'attest, in fact, to its reality' (ibid.) – precisely because the appearing of becoming is not illusory and deceiving ('the senses are not lying when they show becoming'). That is to say, the appearing of becoming is irrefutably self-evident, and 'Heraclitus will always be right' in asserting this self-evidence: and, therefore, in asserting 'that being is an empty fiction'.

Moreover, the existence of a 'true world' renders the world of becoming merely apparent. For if that true world already existed, it would constitute the truth of everything that can appear in the world of becoming. Therefore, the 'creativity' and the 'eternal joy of creating' would not add anything *truly* new to the 'true world', and that very creativity would thus be illusory and merely apparent. 'What would there be to create, after all, if there were gods?', asks Zarathustra. Nothing! However, we *are* creators: this creative force is the ultimate self-evidence. '*Therefore*, there are no gods' (*Thus Spoke Zarathustra*, Second Part, 'On the Blessed Isles'). The text states: '*If* there were gods, how could I bear not being a god myself? *Therefore*, there are no gods.' Zarathustra cannot bear not being a god because he cannot bear the fact that – insofar as a god exists, and insofar as he is not that god – his creative will should be reduced to a mere appearance, and thus have nothing left to create. If god's 'true world' existed, the subject would have nothing left to create; but the creativity of the subject constitutes the ultimate self-evidence; *therefore*, there exist no gods. Positing a 'true world' that differs from this one, which coincides with the very act of the creative subject, means 'libelling, belittling, and casting suspicion on life' (*Twilight of the Idols*, "Reason' in Philosophy', 6). That is to say, it means libelling, belittling and casting suspicion on becoming itself: precisely insofar as becoming is in this way deprived of all truth and reduced to a mere appearance. According to Nietzsche, restoring the 'innocence of becoming' thus means freeing becoming not only from every teleological order, but, first of all, from the 'true world' of any immutable being – of which that order is an aspect – that would render the originary self-evidence of becoming impossible, and reduce it to a mere appearance.

10

This same conceptual structure – according to which becoming is freed from what renders it impossible – is also present in Gentile, and in a more rigorous and explicit form. Indeed, in Gentile's work, the refutation of every immutable being is essentially connected to the fundamental theorem of idealism: namely, to the impossibility of positing – i.e. of thinking – any reality that would be external to the thinking subject, and independent of it. The positing of that reality – that is, of Nietzsche's 'truth in itself' – not only constitutes the absurd and contradictory concept of a reality that is thought as being external to thought itself, but also renders becoming inconceivable and a mere appearance.

According to Gentile's actual idealism [*attualismo*], every reality that is presupposed to thought is an immutable reality that renders the becoming of thought impossible; and, conversely, every immutable reality is a reality that is presupposed to thought – a reality whose positing can have no foundation, and that is, precisely, only presupposed. This means that, according to Gentile's actual idealism, becoming *does* indeed coincide with a 'creative subject', but also that this creative subject consists of present and actual thinking [*il pensiero in atto*]: namely, of reality as it is in its actually and presently being thought. Gentile can object to

Nietzsche – who, with Leibniz, claims that 'consciousness constitutes only one state of our spiritual and psychic world' (*The Gay Science*, 357) – that everything that in this way transcends actual and present consciousness is, once again, a 'truth in itself': that is, a part of the false 'true world' of metaphysics. The world of becoming is the only real world – granted that it should not be regarded as something that extends beyond (or *also* beyond) present and actual thinking. Nietzsche and psychoanalysis understand the world of becoming in this way, insofar as they presuppose that psychic-spiritual processes extend beyond the processual dimension of consciousness. Gentile shows that the world of becoming, thus understood, becomes itself an immutable and self-identical world: one which renders the concrete becoming of thought inconceivable and merely apparent.

11

Gentile defines 'intellectualism' as the conceptual stance that conceives 'the process of spirit as a process that *presupposes* its object as being already realized before the process itself has begun' (*Teoria generale dello spirito come atto puro*, Chap. XVIII, § 3). That is to say, intellectualism regards the 'intellect', or the 'understanding' – the Hegelian *Verstand* – as the ultimate standpoint of knowledge. Every abstract, 'fixed' (*fest*) and self-identical determination – which for the Hegelian *Verstand* is 'something that is and subsist on its own account' (*für sich bestehend und seiend*) – is precisely an 'object' that is presupposed as already being realized (and, therefore, as being fixed and immutable) before the becoming of thought has begun. 'Intellectualism', as described by Gentile, thus coincides with Nietzsche's 'invincible faith' in the 'truth in itself' of things. According to Gentile, too, philosophical thought is, in its entirety, intellectualist – except for Hegel's grand (but not completely successful) attempt at doing away with every form of intellectualism.

According to philosophical intellectualism, reality is 'a presupposition of thought': that is, it is 'a reality to which nothing is added by the development of thought itself'. It is a 'reality that, if thought and conceived, makes it impossible to conceive human thought itself' (ibid., Chap I, § 3). 'Conceiving human thought' means giving it its due; and what human thought is due is the acknowledgement of the irrefutable and ultimate self-evidence of its becoming – namely, of its 'dialecticity': 'Look with steady gaze at the true and concrete reality of actual and present thinking. The dialecticity of the real will then appear as evident and certain as it is evident and certain to each of us that in thinking we are conscious of what thinks' (ibid., Chap. IV, § 18). If the category of becoming is conceived of as the becoming of thought, 'then there will be nothing more evident than that being that is not and that non-being that is, which constitute this category' (*Sistema di logica come teoria del conoscere*, First Part, Chap. IV, 8).

The Greek meaning of becoming – the unity of being and non-being – also persists in Gentile's actual idealism, as well as in Hegel, and in Nietzsche's creative and annihilating activity of the subject. Furthermore, the dialecticity (the becoming) of thought constitutes for Gentile, too, the ultimate form of self-evidence – as long as it is regarded as the becoming of actual and present thinking. By presupposing an object to the becoming of thought, philosophical intellectualism posits a reality 'to which nothing is added by the development of thought', and, therefore, a reality that – in being 'already realized' before this development – renders this very development merely 'apparent' (*Teoria generale*, Chap I, § 3): that is, it deprives it of its 'seriousness' (ibid., Chap. IV, § 14). Precisely insofar as 'ancient philosophy' presupposed reality to thought, it 'never did comprehend history': not even when it regarded reality in terms of becoming and history. The 'seriousness of history' is something altogether 'modern', 'spiritualist' and 'Christian' (cf. *Gli abitatori del tempo*, Emanuele Severino, Milan: Rizzoli, 2009, Chap. 3, 1).

Gentile, too, like Nietzsche and most of contemporary philosophy, does not realize that he is completely immersed in the Greek meaning of becoming. History is 'serious' precisely because events do not pre-exist in an immutable reality, but issue from nothingness. History consists in the arising of the new and of the unpredictable – and is therefore not a merely apparent innovation – only insofar as what arises has been a nothingness. Only what issues from nothingness may constitute an unpredictable novelty. This means that, for the first time, the Greeks have caught a glimpse of the 'seriousness of history' – of that issuing from nothingness and returning to it. At the same time, however, they have then believed they would find shelter from the terror induced by the becoming of history in the invocation of the very immutable dimension of being that, in their view, constitutes the condition for the conceivability of becoming itself. Contemporary philosophy, on the other hand, regards this immutable dimension as being responsible for the suppression of becoming: that is, for the suppression of what may not be suppressed, insofar as the West, from the Greek onwards, regards it as the ultimate form of self-evidence.

12

As part of the intellectualist stance, actual and present thinking forgets its being a creative act: namely, a becoming one. This forgetting entails its not being able to see anything but a reality that has already been thought (a reality that includes thinking itself), conceiving it – i.e. presupposing it – as a reality that is independent of the very act of conceiving it or seeing it. That is to say, this forgetting entails conceiving of reality as a 'truth in itself'. According to Nietzsche, the faith in the 'truth in itself' of things sees these very things as 'congealed' and 'solidified': that is to say, it conceives of them as self-identical, mutually different, immutable and unconditioned substances. In the same way, according to Gentile, the intellectualist stance presents a reality that is 'self-identical' (*Teoria generale*, Chap. IV, § 10) relative to a thought that simply comes to reflect on it without augmenting it or producing it. That is to say, this reality conforms to the 'laws of Aristotelian logic' (ibid.), and, first of all, to the 'fundamental law' of this logic: 'the principle of identity or non-contradiction' (ibid., Chap. IV, § 7). It is a reality that, insofar as it is 'self-identical', it is 'immutable' (ibid.), for it is 'already realized' before the process of thought has begun: it is an 'abstract unity' (ibid.), a 'substance', a 'fixed and definite entity' (ibid., Chap. IV, §3).

All these attributes, as well as the fundamental law that sustains them – the principle of non-contradiction – pertain to a reality that has already been thought. They express the intellectualist error and alienation that take place insofar as reality is separated from the thinking that thinks it, and insofar as this very thinking forgets that it, itself, constitutes the becoming that creates every object of experience. This thinking forgets that it, itself, produces all determinations, but, with the same gesture, consumes them and transcends them in the limitless process of becoming. The 'fiery fluidity' with which, according to Nietzsche, the world 'pours forth' from the 'artistically creative subject' corresponds to the 'flame' of spirit's becoming described by Gentile (cf. for instance ibid., Chap XVI, § 10) – the 'flame' that consumes all determinations that, at the same time, it 'needs' as its own fuel.

According to Gentile, outside of the intellectualist alienation, thinking knows that each and every 'fixed and definite entity' has completed its becoming, and is therefore destined to perish: in the same way in which, according to Nietzsche, the knowledge of the 'genesis of thought' (*Human all too Human*, vol. I, 18) realizes that every 'object in itself, ... as being self-identical, self-existent and at bottom always the same and immutable' is something that has completed its becoming. The 'belief' in this form of objects constitutes the 'originary error' that has allowed humans to survive.

13

According to Gentile's actual idealism, the intellectualist stance presupposes reality to thought, and thus conceives of reality itself as an immutable being – an already realized totality – that renders inconceivable what, in fact, is originarily self-evident: the becoming of thought. This is the case – as we have mentioned – even when what is presupposed by intellectualism to actual and present thinking (from Plato's dialectics to Hegel's) is becoming itself (the becoming of nature or the becoming of mind – in the latter case transforming mind itself into nature). From the standpoint of actual idealism, not even Nietzsche succeeds in freeing himself from an intellectualist conception of becoming – precisely because he does not achieve a rigorous identification of becoming with thinking. Gentile writes: 'Becoming may not be comprehended as the law of reality unless reality itself has been identified with thinking' (*Sistema di logica*, Third Part, Chap. V, 6).

All philosophies of language and all hermeneutical philosophies – which believe to have done away with every 'philosophy of consciousness', and which regard language as the authentic site of becoming – still need to confront this principle of actual idealism. Even the becoming of language – if separated from thought and presupposed to it – becomes an immutable reality. According to actual idealism, every form of becoming that is presupposed to the becoming of actual and present thinking appears as a process to which thinking itself must conform. Therefore, it appears as a 'process of reality that has been logically exhausted', that is already 'everything that it can be, even though it is not completely actualised in time', and that, therefore, 'is not free to determine itself according to new and unpredictable manifestations' (*Teoria generale*,

Chap. III). The creative and unpredictable innovation of thought is evident as the becoming of actual and present thinking or experience; even becoming, if presupposed to thinking, becomes an immutable being that renders inconceivable the evident and certain becoming of thought.

14

Actual and present thinking, as a creative and unpredictable innovation, leaves behind every certainty that originates from the stability and identity of thought reality, and recognizes that its own becoming would be impossible without any pain, evil, or error. Gentile writes: 'Spirit's real need is not that error and evil should disappear from the world, but that they should eternally be present' (ibid., Chap XVI, § 10).

Every negative aspect of life (every dread, unpredictability, uncertainty, pain, or problematic dimension) may indeed be traced back to the nothingness that is linked to being as part of becoming. The impossibility of separating pain from life is first of all stipulated by Greek ontology, before being demanded by Hegel and by all those who, like Nietzsche and Gentile, draw from him in different ways. Gentile writes: 'Spirit's non-being: this is what pain is' (ibid., Chap. XVI, § 7). Spirit 'is while not being and it is not while being': it coincides with becoming itself; it constitutes the authentic dimension of the Greek meaning of becoming.

Nietzsche himself attributes to the Greek Dionysian spirit what he does not ascribe to Greek philosophy itself: to have realized that, together with the 'eternal joy of creation', 'there must also exist the eternal "agony of the birth-giver"'. In a fragment from 1884, Nietzsche writes that, as the 'danger' of existence recedes, 'a joy in insecurity is born' and, therefore, one in unpredictability. There comes to light a 'happiness in being able to find uncertainty and recklessness anywhere' (Fragment 26 [280], Summer–Autumn 1884). This happiness belongs to the '*Übermensch*', who, in saying 'yes' to becoming, develops a 'predilection for terrible and questionable things' (Fragment 10 [168], Autumn 1887), and 'can allow himself not only the sight of what is terrible and questionable, but even the terrible deed and every luxury of destruction, decomposition, annihilation' (*The Gay Science*, 370).

This destruction, however, as part of the Dionysian 'yes' to becoming, does not have nothingness as its ultimate goal, but it 'is the expression of an overflowing, generative and procreative force' (ibid.): it is the destruction that is required by creation. Hegel had indeed excluded that the result of the contradiction of the abstract determinations of the understanding could be pure nothingness: that is, he had excluded 'nothingness as a result' (*das Nichts zum Resultate*. Cf. *Gli abitatori del tempo*, Chap. II, §§ 1, 2). Already according to the Greeks, becoming is inexhaustible insofar as the annihilation of beings constitutes the condition for the creation of other beings. The becoming of becoming, Aristotle says, is impossible.

In the same way in which, according to Nietzsche, pain and annihilation always breed becoming, according to Gentile, spirit's non-being coincides with the pain that makes the very becoming of spirit possible. Gentile writes: 'If spirit (reality *qua* concept) *were to be*, in the sense in which Parmenides' Being *is*, there would no longer be any place for pain. But spirit is the negation of Being precisely insofar as it is the non-being of Being, and is, therefore, self-production *qua* thinking. Thus, spirit is while not-being: it fulfils its own nature insofar as this is not already realised and must realise itself. And hence spirit finds itself before itself as opposed to its own negation [but perhaps this is to be understood: as its own negation]: and here is the providential pain which spurs us on from task to task, and which has always been recognised as the inner spring by which spirit progresses, and lives on condition of progressing' (*Teoria generale*, Chap XVI, § 7).[2]

Nietzsche, too, finds in Parmenides – but 'even the Eleatics' adversaries' may be traced back to Parmenides – a will to avoid becoming in order to avoid pain (*Twilight of the Idols*, '"Reason" in Philosophy', 1–5). Indeed, according to Nietzsche, Parmenides' Being constitutes the most rigorous expression of the faith in a 'truth in itself' (that is, of the faith as part of which the creative activity forgets itself); in the same way, according to Gentile, Parmenides' Being constitutes the most rigorous expression of the intellectualist presupposition of reality to the becoming of thought. Neither of them suspects that the eternity of Being may have a meaning that differs from the naturalistic-intellectualist presupposition or from the desire to be safe from the dangers of life.

(Moreover, Parmenides may assert the illusory nature of becoming only insofar as he understands what it means 'to become'; as far as we know, this understanding explicitly appears for the first time in Parmenides' Poem. For the first time, Parmenides invokes the notion of an emergence from nothingness and of a return to it, but, with the same gesture, he posits this process as illusory. He invokes it for the first time, but ascribes it to prior forms of thinking.)

15

According to Nietzsche, metaphysical-moral-Christian nihilism turns life into a form of nothingness. For, indeed, the becoming of life is nullified insofar as it becomes the appearance of a 'true world' that is in itself immutable. Gentile, too, identifies (*Teoria generale*, Chap. I, § 4) intellectualist presuppositions with a 'nullification of thought': namely, with a nullification of concrete becoming. Relative to an immutable and in itself complete reality, 'thinking is, strictly conceived, nothing' (ibid.). However, in Nietzsche and Gentile's thinking – not to mention in other forms of contemporary philosophy – it does not fully come to light that the positing of an immutable being annihilates becoming because it does not respect the nothingness of the nothing that, as part of becoming, is united with being. Indeed, if there existed an immutable dimension in the totality of being, it is not only the totality of what is that would have to conform to that dimension, but also the totality of what is still nothing. Thus, what arises as part of becoming must conform to the law constituted by the immutable, and it therefore may no longer arise from nothingness, but only from a nothingness that heeds and attends to that law – and which is therefore a being.

It thus follows that what should issue from nothingness as part of becoming ends up issuing, in its fundamental essence, from the ultimate Meaning of the Whole formed by the immutable. It thus follows that, in the tradition of metaphysics, this issuing from nothingness constitutes an *ex nihilo nihil fieri*. The immutable being turns nothingness – which according to the Greek meaning of becoming is united with being – into a being. Without being aware of it, contemporary philosophy (and the entirety of contemporary culture and civilization) expresses, by destroying every immutable being, a most rigorous faithfulness to the Greek meaning of becoming.

16

Nietzsche's *Übermensch* and Gentile's actual and present thinking take on the task of acknowledging becoming: of protecting it, freeing it and saving it from the immutables that turn it into something impossible. That every object and every theory should be an 'interpretation' – as the later Nietzsche remarks – constitutes a radical way of dissolving the forms of stability that render becoming inconceivable. In the same way, according to Gentile, history is not a datum of experience or a 'fact' – namely, once again, something stable – but it is produced and 'created' by spirit. In a fragment from 1887, Nietzsche writes that the positing of any immutable being constitutes a 'faith' – 'a faith in what is' – and that this faith is a 'consequence' of the 'astonishment experienced in front of becoming' (Fragment 9 [60], Autumn 1887). According to Gentile, too, intellectualism is a 'presupposition' – namely, a faith – which would not have been possible if thought had recognized the 'seriousness' of becoming.

It is instead precisely Greek thought that invokes becoming for the first time, and recognizes its extreme seriousness (and its extreme danger). Furthermore, Greek thought perceives becoming for the first time as the ultimate and irrefutable form of self-evidence. Even according to the Eleatics, the becoming of beings appears – it is evident; and it is this self-evidence that is posited by the *lógos* as an illusion: that is to say, the *lógos* does not erase the appearing and self-evidence of becoming, but incorporates them in the form of an illusion (cf. *Essenza del nichilismo*, pp. 300–302). Greek thought invokes becoming, and, in it, finds life itself; however, it also finds an extreme form of danger, and attempts to protect itself by invoking the immutable structures that, in suppressing the danger of becoming, end up suppressing becoming itself. The will to be protected from the pain and the unpredictability of becoming, however, exists only and precisely insofar as the irrefutable self-evidence of becoming is first of all acknowledged.

If becoming exists, the invocation of the immutables is certainly a faith. The belief that within or beyond becoming there may exist an immutable being is only a faith. However, what constitutes the faith as part of which the entirety of the civilization of the West has appeared, and which has today reached the culmination of its coherence and of its power in the civilization of technics, is the conviction that becoming exists, and that it is the ultimate and ultimately irrefutable self-evidence. The critical spirit of our culture questions everything, but does so while remaining within this faith – and doing away with anything that appears to be irreconcilable with it. This faith is all the more radical and dominant the more one believes to have nothing to share with Greek

70 BEYOND LANGUAGE

thought. Perhaps the time has come to realize that the Greek meaning of becoming – the ultimate self-evidence of the West – is but a faith: and that *this* is the truly 'invincible' faith, from which every other faith originates. Perhaps the time has come to understand what the soul of this faith harbours within itself.

2 PROBLEMATICISM AND ACTUAL IDEALISM

1

Ugo Spirito's problematicism moves towards the same goal as the entirety of contemporary philosophy: to free the becoming of reality from what makes it impossible. In order to grasp the meaning of this assertion, it is necessary to keep in mind the singular relation that links Spirito to his mentor Gentile. Gentile had reformed the Hegelian dialectics. Dialectics is the theory of becoming.

The first few pages of *Vita come ricerca* (Firenze: Sansoni, 1937) aim to highlight the 'antinomy' that thought is unable to leave behind.

The first side of that antinomy consists in the acknowledgment of the existence of becoming. Every thought is confronted with an objection. This confrontation constitutes the very 'development of history' – that is, the transition from the past to the future: from the past 'in which none of the things of today existed, and other things existed that today no longer exist', to the future, 'in which the things of today will no longer exist, but new ones will', until all things 'will vanish into nothingness'. 'Everything becomes, and everything is nullified by this infinite flowing'. The annihilation and nullification of things are the objection to the very thinking as part of which they appear, and objections constitute the annihilation and nullification of every form of thought that would claim to posit itself as definitive and conclusive.

The second side of the antinomy consists in the realization that – given that everything is null as part of this 'eternal becoming' – the very 'principle' of becoming may however not itself be null. Therefore, everything that becomes, and which is altogether nullified, is, at the same time, altogether saved from its nullification, and appears 'as being absolutely necessary'. Life is nullified, and, at the same time, it may never be nullified. While this is, according to Spirito, the 'most immediate and elementary guise of the antinomy, this is essentially the antinomy that turns into the most difficult obstacles for contemporary dialectics'. These are the obstacles that Hegel, and later Marx – and, above all, Gentile – have had to confront: and they are difficult and dramatic obstacles, Spirito writes, because, as part of actual idealism, 'the culmination of anti-intellectualism turns into the culmination of intellectualism itself' (*Il problematicismo*, Firenze: Sansoni, 1948, p. 45).

2

As already discussed, Gentile, in *Teoria generale dello spirito come atto puro* (Chap. XVIII, § 3), defines intellectualism as the theoretical stance according to which 'the process of spirit . . . *presupposes* its object as being already realised before the process itself has begun'. Intellectualism thus constitutes a realist-naturalist presupposition that conceives of reality as being external, independent and in itself realized relative to the subject that thinks it. The theoretical strength of idealism – and, in particular, of actual idealism – consists precisely in showing that every form of intellectualism constitutes a 'presupposition' and an unjustified assumption; this assumption is, in fact, 'absurd', for it believes to be able to think what it regards as being external to thought itself.

In the definition of intellectualism given by actual idealism, however, there appears the distinctive feature that we have discussed in par. 11–14 of the previous chapter (cf. also *Gli abitatori del tempo*, Chap III, § 1). This feature, however, is never brought to light, and remains hidden even in the way in which Spirito presents the philosophy of actual idealism.

In the passage quoted above from the *Teoria generale* – in which intellectualism is argued to coincide with a form of realist presupposition – Gentile adds that the intellectualist stance conceives of the object as an 'external limit to the subject: *a limit that, once posited, makes it impossible to conceive the subject itself* (emphasis added). The intellectualist stance renders the subject *inconceivable*. The passage under consideration is found in the last pages of *Teoria generale*, but its meaning is determined in the first chapters of that work.

The fundamental reason why, according to Gentile, the intellectualist stance renders the subject inconceivable may briefly be retraced as follows.

The 'subject' coincides with 'present and actual thinking': namely, with becoming in its concreteness, certainty and self-evidence. However, by presupposing reality as being external, independent and already realized relative to thought, the very becoming of thought becomes illusory and merely apparent: for it is only apparently and illusorily that it constitutes a creative and innovatory process. On the other hand, becoming, if conceived of as the becoming of thought, constitutes the ultimate and originary form of 'self-evidence'. Insofar as intellectualist presuppositions refute the self-evidence of becoming and render the creativity of the subject illusory, they are something absurd.

Reality, if presupposed to thought as having already been realized, takes the form of an immutable reality; in turn, every immutable being constitutes a reality that is presupposed to the becoming of thought. Therefore, the self-evidence of the becoming of thought entails the impossibility of every immutable reality.

The destruction of the immutables carried out by actual idealism is one of the most rigorous forms of destruction of the immutables that lies at the heart of the contemporary philosophy – and of the culture and of the very civilization of the West – of the last hundred and fifty years.

3

Let us read again: 'Look with steady gaze at the true and concrete reality of actual and present thinking. The dialecticity of the real will then appear as evident and certain as it is evident and certain to each of us that in thinking we are conscious of what thinks' (*Teoria generale*, Chap. IV, § 18). The 'dialecticity of the real' coincides with becoming itself. Becoming, in turn, is 'evident' and 'certain' only insofar as it is conceived of as the becoming of the one, true and concrete reality constituted by actual and present thinking. The existence of becoming is the ultimate self-evidence of Western civilization. What varies through the history of the West is not the *meaning* of becoming – the meaning that is invoked for the first time by Greek thought – but the dimension or the domain in which that meaning is each time instantiated. The Greeks conceive of becoming as the 'unity of being and non-being' – *eînai te kaì mè eînai* (Plato, *Republic*, 477 a). It is only because the Greeks think the radical meaning of being and non-being – only because they think the infinite opposition between being and non-being – that they are able to think becoming as a unity of being and non-being: that is, as a unity of what is infinitely opposed. Only the Greeks begin to think what, for a long time now, has become a commonplace, *the* common-place of our entire culture: that things in the world issue from nothingness and there they return – that at first they are not, then they are, and then, once again, they are not. This is the place that is common to the entirety of Western civilization. It constitutes the Greeks' unheard-of thought – a thought that, by now, gathers together every thought and every action. In the world, according to Plato, 'things come into being, not having been before' – *tà mè próteron ónta hústeron gígnesthai* (*Sophist*, 265 b–c). Becoming is precisely this unity of being and non-being. What becomes, Plato writes, is 'a being and, at the same time, a non-being', *háma ón te kaì mè ón* (*Republic*, 478 d). The same definition of becoming appears in Hegel; and, therefore, in Gentile. It is therefore inevitable that Ugo Spirito, in considering his 'antinomy', should speak of a time 'when none of the things of today existed', and of a time 'when the things of today will no longer exist' and 'will vanish into nothingness'. Spirito's antinomy may be established only insofar as Spirito's problematicism, too, belongs to the place that is common to all the inhabitants of the West.

4

As we have already remarked, however, according to actual idealism, becoming is 'certain' and 'evident' only if it is conceived of as 'actual and present thinking' – as 'thought in act': namely, as the act of the thought that posits the world rather than as the dynamic unfolding of a reality that is external to thought and independent of it. Insofar as becoming is conceived of in this latter way, according to Gentile, it does not appear as a creative innovation, as part of which being 'is while not-being, and is not while being' (*Sistema di logica*, First Part, Chap. IV, § 7). On the contrary, it appears as a system that is already realized: one that is 'logically exhausted' and 'ideally actualised', even if 'not completely actualised in time' (*Teoria generale*, Chap III, § 3). That is to say, it does not appear as a development, but as a self-identical world, which is thus immutable 'at least in relation to the thought that thinks it' (ibid., Chap. IV, § 10). Insofar as becoming is regarded as being prior to thought – as something to which thought must conform – becoming turns into an immutable being; in relation to this immutable being, the creative development of thought becomes merely apparent insofar as it does not add anything new.

However, since this development is not merely apparent, but 'evident' and 'certain' (i.e. since thinking is what posits itself as being that is while not-being, and which is not while being), and since there is nothing 'more evident than that being that is not and that non-being that is' in which the becoming of thought consists (*Sitema di logica*, First Part, Chap. IV, § 8) – it must be concluded that what is merely apparent and non-existent is the becoming that has been presupposed to thought. Thus presupposed, it 'remains a mere postulate' (*Teoria generale*, Chap. IV, § 12). This is 'why ancient philosophy never did comprehend history' (ibid., Chap IV, § 13). The 'seriousness of history' (ibid., Chap IV, § 14) coincides with the creative, free and unpredictable innovation of becoming, and this innovation is possible only if becoming is conceived of as the manifest development of thought itself.

When Gentile writes that 'becoming may not be comprehended as a law of reality unless reality itself has been identified with thought' (*Sistema di logica*, Third Part, Chap. V, § 6), he does not leave behind the *content* that Greek thought has assigned to that law once and for all – he does not leave behind Greek ontology and the notion of a 'unity of being and non-being' – but he only leaves behind the *realist instantiation* of becoming, insofar as this prevents becoming from constituting the manifest law of reality. By radicalizing the principle of modern philosophy, actual idealism no longer locates the Greek meaning of becoming in a reality that is external to thought, but in the very dimension constituted by thinking itself.

The fundamental – and yet often unknowing – reason why, today, the philosophies of language stand in different ways in opposition to the philosophies of consciousness is given by the conviction that language – rather than consciousness or thought – constitutes the authentic site or dimension of becoming. This is the dimension that allows becoming to be alive, and that frees the Greek meaning of becoming from what renders it impossible.

According to the standpoint of actual idealism, naturalist presuppositions render the manifest becoming of thought merely apparent – even when the reality that is thus presupposed is becoming itself. Even becoming, if presupposed to thinking, is an immutable relative to that very thinking. (It can therefore be understood how, according to Gentile, the most rigorous form of realist-intellectualist presupposition is Parmenides' immobilism – cf. *Sistema di logica*, First Part, Chap. IV, § 2).

In any case, if a reality is presupposed to thought, which may thus only mirror that reality, it already contains everything that will appear as part of the development of thought itself: that is to say, that reality is immutable, and that development is a pure appearance devoid of all 'seriousness'. However, according to the standpoint of actual idealism, the 'seriousness' of the becoming of thought constitutes the ultimate 'self-evidence': therefore, any reality that is presupposed to thought must be refuted, for it denies the self-evidence of the 'seriousness' of becoming. This is the self-evidence of the process as part of which what is born constitutes an absolute and unpredictable novelty – namely, something that has been created and that issues from nothingness – and what perishes is radically and conclusively destroyed – that is to say, it turns into nothing. According to the intellectualist stance, reality is 'a presupposition of thought, a reality to which nothing is added by the development of thought'; therefore, relative to thought, it is an immutable and self-identical reality – 'a reality that, if thought and conceived, makes it impossible to conceive human thought itself' (*Teoria generale*, Chap. I, § 3). It thus becomes impossible to posit what, instead, constitutes the ultimate self-evidence and concrete experience of becoming: the 'development of thought' – which is, precisely, a creation and an 'addition' or 'increase' of reality: an act that lets reality issue from nothingness.

The elimination of every intellectualist-naturalist presupposition carried out by actual idealism thus constitutes one of the most rigorous forms of the process of destruction of the immutables – a process that determines philosophical thought after Hegel.

5

After having invoked the ontological meaning of becoming, the Greeks – and then the whole philosophical tradition up to Hegel – believe that becoming itself is inconceivable without the positing of the existence of an immutable being. And yet, it is precisely the Greek meaning of becoming that inevitably leads to the destruction of every immutable being.

For, indeed, becoming – as unity of being and non-being – is an absolute innovation and unpredictability. What arises, as part of becoming, is radically new and unpredictable in that it issues from its own nothingness. Issuing from nothingness, it may not in any way be anticipated and predetermined by what already exists. Asserting that there exists an immutable being beyond becoming entails that this very immutable being anticipates and predetermines everything that may arise as part of becoming. The immutable coincides precisely with the ultimate and unchangeable Meaning of the Whole, to which everything that arises must conform; it is the Measure and the Yardstick of every future.

This entails that, if there exists an immutable being, what arises may not constitute a radical novelty and unpredictability: on the contrary, it is essentially anticipated and predetermined by the immutable Meaning of the Whole. Its issuing from nothingness thus becomes an illusory appearance, for, in truth, it originates from that immutable Meaning, and there it returns after having perished. Precisely for this reason, this process of issuing from nothingness and returning to it is, for the Greeks, at the same time an *ex nihilo nihil fieri*.

The existence of an immutable being deprives the notions of birth and death of their 'seriousness'. However, it is precisely Greek thought that has explicitly presented, for the first time, the extreme seriousness of the notions of birth and death – precisely insofar as it has conceived of them as an issuing from nothingness and a returning to it. It is therefore precisely the extreme seriousness with which Greek thought has conceived of becoming and of history that has led to the destruction of all immutable beings – that is, of those beings that Greek thought, and then the whole philosophical tradition, have had the illusion of being able to reconcile with becoming.

For, indeed, the seriousness of becoming and history depends on a reflection on the unity of being and non-being within becoming, and on the conviction that this unity is manifest. Rather than stating that ancient philosophy never did comprehend the seriousness of history, it should be held that it is precisely because it *did* comprehend it – and did so for the first time – that the destruction of every meta-historical reality that philosophy and tradition have attempted to reconcile with history has become unavoidable. One of the fundamental meta-historical realities discerned by contemporary philosophy is then precisely that of a reality presupposed in an intellectualist way. Intellectualism conceives of becoming itself – of the very unity of being and non-being – as being external to actual and present thinking, and independent of it. With the culmination of anti-intellectualism, actual idealism's refutation of every intellectualist presupposition reaches one of the most rigorous and self-aware forms of the destruction of every meta-historical and immutable being.

6

Ugo Spirito's problematicism originates from the conviction that actual idealism – namely, 'the culmination of anti-intellectualism' – 'turns into a culmination of intellectualism itself', and that 'a most conspicuous contradiction thus besets the entirety of thought' (*Il problematicismo*, p. 45). According to Spirito, this contradiction essentially arises insofar as not even actual idealism may avoid constituting a dialectical theory, and ascribing a non-dialectical character to its own theory.

Spirito remarks first of all that, according to Gentile (but already according to Hegel), asserting that reality becomes – namely, that 'it is and it is not' (ibid., p. 48) – entails asserting that 'no philosophy may claim to be conclusive'. According to Spirito, this very conclusiveness would prevent any 'additional development, and would thus conclude the spiritual process itself, marking the end of life' (ibid.). This conclusiveness would therefore render becoming impossible. Spirito, too – alongside Gentile, Hegel, and the entire culture of the West – asserts that becoming (that is, the Greek meaning of becoming) may not be refuted, that a 'development' must be secured, that the 'spiritual process' must remain open, and that 'life' must continue.

According to Spirito, Hegel and Gentile's contradiction does not lie with their attempt at saving becoming: according to Spirito, too, becoming – 'reality comprehended as becoming insofar as it is and it is not' (ibid., pp. 47–48) – constitutes the ultimate and irrefutable form of self-evidence. Actual idealism, Spirito reiterates, excludes any conclusive philosophy, for it 'excludes that anything may be defined without introducing death in the place of life'. 'Life' is, precisely, becoming; anything that is immutable is 'death'. According to Spirito, too, it is therefore irrefutable that becoming is to be freed from every form of 'death': namely, from everything that renders it impossible. It must be 'freed' because it stands before us as 'certain' and 'evident': in fact, as what is most evident. Not even Ugo Spirito's radical problematicism puts into question the fundamental faith of the West: the faith in the existence of becoming.

7

The fact that this faith also constitutes the non-problematic foundation of Spirito's problematicism follows from his leaving idealism and actual idealism behind precisely insofar as – despite all their intentions to free becoming from what renders it inconceivable – they end up rendering becoming radically inconceivable. Indeed, Spirito writes: 'the dialectician' – namely, the advocate and rescuer of becoming – 'after having achieved a consciousness of the dialecticity of life, hypostasises it in the form of a conclusion that, unlike all others, stands outside of the process and becomes its guarantor. This is the conclusion that defines the Absolute, and that once again posits Being as prior and opposed to becoming' (ibid., p. 48).

Consciousness – the theory of dialectics, the theory of becoming – is thus once again established as the immutable Being to which the becoming of thought must conform. Becoming must conform to the non-becoming consciousness of becoming. Spirito writes: 'Tomorrow, spirit will be able to resume and renew every past and every future through an unpredictable creative act; however, it will always have to confirm its own dialectical *nature*, and to eternally re-affirm this self-knowledge that it has just attained: that it, itself, is a dialectical act, a synthesis of opposites, an absolute creativity [...]. Spirit will be able to create everything, but not the self-knowledge of its own creative ability' (ibid., p. 78). According to actual idealism, authentic becoming must be conceived of as an unpredictable and creative act of thought; however, its self-knowledge – that is, actual idealism's theory of becoming – turns into an immutable Being or Essence to which the development of thought must conform (in the same way in which, from the standpoint of intellectualism, the development of thought must conform to a presupposed reality).

The contradiction that Spirito detects in the stance of actual idealism is thus the same one that actual idealism detects in the intellectualist stance: that of rendering impossible the becoming of thought – a becoming that, on the contrary, is 'evident' and 'certain'. According to Spirito, too, the task is therefore to free becoming from what renders it impossible: to think becoming freed from all contradictions.

8

The crisis of actual idealism, Spirito writes, 'reaches an extremely critical stage because the principle of intellectualism – that is, of a reflection on a presupposed reality – turns back precisely on becoming itself: on the process, on the self-production of the subject, and on the spiritual activity – of which it is at the same time asserted that they may never be presupposed, insofar as they constitute the one and only self-positing of reality. A most conspicuous contradiction besets the entirety of thought, and the culmination of anti-intellectualism turns into a culmination of intellectualism itself: precisely of an intellectualism that turns the subject itself into an object of reflection, and that comes to define spirit on a par with nature' (ibid., p. 45).

The meaning of this passage may be unfolded as follows. Authentic becoming coincides with the subject or spiritual activity. According to actual idealism, only this subject does not constitute a presupposed reality, for it is the 'self-positing' (the self-production or self-creativity) of reality itself. Except that, from the standpoint of actual idealism, the self-knowledge (the theory) of this self-positing of the subject conceives of itself as something that does not become: that is to say, as part of this self-knowledge, becoming – the self-positing of the subject – appears as an unchangeable essence and 'nature', and this 'essence' or 'nature' of becoming comes to be presupposed to becoming itself.

Strictly speaking – even though the passage quoted from Spirito does not make this aspect explicit – the *essence* of that self-positing of the subject appears as a presupposition relative to *both* the general self-positing of the subject *and* to the specific form of self-positing constituted by the self-knowledge or consciousness that has, as its content, the self-positing of the subject. This self-knowledge thus appears as a 'reflection on a presupposed reality': that is, precisely on the presupposed reality that consists of the very self-positing of the subject. The subject – i.e. authentic becoming – thus becomes the object of an intellectualist reflection.

In other words, actual idealism removes the thought of becoming from the becoming of thought (it removes the self-knowledge, consciousness or theory of the process of spirit from that very process). On the one hand, thought, *qua* result of thinking, becomes in this way an immutable essence – a presupposition to thought *qua* thinking (that is, it becomes an 'object'); on the other hand, thought, *qua* thinking, becomes an intellectualist reflection on the presupposed reality constituted by the very 'essence' or 'nature' of the becoming of thought.

Spirito thus holds that, according to the standpoint of actual idealism, the becoming of thought becomes itself illusory and merely apparent – and so does the unpredictable innovation, creativity and freedom of thought – insofar as the becoming of thought must conform to its own immutable essence, in the same way in which, according to the realist-intellectualist stance, the becoming of thought must conform to a reality that is external to that very thought, and independent of it. According to Spirito, actual idealism thus turns into a most conspicuous contradiction: for with one and the same gesture with which it aims to safeguard becoming in the most uncompromising way, it ends up refuting this very becoming in just as uncompromising a way. The contradiction detected by Spirito as part of the standpoint of actual idealism is the contradiction that arises in rendering becoming inconceivable at the very moment in which one aims to free becoming from what renders it inconceivable.

9

Spirito understands problematicism as the length that modern criticism must necessarily traverse after having 'reached the extreme form of intellectualism' (ibid.). Contrary to the dialectician, who, after 'having achieved a consciousness of the dialecticity of life, hypostasise it in the form of a conclusion that, unlike all other conclusions, stands out of the process [...], the problematician, on the other hand, after having achieved a consciousness of the dialecticity of life, does not find it warranted to take the step necessary for regarding this very dialecticity as the essence of reality. On the contrary, the problematician holds that this step, insofar as it leads to an a-dialectical conclusion, is unwarranted and contradictory. This entails that dialectics, far from rising to a conclusion, remains the very problem of life in its antinomic tragedy' (ibid., p. 48).

Thus, problematicism, too, 'achieves a consciousness of the dialecticity of life'. Strictly speaking, however, it does not 'achieve' it, but *remains* within the configuration of the Greek faith in the existence and self-evidence of becoming that is found in idealism and actual idealism. The existence of becoming is evident for problematicism, too: what is 'unwarranted and contradictory' is to regard becoming as 'the essence of reality', and to present the problem itself as a solution.

Becoming constitutes a problem, for becoming is the development of thought, in which every claim of conclusiveness of what is thought comes to be progressively annihilated – precisely insofar as this conclusiveness would render the creative and unpredictable innovation of thought impossible. According to the standpoint of problematicism, however, the problem itself may not turn into the solution – that is, becoming may not constitute the 'essence of reality' – because, as already discussed, the 'essence' of becoming constitutes an intellectualist presupposition of becoming itself, and the solution (namely, the problem raised to the rank of solution) constitutes an intellectualist presupposition of the problem itself.

In opposition to this 'metaphysical dialecticity', Spirito thus posits a 'problematic dialecticity': namely, an acknowledgement of the dialecticity, or becoming, of life, which does not unknowingly presuppose an a-dialectical Absolute, but 'explicitly tends to it'.

Metaphysical dialecticity is contradictory without being aware of it; problematic dialecticity consists in an acknowledgment of this contradiction, and in a desire to find a way out of it. When Spirito writes that problematicism 'explicitly tends to an a-dialectical Absolute' (ibid.), he does not imagine a path in which, after having reached God, it becomes clear that humans (i.e. becoming) have never existed; on the contrary, he imagines a path in which, after having reached God (i.e. the immutable), the contradiction and the problem of human beings are resolved. That is to say, the tragic antinomicity of becoming is resolved, and the originary self-evidence of becoming *is acknowledged*: it is acknowledged that becoming (however antinomic it may be) constitutes the inescapable starting point of a path that, in being possible and hoped for, leads to God.

According to Spirito, problematic dialecticity 'explicitly tends to an a-dialectical Absolute, without knowing whether this Absolute is compatible with dialectics itself' (ibid., pp. 48–49) – that is, without knowing whether the immutable is compatible with becoming. Spirito thus fails to see that the immutable to which he tends *is* incompatible with becoming, and that his apparently radical critique of actual idealism takes *a step backwards* relative to actual idealism itself – in the same way in which a step backwards has been taken by all those who, grounded in the standpoint of actual idealism, have believed to be able to reach, in admittedly different ways, the God of Christian theology. This is the last point that is left to elucidate.

10

Problematicism leads the standpoint of actual idealism back to the sceptical one, and finds it unable to withstand the 'logic of the argument against the sceptic'. Actual idealism would thus incur in 'a most conspicuous contradiction', insofar as it posits the assertion, according to which there exists nothing conclusive and immutable, as being itself conclusive and immutable.

However, the scepticism described by Spirito (and by many others) is just an abstraction, rather than a historical occurrence. No philosophy in the history of the West has refuted every conclusive truth without any reason. Scepticism, in its concrete historical configuration, does not consist of an arbitrary will to refute truth. All the forms of scepticism that have appeared in history – thus including most of contemporary philosophy – maintain, in different ways, the impossibility of any conclusive truth *that would claim to stand above and beyond the becoming of the world, and account for it.*

This means that every form of scepticism that has appeared throughout the history of the West does *not* put into question the faith in the existence of becoming. On the contrary, standing within this faith (which therefore never appears as a faith, but always as the ultimate form of self-evidence), all forms of scepticism hold that this faith is incompatible with any *other* conviction that would appear as a definitive truth or as the ultimate and definitive Meaning of the becoming of the world (namely, as a Meaning that would prevail over the meaning that becoming has in its own right as part of its manifest appearing). This process achieves an extreme intensity with contemporary thought. Actual idealism itself perceives, in a particularly rigorous and self-aware way, the necessity of saving becoming from any immutable truth, which, *qua* immutable, would render becoming impossible. Spirito's problematicism leaves the standpoint of actual idealism behind insofar as actual idealism itself is claimed to render becoming inconceivable. It is then necessary to realize that the move from actual idealism to problematicism constitutes a step *backwards* relative to the internal coherence of the faith in the existence of becoming.

11

Regardless of the actual ways in which contemporary thought refutes every form of definitive truth and *epistéme*, the fact that the faith in the existence of becoming should lead to the destruction of every immutable being – whether this being be part of that faith or not – is, let us repeat, *something necessary*. For, indeed, the immutable being anticipates within itself the Meaning of the Whole, thus rendering predictable what, in arising from nothingness as part of becoming, is instead radically unpredictable. By anticipating the Meaning of the Whole, the immutable determines the Meaning to which the nothingness from which things originate as part of becoming must conform. The immutable thus transforms nothingness into a heeding and observance of Being: that is to say, it transforms nothingness into a being. What issues from nothingness, however, may not be compelled to submit to the Meaning of what already exists: for, otherwise, what arises would not be issuing from nothingness – i.e. from an absolute absence of meaning – but from the Meaning of what already exists. If there exists an immutable being, it compels not only everything that exists, but also everything that arises to submit to a definitive Meaning – precisely insofar as the immutable is the conclusive Meaning of everything that is, has been and will be. The existence of an immutable thus transforms nothingness – the nothingness from which things originate as part of becoming – into the non-nothingness constituted precisely by the definitive Meaning of the Whole. If there exists an immutable (God, the absolute laws of nature, of society, of history, of human beings, of science, of knowledge, of art), there may not exist any form of issuing from nothingness: that is to say, there may exist no becoming as it has been conceived once and for all by Greek philosophy. If there exists an immutable being, there may exist no unpredictable innovation *qua* it pertains to every form of issuing from nothingness. Starting with the Greeks, however, this innovation constitutes the ultimate self-evidence of the West. Therefore, no immutable being may exist.

Now, the tenet of actual idealism, according to which everything that exists constitutes a form of becoming, is certainly regarded by actual idealism itself as a definitive truth: that is, as an immutable. Through this tenet, the faith in the existence and self-evidence of becoming realizes that the existence of an immutable being – which would attribute to becoming an *additional* meaning relative to the one that becoming shows in and of itself – is impossible. This tenet of actual idealism – according to which everything is a form of becoming – certainly constitutes an immutable; however, it is the *one* immutable that allows becoming to retain the openness that pertains to it *qua* becoming.

For, indeed, actual idealism refutes every reality that is presupposed to thought in an intellectualist way, insofar as thought may not truly produce the content of that reality, and, relative to it, it may not truly become. This content already immutably is, anticipates, predetermines and renders predictable everything that thought is supposed to become. Actual idealism's assertion, too, that all reality is a form of becoming – in other words, the positing of an 'essence' or 'nature' of becoming, too – certainly constitutes an immutable that anticipates and predetermines becoming, rendering it predictable; the content of this assertion, however, anticipates and predicts that everything that arises is to issue from nothingness: that is to say, it anticipates and predicts that what arises may not be anticipated or predicted. The unpredictable act of thought is rendered predictable to the extent that it will have to eternally be an unpredictable act. It will have to conform to its own 'essence' or 'nature' to the extent that it will never have to conform to any essence or nature.

The standpoint of problematicism remarks that if, according to actual idealism, thought is able to renew and reconstitute every past and every future through a creative and unpredictable act, it will nevertheless have to eternally confirm that it, itself, is a creative and unpredictable act; it will have to eternally confirm its own immutable essence: its being a form of becoming. However, this conformity of becoming to nothing but its own immutable essence is precisely what allows becoming to be becoming. The immutable essence of becoming, posited as the content of a definitive conclusion, is the one immutable being that guarantees that becoming is not a mere appearance. That immutable being is precisely the one anticipation that acknowledges and safeguards the originary nothingness of what arises, without transforming it into something that already exists – that is to say, without transforming it into a heeding and observance of a definitive Meaning of the Whole, which would claim to stand beyond the meaning and the essence of becoming itself.

Precisely in order to uphold the self-evidence of becoming (that is, of an issuing from and returning to nothingness), it is therefore necessary to assert that everything becomes *except* for the content of this very assertion. The content of this assertion is the one immutable being that is not destroyed by the self-evidence of becoming, for its destruction would coincide with the positing of the immutables that render becoming inconceivable. For, indeed, if the assertion of the becoming of the Whole did not constitute a definitive truth – an immutable – the possibility would arise that, beyond becoming, there could exist an immutable being that differs from the assertion of the becoming of the Whole, and that would thus render becoming inconceivable.

12

Thus, if by 'scepticism' one understands the assertion of the non-existence of any definitive truth, scepticism is certainly self-contradictory. Actual idealism, however, does not refute the existence of every definitive truth, but, rather, asserts that the only definitive truth is that everything becomes and everything is devoid of any definitiveness: everything *except*, precisely, for the theoretical comprehension of the Whole – the *theory* of spirit. While intellectualist presuppositions render becoming impossible, the definitiveness of the comprehension of becoming achieved by actual idealism guarantees and safeguards becoming itself. It therefore may not be regarded – according to what, instead, Spirito claims – as the very form of intellectualism in which the culmination of anti-intellectualism turns into a culmination of intellectualism itself. Actual idealism remains 'the culmination of anti-intellectualism' – the culmination of the faith in the existence of becoming.

Spirito's problematicism, on the other hand, by striving towards an a-dialectical Absolute, remains within the philosophical-theological tradition of the West, insofar as the latter posits, as a possibility or as an actual reality, the existence of an immutable being that renders becoming inconceivable and merely apparent. The a-dialectical Absolute – the God towards which Spirito strives – certainly constitutes a 'hope', and not a 'possession'. However, since the faith in the existence of becoming constitutes the foundation of problematicism, too, that 'hope' is destined to be disappointed: for, if what it hopes for were to exist, it would render its own foundation – namely, the faith in the existence of becoming – impossible and merely apparent. The difference between a 'hope' and a 'possession' becomes irrelevant also because given that, according to Spirito, the standpoint of actual idealism coincides with a most rigorous assertion of the becoming of the Whole, and given that this assertion is itself contradictory, it remains unclear why he should have settled for a 'hope' for the existence of an a-dialectical Absolute (namely, of the immutable God of Christian metaphysics and theology), rather than positively *asserting* that existence. The conceptual structure of classical metaphysics consists precisely in the positing of the existence of an immutable being – a positing that takes place on the basis of an acknowledgment of the contradiction that ensues from the identification of the dimension of becoming with the Whole. Spirito, however, presupposes precisely that the positing of the becoming of the Whole asserted by actual idealism is itself contradictory.

Through these remarks, we are certainly not claiming that actual idealism is free from all contradictions. The contradiction of actual idealism, however, is to be sought in a place that lies far deeper than the one in which Ugo Spirito, and the other critics of actual idealism, have believed to have found it: it is to be sought in the original dimension in which every form of civilization of the West appears; that is to say, it is to be sought in the faith in the existence of becoming – the faith that, throughout the history of the West, dominates the invocation *as well as* the destruction of every immutable being.

3 SOCRATES, SILENUS, AND VIRTUE

1

The invocation of the immutables dominates the philosophical tradition of the West; precisely for this reason, however, it subordinates to itself the rival stance, which is also present in the tradition of the West, and which does not posit through the *epistéme* an immutable dimension above becoming. The non-Platonic Socrates of the *Apology* may be included as part of this stance.

When Nietzsche sets Silenus' Dionysian wisdom in opposition to Socrates' scientific spirit, he turns his back on an immemorial tradition that, instead, links Socrates and Silenus – not only for what concerns their hideous appearance, but also for what concerns their shared 'irony'. Effectively, their paths cross, only to then diverge from one another.

After a long silence, Silenus at last bursts into laughter, and replies to King Midas, who wished to know from him what the best and most desirable thing for humans is: 'Wretched, ephemeral race, children of chance and tribulation, why do you force me to tell you the very thing which it would be most profitable for you *not* to hear? The very best thing is utterly beyond your reach: not to be born, not to *be*, to be *nothing*. However, the second-best thing for you is: to die soon' – (that is, to return as soon as possible to nothingness). Assuming that we may speak of a Silenus that is able to think the notions of being and nothingness, he states that it is 'most profitable' for humans 'not to hear' what is best for them. What is best for them is so dreadful that ignoring it is most profitable. What is best is ignoring what is best. However, since humans wish to know – and in this respect, too, be 'children of tribulation' – what is best is then 'not to be, to be nothing'; and, since it is impossible for those who are alive to not have been born, the best that can actually be achieved is to die soon: to return as soon as possible to nothingness.

In the *Apology*, Socrates states that he does not fear death, and that he has 'good hope' (*pollè elpís*, 40c) that death is something 'good'. Plato lets here his mentor speak. In the *Phaedo*, on the other hand – where Plato lets Socrates present the seminal 'proofs' of the immortality of the soul – things stand in a different way. Socrates hopes right away to be able to deliver 'a more persuasive argument' than the one he presented before the judges – that is, more persuasive than the one included in the *Apology*. It is precisely as part of this *less persuasive* argument, however, that Socrates' path crosses Silenus'.

2

'To fear death', Socrates states in the *Apology* (29 a–b) 'is nothing else than to think oneself wise when one is not, to think to know [*eidénai*] what one does not know'. The knowledge of which Socrates speaks here is the *epistéme*. Humans 'fear death as if they knew that it is the greatest of evils', while it could instead be 'the greatest of all blessings'. Socrates, however, states that he knows nothing – and, therefore, that he does not know whether death is something good. Precisely for this reason, he may not fear it and flee from it in the same way in which one flees and fears the things that may be known to be evils. The Socrates of the *Apology* – who is perhaps closer to the 'joy in adventure' of Nietzsche's *Übermensch*, and who is certainly at odds with the underlying stance of Greek thought – thinks that ignorance and a lack of knowledge constitute the foundation on the basis of which it is possible to free oneself from the fear of death.

Silenus' wisdom does not coincide with the *epistéme* (or, in any case, it only belongs to the 'base' of the *epistéme*, in the sense indicated in *Il giogo*, Emanuele Severino, Milan: Adelphi, 1989, Second Part, Chap. II, par. 3): his wisdom consists in knowing that humans proceed by chance out of nothingness, and there they return, always accompanied by a feeling of tribulation – and that, therefore, the best and most desirable thing for them would have been to remain nothing. Silenus certainly claims that it is 'most profitable' for humans 'not to hear' (that is, not to know what is best for them), insofar as he knows that humans, and first of all the Greeks, are convinced that not being – the not-being that follows death – is the greatest of all evils. Nevertheless, remaining nothing is regarded as what would have been best for humans insofar as it is believed that the greatest of all evils is, precisely, for those who are alive to definitively return to nothingness. The mode of thinking beyond which Silenus aims to move lies at the foundation of his own wisdom. Insofar as we are unable to have remained nothing, and rather than feeling the anxiety induced by death (and by the pain that anticipates it), what is best is to no longer be or feel anything.

In any case, according to both Silenus and Socrates, ignorance itself is profitable – even though, according to Silenus, it is profitable for those he regards as fools (namely, those who regard nothingness as the greatest of all evils), whereas, according to Socrates, ignorance is profitable for the wise ones, who ignore whether death is the greatest of all evils.

Nevertheless, it is not only Silenus who knows that being nothing is the best and most desirable thing for humans. The Socrates of the *Apology*, too, knows this. Together with Silenus, he leaves behind all fools, including the entire philosophical knowledge of origins – the knowledge that finds in truth, and in the content of the *epistéme*, a remedy against the pain and sorrow of death.

Towards the end of the *Apology* (40 c ff.), Socrates introduces a sort of argument in support of his 'good hope' that death may be something good. Death, he says, 'is either a no longer being anything' (*medèn eînai*) and a 'no longer perceiving anything' (*aísthesin medemían medenòs*), or it is a 'migration of the soul' to a different place. In the first case, death would be a 'wonderful gain', for no one would 'easily' find a night or day of their life that may be 'happier and more pleasant' than the night of death – in which one falls into 'so profound a sleep as to not even have the faintest dream'. Were death, on the contrary, to consist in a migration of the soul – a migration that, without annihilating the soul, would lead it outside of a world so devoid of happiness – then, there would be no greater good than death.

3

Thus, 'no longer being anything' and 'no longer feeling anything' are a 'wonderful gain' – in the same way in which, according to Silenus, what is best is 'to not be, to be nothing', and, therefore, to die as soon as possible. Nothingness is to be preferred over the hardship and pain that humans have to experience day and night: nothingness is to be preferred over the anxiety induced by nothingness itself. 'Oh, if only death, bringing everlasting sleep, were to come swift, painless, and spare us the bed of agony' (cf. *Interpretazione e traduzione dell'"Orestea' di Eschilo*, Emanuele Severino, Milan: Rizzoli, 1985).

If Silenus had run into the Socrates of the *Apology*, instead of King Midas, and had said to him: 'Even if for you it would be most profitable not to know this, the best thing for you is to be nothing', Socrates would have replied: 'I agree with you: if death is not a migration of the soul (a possibility that I, contrary to you, take into serious consideration), but a no longer being and feeling anything, then, certainly, death is for me the best and most desirable thing: a wonderful gain. Knowing this is therefore most profitable for me, as I think differently from everyone else'. For, indeed, he sails against the tide – the Tide being the way of thinking that regards the annihilation of humans as the origin of fear and anxiety. Unlike the Socrates of the *Apology*, this way of thinking does not find a remedy in a form of non-knowledge, but in a knowledge that is incontrovertible: in the *epistéme*, which reveals the destiny of humans in the world, and their power to prevail over nothingness, chance, and pain.

At the same time, however, Silenus' wisdom effectively constitutes only a part of the Socratic alternative (as to whether death is a form of annihilation or migration). Together with the possibility of a migration, the possibility of no longer being anything sustains the 'good hope' that death may be something good. The thought of death keeps Socrates suspended between the possibility of nothing and that of everything (that is, of the land of happiness to which the soul migrates), but the ultimate peace of mind does not dawn on him from that positive possibility (to dwell in the land of happiness), but from the fact that, in his view, both the 'positive' possibility and the 'negative' one (the annihilation) are in fact positive possibilities.

Kierkegaard has identified in this peace of mind the distinctive feature, as well as the limit, of the Socratic 'irony': that is, of the look that recognizes the nothingness of things, and finds peace in it. Later, however, Kierkegaard no longer sees in Socrates a master of irony, but a 'martyr' that is able to take a risk – namely, that is able to have faith: 'Socrates did not try to gather some proofs for the immortality of the soul'. This was so important to him that he staked his own life on it: 'His life is a proof of the immortality of the soul' (*Journals and Notebooks: Volume 7*, Stanford: Stanford University Press, 2014). Such is the risk of faith.

It is indeed Socrates' *faith* that once again distances him from Silenus. For what concerns the dimension of knowledge, Socrates keeps oscillating between the whole and the nothingness of death; through faith, however, he breaks away from that oscillation, and comes to *believe* that death is not a form of annihilation, but a migration to a land of happiness. It is for this faith that he has staked his life. He has thus anticipated the Christian faith at the very moment in which Greek thought makes an immense attempt at freeing itself from the fear of death through reason – and at moving, through the *epistéme*, beyond the dimension of faith. The Socrates of the *Apology* comes both too soon and too late. Too soon does he turn his back on his attempt, and too late does he once again advance a form of faith and myth: a form of the stance from which philosophy, in being born, has distanced itself.

4

The Socrates of the *epistéme*, according to whom the immortality of the soul is the content of a 'true and firm' *lógos* (*alethès kaì bébaios lógos*, *Phaedo*, 90 c), prevails instead in the *Phaedo*. In aiming to provide a 'more persuasive argument' than the one he delivered before the judges, Socrates adds that if he were not convinced by a true and firm *lógos* that dying means going to a better place he would be mistaken (*edíkoun án. . .*) in not being troubled by death (*ouk aganaktôn tô thanáto*) (63 b). This is a retraction of the fundamental stance of the *Apology*.

'Those who correctly philosophise [*orthôs philosophoûntes*]', Socrates states in the *Phaedo* 'practice [*meletôsi*] death, and they fear death least of all men' (67 e). The whole philosophical tradition expresses this idea, mirroring one of Socrates' most well-known concepts. Pierre Hadot, among others, has considered this concept (in his *Exercices spirituels et philosophie antique*) and claimed that, in relation to ancient Greek and Roman philosophy, it is also one of the most authentic and deeply rooted concepts of our culture. It is commonly said that 'one should be philosophical about life'. Beyond the level of banality, it is often believed that a philosopher is first of all someone who is able to live. Epictetus calls philosophy 'the art of living'; Hadot – following Bergson, Nietzsche, Kierkegaard and existentialism – emphasizes that philosophy has the character of an 'art', and of a 'spiritual practice' that allows individuals to think and live in a way that deviates from the ordinary one. A philosopher is not just an erudite, a scientist or a mentor; the primary task of philosophers is not the construction of a system or the communication of a doctrine, but a 'total metamorphosis' through which they are able to confront life itself.

These are, by now, old motifs of modern European culture. According to Hadot, however, these old questions are in fact age-old – so old that they can be traced to no less than the origins of philosophical thinking. For, indeed, Socrates states that philosophers 'practice': in view of what? In view of death. Hadot's historical scrutiny confirms, in its own way, that the fundamental meaning and task of philosophy in our civilization has been to pre-arrange a remedy against the anxiety induced by death – as well as by pain, insofar as pain, as Edmund Burke has stated, is such because it is regarded as the 'herald of the queen of all dreads': death. Practicing death thus means obtaining a remedy that may render the anxiety over one's annihilation bearable. For, indeed, (as La Rochefoucauld warns in one of his maxims) 'one may stare directly neither at the sun nor at death': neither at an excess of light nor at an excess of darkness. And, indeed, according to Plato, it is necessary to practice both in order to gaze at the sun of truth and to gaze at death.

Why, however, has philosophy succeeded, for a long time, in being a form of remedy and consolation? Because, in its traditional form, it has aimed to reveal the *immutable truth* of the Whole. Humans protect themselves from the becoming of the world by creating a connection with the immutable. Precisely for this reason, in the *Phaedo*, Socrates states that death is not intimidating for those who 'correctly' philosophize: that is, for those who philosophize with truth and by looking at truth. Correct philosophizing coincides with the *epistéme* – with a knowledge of the unerring and incontrovertible truth; with a 'true and firm *lógos*'. Philosophers may be freed from their fear of death only if it is true that the soul, in contemplating the Eternal, is itself eternal.

This means that, starting with ancient philosophy, and then through the whole philosophical tradition, every 'spiritual practice' is indissociably linked to the knowledge of truth, and that, without this knowledge, that practice most radically fails. In fact, the authentic practice that allows one to confront death is the very knowledge of truth: the *epistéme*. Even though Hadot struggles to realize it, knowledge, doctrines and systems – that is, the contemplation of truth – belong to the essence of the philosophical tradition. Hadot is fascinated by a Socrates who claims to know but one thing: that he knows nothing. Plato, however, certainly does not attribute to Socrates this 'negative' knowledge when he lets Socrates state that he does not fear death.

It would then be necessary to establish whether this 'I know that I know nothing' – together with other forms of Greek thought, such as scepticism and Silenus' wisdom – forebodes a content that is radically different from the one that the philosophical tradition has brought to light: a content, characteristic of contemporary culture, that consists in a lack of any patience for 'Truth' – that is, in a lack of any patience for the old remedy against death.

5

The Socratic 'I know that I know nothing' does not anticipate the destruction of the immutables and of epistemic truth that is carried out by contemporary thought. Socrates does not rule out the possibility of the *epistéme*: he only attests its absence (the *Apology* contains the word *sophía*, which, however, is understood as a synonym of *epistéme*, as for instance in *Protagoras*, 352 d). Socrates, however, knows what the existence of the *epistéme* would entail for human life. He knows that the existence of the *epistéme* would necessarily entail a notion of 'virtue', as well as the notion of an absence of it – a notion of 'ignorance' (*amathía*; *amathía* is the action performed without *epistéme*, *áneu epistémes*, *Protagoras*, 357 e): that is, of vice.

However, is there a contradiction between the claim that vice coincides with ignorance and the principle of the *Apology* according to which it is an ignorance concerning death that allows Socrates not to fear death itself ('I have no knowledge of things in Hades, and nor do I think I have it', 29 b)? Thinking together the principle of the 'I know that I know nothing' and the principle that vice coincides with ignorance (that is, with a form of not-knowing), it should be remarked that Socrates does not regard his not knowing what death is as a vice. At the same time, insofar as he asserts that his knowledge consists in his knowing to know nothing, is he not asserting that his virtue consists in knowing that he is not virtuous?

If, according to Socrates, every vice were a form of ignorance (of not-knowing), but not every form of ignorance were a vice – a vice being a form of ignorance concerning what is to be done: that is, an absence of the *epistéme* in human decisions – there would be no contradiction in claiming that not knowing what death is does not make one fear it, and, at the same time, that a vice is a form of ignorance concerning what is to be done. That is to say, there would be no contradiction in claiming, on the one hand, that the ignorance concerning death entails that lack of fear of death that Socrates does not regard as a vice, and in claiming, at the same time, that a vice is a form of ignorance concerning what is to be done. In the *Euthydemus* (and elsewhere), however, Socrates states that what are usually called 'goods' are not such 'in themselves' (*kath'hautá*), but only if they are ruled by 'science' (*sophía*): for, if they are ruled by ignorance, they are in fact 'greater evils than their opposites'. Accordingly: 'science is good, and ignorance is bad' (281 d–e; for the same concept, see *Phaedo*, 68–69, where the word *phrónesis* appears instead of *sophía*). That is to say, there is no form of ignorance that is not an evil – namely, a vice. Every form of ignorance is a vice.

Furthermore, the fear of death, too, constitutes a form of doing: faced with death, what are we to do? Are we to fear it, or not? And not knowing whether death is to be feared constitutes a form of vicious ignorance: thus, of this form of not-knowing, too, it may be said that it is 'the most reprehensible form of ignorance' (*amathía estìn haúte he eponeídistos*, *Apology*, 29 b) present in those who, like Socrates, claim to not fear death – 'the most reprehensible form of ignorance' being that of 'believing that one knows what one does not know' (*oíesthai eidénai hà ouk oîden*, ibid.).

It is precisely this last formulation, however, that indicates how Socrates' understanding (to the extent that the unity of those two principles may be regarded as his understanding) may be considered to be free from that contradiction. For, indeed, vice does not coincide with not-knowing as such, but, precisely, with *believing* to know what one does not know. A lack of fear of death is not a vice: but not because Socrates, despite not knowing what death is, does not fear it – for, in fact, according to Socrates' logic, not fearing death without knowing what it is (and, thus, without knowing if it is to be feared) constitutes a vice. Rather, a lack of fear of death is not a vice because Socrates knows that he does not know what death is: insofar as he knows this, he therefore cannot fear it *in the same way in which* it is feared by those who believe to know what it is. This means, however, that his not fearing death is different from the lack of fear of those who do not fear death while believing to know what it is, or while truly knowing what it is and thus knowing that it is not to be feared. In the same way, Socrates, in asserting that his knowledge consists in knowing to know nothing, asserts that his 'virtue' consists in knowing that he is not virtuous *in the way in which* those who know, or believe to know, are virtuous.

The lack of fear of death of the Socrates of the *Apology* has an, as it were, 'transcendental' or 'formal' character – and not an epistemic one. On the other hand, for the Socrates of the *Phaedo*, this lack of fear has an epistemic character, but not a 'transcendental' or 'formal' one – this 'transcendental' or 'formal' peace of mind (and 'virtue') constituting the 'positive' figure of the symmetrical 'negative' one of the 'anxiety' that, in Heidegger's thinking, is not directed at any determinate dimension of being.

6

There exists a (historical, or even just 'ideal') *place* where the Greek invocation of becoming brings about the most extreme form of anxiety: the anxiety induced by nothingness – the nothingness to which humans and things fall prey. The anxiety indicated at the end of the previous paragraph constitutes an *internal* configuration of the Greek anxiety: for, indeed, 'Being' – regarded as a 'Nothing' *of beings* (according to Heidegger's notion) – induces anxiety insofar as it is not a ground that succeeds in withholding beings within *being* (understood as the negation of the *nihil absolutum*), but lets them be swept over by *nothingness* (*nihil absolutum*). Thus, Heidegger's 'Being' is an *Abgrund*.

Silenus' 'Dionysian' wisdom dwells in that place, and so does *one* of the two sides of the Socratic alternative of the *Apology* (see above, par. 2–3): namely, the one in which Socrates asserts that, if death is a total annihilation, he would prefer the 'infinite time' (*ho pâs chrónos*, 40 e) of the 'sleep' of death – in which, 'the sleeper does not even dream' (40 d) – to the pain and the anxiety through which he has to go in life. In the same way, the hopeless chorus of Aeschylus' *Agamemnon* invokes 'a death that may bring an everlasting sleep'.

These, however, are the words of those who have lost sight of the saving truth (cf. *Il giogo*), and, contrary to the Socrates of the *Apology*, do not believe in the possibility that death may be a migration of the soul to a land of happiness (this is the second side of the alternative). The hopeless chorus of the *Agamemnon* isolates the first side of the alternative from the second one. It is in this respect that one should understand the proximity between the Socrates of the *Apology* and Silenus' Dionysian wisdom (granted that the possibility of reflecting over the notions of *being* and *nothingness* has been retroactively attributed to Silenus).

7

Why do humans do evil? It is said that it is because their instincts make them stray from the norms that govern them, in such a way that the will to respect those norms capitulates. In every form of society, the norms that govern life represent the 'good': individuals know these norms, but, often, overcome by their passions, they violate them. This is the predominant answer provided by our culture.

Christianity belongs to this mode of thinking. Jesus tells the Pharisees: 'If you were blind, you would have no sin' (*John* 9:41). The 'blind' *do not see* – that is to say, they do not know the norm to which they must conform. If they do not see this norm – if they ignore it – then, regardless of what they do, they do not commit a sin: they are not responsible. A sinner *sees* the norm, and recognizes its rightness – and, despite this, violates it.

Before Christianity, Ovid lets Medea, overcome by passion, express this same concept: 'I see what is best, and I approve of it; but I follow what is worse' (*Video meliora proboque, deteriora sequor*). In the *Epistle to the Romans* (7, 15), Paul the Apostle echoes Medea's words: 'For what I want to do I do not do, but what I hate I do'. However, well before Christianity and Ovid, this motif appears in the most ancient forms of Greek thought. And it is *against* this motif that Socrates turns.

According to Jesus, those who are 'blind' may not sin; according to Socrates, on the contrary, one sins *precisely because* one is 'blind': that is, because one ignores the norms that govern human life. Humans do evil out of ignorance (and, moreover, while believing not to be ignorant). As early as in Socrates' time, in the fifth century BC, his thesis sounds paradoxical and unacceptable. Humans do not do evil because they are overcome by passions and, led by their instincts, stray away from what they nevertheless recognize as being good; they do evil because they ignore what the good is – while nevertheless believing to know it. This thesis of Socrates' appears in a clearest and most compelling way in the grand conclusion of the *Protagoras*.

Aristotle has devoted a great deal of attention to the Socratic doctrine that humans do evil out of 'ignorance', and that 'virtue' thus coincides with 'science'. Aristotle, too, however, disagrees with Socrates. The latter, according to Aristotle, makes the mistake of 'thinking that each virtue is a kind of science'. According to Aristotle, this claim is unacceptable, for 'science' is an act of reason, and, by identifying 'truth' and 'science', evil and ignorance', one ends up 'doing away with the irrational part of the soul': namely, the will, 'as well as passions and moral characters'. In order to perform a good deed, it is not sufficient *to know* that it is good: one must also *wish* to perform it. One may *see*, or know, that it is a good deed, and, despite this, one may *not* wish to perform it. Once again, Aristotle and Christianity are in agreement.

And yet, Socrates' thinking concerning the nature of evil is not so easily dismissed; its complexity and power may be inferred from Aristotle's own words.

8

The whole issue concerns the term 'science'. This word does not indicate what we are used to thinking when we refer to modern science. In the context discussed here, the word 'science' translates the Greek word *epistéme*, which indicates the soul and the essence of what philosophy has, since its beginning, aimed to be: a *stability* (*-stéme*) of knowledge – a capacity for *standing* that prevails *over* (*epí-*) everything that may attempt to make it sway and yield. The *epistéme* thus indicates something altogether different from common sense. It indicates a knowledge that may not in any way be refuted: not today, not tomorrow, not ever; neither by humans nor by a God. It thus indicates a knowledge that differs from everything that humans commonly know and believe. For the first time in human history, philosophy has invoked the *idea* of this extraordinary knowledge, and has taken the first steps towards concretely determining what the form of knowledge that deserves the name of *epistéme* actually is.

What does then Socrates mean, when he asserts that virtue coincides with 'science', and that humans do evil out of 'ignorance'? In the *Protagoras*, Socrates states that when we eat something that could be harmful, despite knowing that it might be harmful, we do not eat it because it is harmful, but because it tastes good. If we eat it despite knowing that it is harmful, we do this because we believe that that future harm is inferior to this present pleasure. And yet, it often happens that the future harm is *greater* than the present pleasure. What does it mean to have been won over by passions – gluttony, wrath, envy, lust, pride? It means that one has not been able to 'measure' present pleasures and future evils, or present evils and future pleasures, thus remaining in the end with a greater share of evils than of goods.

For, indeed, if the one who acts possessed 'science' – the *epistéme* – and if the *epistéme* were to indicate, *in an absolutely incontrovertible way*, that the choice of a certain pleasure would inevitably come with a much greater pain (a pain that the one who chooses would never wish to suffer), this person would never choose to relish the present pleasure. If, while reaching out with your hand to grasp what you desire, it irrefutably appeared to you – through the light of the *epistéme* – that the enjoyment of this pleasure carries along an unbearable pain, you would immediately withdraw your hand and flee away – and thus be 'virtuous'. If you decide not to flee, but to relish that pleasure, this is because you do not see that light, and you choose the present good in the hope that the future evil will somehow be bearable. Evil is precisely an unbearable pain. Thus, those who do evil do so out of 'ignorance': that is, out of a lack of 'science' – by ignoring the connection that links this present pleasure to that unbearable pain. This is the reason why, according to Socrates, virtue coincides with 'science', and vice with 'ignorance'.

If you were blind, you would not sin; if you sin, it means that you see what you ought to do – thus reads the Gospel. You see what is better, but follow what is worse – thus state Medea and Paul the Apostle. Socrates objects: this kind of 'seeing' proceeds through shadows and haze; it is not the true seeing that gazes into the light of 'science'. If you were to truly see, through that light, what the consequences of your action are – if you possessed 'science' – you would never sin. According to Socrates, and contrary to what is described in the Bible, humans sin precisely because they have *not* tasted the fruits of the tree of the science of good and evil.

Socrates knows that he knows nothing, but this lack of knowledge does not compel him to ignore the consequences that a lack of knowledge entails for the human will. He does not know the *content* of 'science', but he knows what 'science' means, and it is on the basis of this knowledge that he is able to assert that 'virtue' coincides with 'science'.

In any case, Socrates' 'ethical intellectualism' does not erase the dimension of the will. 'Ethical intellectualism' and 'voluntarism' share an acknowledgement of the existence of the will: that is, of the human or divine 'principle' that lets beings oscillate between being and nothingness. This 'principle' appears today in its most rigorous form: as the apparatus of science and technics.

PART THREE

1 ON IDENTITY AND DIFFERENCE

1

Let us consider the beginning of the *De Interpretatione* (16a 3–8), in which Aristotle establishes the relationship between 'spoken sounds', 'affections of the soul' and 'things'. Spoken sounds (which, in turn, are indicated by written letters) are signs (*súmbola, semeîa*) of the affections of the soul (*pathémata tês psuchês*), and these affections are images (*homoiómata*) of things (*prágmata*). Contrary to sounds and written letters, which 'are not the same [*tà autá*] for all [*pâsi*]', 'the affections of the souls are the same for all, and so are the things of which these affections are images'. There exists a unique world for humans, and the images that, in the soul, mirror that world are the same for everyone. That is to say: not all images are the same for everyone, but, among those that are, we primarily have – even though not solely – those that succeed in having a content that is similar to the one of the world; Aristotle calls these images *homoiómata*. Spoken sounds and written letters, on the contrary, are not the same for all: they *change* from place to place (from region to region), and they even change within the same place. In the *Seventh Letter* (342a ff.), Plato advances – albeit in a different way – the same thesis of this passage of the *De Interpretatione*, and he explicitly affirms the *change* of what Aristotle calls written letters and spoken sounds, i.e. of what Plato himself calls 'names' (i.e. something 'spoken') and 'definitions' (*lógos*, understood – as in *Sophist* 263a – as a sensory collection 'consisting of names and verbs'). Within the names and definitions that we 'pronounce' (*ephthégmetha*, 342b), 'there is nothing fixed with sufficient firmness' (*medèn hikanôs bebaíos eînai bébaion*, 343b). Their radical instability consists precisely in the radical change that they undergo from place to place and from time to time: for, indeed, 'nothing prevents [*kolúein d'oudén*] the things that are now called "round" from being called "straight", and those that are now called "straight" from being called "round"' (ibid.). As a result, not only are names (as well as verbs) and definitions (i.e. written letters or spoken sounds) not the same for everyone, but they are not even the same for the same person.

In the philosophical tradition of the West, *what is the same for everyone* is conceived of in different ways; precisely for this reason, however, what remains unquestioned throughout the unfolding of that tradition is that there is something that is the same for everyone – and that is the same for everyone in that it does not change or become. The fact that words refer to something that is not itself a word (but which is a 'thing' or an 'affection of the soul') is a tenet that, in the last instance, is grounded in the conviction that there exist immutable things and immutable kinds of knowledge (that is to say, ones that are identical for everyone). It is indeed the case that, according to Plato and Aristotle, as well as to the entire philosophical tradition, words also indicate the world of becoming; nevertheless, they do so to the extent that there is something in that world that does not become: namely, to the extent that the immutable is mirrored in the world of becoming. What is the same for everyone in the world of becoming is what, in relating to each person, does not itself change: i.e. it is immutable.

After Hegel, and in an ever more definitive way, contemporary thinking comes to refute the existence of every immutable being. The 'linguistic turn' of contemporary thinking refutes every immutable because it refutes the principle according to which words refer to something that is not itself a word: that is, in that it asserts that it is not possible to break out of language. Language itself is certainly not regarded as a simple collection of written words and spoken sounds, but as a reference to a meaning. And yet, this is a reference as part of which meaning – i.e. the thing – once again appears in the form of a word, thus failing to rise above the change, becoming and historicity of the word itself.

In other words: according to the philosophical tradition, words refer to a thing that is not itself a word, because, in the last instance, there exists an immutable thing; the 'linguistic turn' comes to refute every immutable thing insofar as the thing that is referred to by the word (i.e. by a form of becoming and historicity) is, once again, regarded as a word. It is no coincidence that Heidegger, in reflecting on the Aristotelian passage from which we set out in our discussion (Martin Heidegger, *On the Way to Language*, New York: Harper & Row, 1971, p. 114), should remind us of Humboldt's notion of an 'influence' of language 'on the spiritual development of mankind' – as well as of Humboldt's principle that 'language, conceived of in its real essence, is something that persistently and in every moment *becomes*'; 'it is not *érgon*, but activity (*enérgeia*)'. Gentile, too, at the end of the second chapter of *Teoria generale dello spirito come atto puro*, recalls the same passage by Humboldt. Gentile, however (who, unlike Heidegger, is in agreement with Humboldt's idealism), does not refute all immutables because it is not possible to break out of language, but because it is not possible to break out of the becoming – i.e. the 'self-production' – of spirit (language being precisely a form of spiritual reality). Heidegger, on the other hand, insists that language should not be regarded in relation to anything other than itself (in this case: in relation to spirit), but that it should be 'experienced in its own terms – that is, in terms of language' itself (*On the Way to Language*, p. 117). The originary and insurmountable situation is given by a 'listening to language itself' (ibid. p. 123).

2

In his *Sophist*, Plato states that *diánoia* (thought) and *lógos* (speech) are 'the same' (*tautón*), 'except' (*plén*) for this: that 'thought' is an 'inner and voiceless conversation [*diálogos*] that the soul entertains with itself' (263 e), 'silently' (264 a), whereas 'speech' is a 'stream of sound that flows from the soul and goes through the mouth' (263 e). The notion of *diánoia* mentioned here by Plato corresponds to that of the 'affections of the soul' discussed by Aristotle. It is indeed the case that, at the beginning of the *De Interpretatione*, Aristotle lays emphasis on those affections that are the same for everyone in that they are 'images' (*homoiómata*) of things, and are therefore the most stable kind of images; this, however, does not preclude the existence of affections (such as pain, pleasure and opinions) that are the same for everyone as to their formal structure, without however being (true and stable) images of the world. Plato's use of the term *diánoia* (264 a–b) refers to both these kinds of affections. In the *Sophist*, on the contrary, the term *lógos* (speech) indicates both names and the *lógos* discussed in the *Seventh Letter*. *Lógos* (speech) and *diánoia* are 'the same' in the sense that they represent the same content, but according to two different forms: as a conversation that is internal to the soul (*diánoia*) – a conversation that may be more or less 'close' to the immutable thing (*Seventh Letter*, 342 b) – and (*lógos*) as the expression of that conversation through a 'stream of words'. It is to this 'conversation that the soul entertains with itself' – namely, to the collection of the 'affections of the soul' – that we now wish to turn our attention.

This conversation, Plato states, is 'voiceless' (*áneu phonês*): 'it takes place in silence'. These voices and sounds are the voices and the sounds of historically determined languages. The notion of the determined historicity of a language is anything but transparent; here, however, we aim to remark that – taking that notion in its ordinary usage (but the notion of 'ordinary usage', too, is anything but transparent) – when Plato refers to the silent conversation that the soul entertains with itself, he aims to say that, in that conversation, the determined historicity of language falls silent. The soul, insofar as it dialogues with itself, *does not speak* any historical language, but *thinks*. This is what constitutes the model of what the Western tradition understands as 'thinking'.

This model, however, also *negates* what appears. For it appears that the 'soul', even when it dialogues with itself, keeps speaking a historically determined language, and that this language may be interpreted as a 'historically determined language'. Thus, it *manifestly appears* that thought thinks in the form of language: namely, that it dwells in the element of language – and, therefore, that words constitute the form of what thought thinks.

This does not yet mean that 'man always speaks', and that 'it is as one who speaks that man is – man' (Martin Heidegger, *Poetry, Language, Thought*, New York: HarperCollins, 1971, p. 187.) Asserting that humans *always* speak, and that *there may not be* any human without language, entails positing a *necessary* - epistemic – *connection* between humans and language. Contemporary philosophy, however, insofar as it consists in a refutation of every immutable being and incontrovertible or epistemic truth, is not entitled to posit such a necessary connection. (What we are stating, however, is grounded *neither* in contemporary *nor* in traditional philosophy.)

Beyond the understanding that contemporary thinking has of itself, the faith in the existence of becoming necessarily entails the non-existence of every immutable being, or definitive truth, which would exist above and beyond becoming (cf. *Destino della necessità*, Chapter II.) However, it is precisely on the basis of that faith that it is possible to refute the absolute character of thought, as well as, therefore, its capacity to extend outside the becoming of language; it is not on the basis of an alleged attestation of a *necessary connection* between thought and language that contemporary philosophy (*qua* refutation of every form of *epistéme*: i.e. of every necessary connection) is able, by presupposing the becoming of language, to ground the non-absolute character of thought. Contemporary philosophy may not posit that necessary connection. On the contrary, contemporary philosophy – based on the faith in the existence of becoming, which rules out the existence of all immutable beings – may rightfully assert that the inseparability of thought and language expresses their inseparability from becoming itself. For, indeed (on the basis of that faith), the only necessary connection that pertains to beings is precisely their being inseparable from becoming: that is to say, their shared belonging to becoming and their shared inability to withdraw from it. (At the same time, becoming itself invariably separates beings from one another, in such a way that the only necessary connection that exists between them is the absolute lack of necessary connections that constitutes their becoming: i.e. their issuing from nothingness and their returning to it.)

And yet, *as a matter of fact*, there appears no 'conversation of the soul with itself' that does not take place in a language that may be interpreted as a 'historically determined language'. As it is often said, we always find ourselves thinking in our mother tongue. (And even when one states that the interior conversation of the soul *appears*, this '*apparire*' is a word of what is interpreted as the 'Italian language' – a language that, according to a specific set of interpretative rules, is claimed to derive from Latin, and, through Latin, from the original Indo-European linguistic systems.) Certainly, something like 'a mother tongue', or 'a historically conditioned language', does not appear as a datum of experience, but it appears (and, in this respect, it is 'given' [*dato*]) as part of an interpretation that situates the linguistic element in which thinking de facto appears (and in which that appearing appears) in a historical dimension. And yet, as a matter of fact, thinking appears in and through a linguistic element that becomes (and, in this sense, is 'historical') even independently of its being included by an interpretation in a 'historical context'.

In order to determine whether something may appear outside of any language, it is necessary to turn to what effectively appears; and yet, it is precisely in this turning to what is manifestly present that the problems and the difficulties proliferate. In any case, looking at what appears, it remains a problem whether something appears outside of every language (this is the problematic character that besets the claim that 'we are always speaking': i.e. the Heideggerian tenet, shared by most of contemporary philosophy, according to which nothing appears outside of language). There is no doubt, however, that a reflection that aims to determine the relation between the word and the thing (and, therefore, the possibility for the thing to appear outside of the word) is itself found to be expressed in and through a word – and, more precisely, in and through those words to which we refer as our 'mother tongue'. 'There is no doubt' means: 'it appears'. It appears that such a reflection is found in a self-differentiating and developing determined language. The interpretation of the meaning of this language compels us (but 'we ourselves', who are thus compelled, are in turn something that appears in and through a word) to recede further and further along what we call 'history', and to move further and further away from the centre in which the meaning of words seems to be at its clearest. That very same 'appearing', however, appears in and through the words that express it – words whose meaning, like the meaning of every word, refers to other words: *ad infinitum*. A reflection on the relation between the word and the thing never leaves the domain of the word and of its historical character. (The latter, however, appears as part of an interpretation that posits as historical the word with which thinking appears to be united.)

Having acknowledged this, however, are we not perhaps admitting that – precisely insofar as there is no definitive word – *no single thought* may itself be definitive and incontrovertible? In fact, since the aim of 'thinking' is to let the thing appear outside of its relation with the word, are we not perhaps asserting that 'thinking' itself is impossible – and, all the more so, that thinking which asserts the eternity *of every thing*, i.e. every thing's being removed from a becoming that would drive it from nothingness into being and from being into nothingness? (Cf. *The Essence of Nihilism, Destino della necessità*). We are going to show why this question must receive a *negative* answer.

In the meantime, let us reiterate that it certainly appears that the word constitutes the form of what thought thinks, but also that the historically determined character of this form does not appear as such, but is the result of an interpretation (i.e. it only appears as the content of that interpretation.) Thinking appears in and through a word; the historicity of this word, however, is a consequence of an interpretation that includes this word in what we call a 'historical context' – in the same way in which an interpretation includes all the other appearing determinations (for instance: my body, other people's bodies, objects, nature, etc.) in that same context. The linguistic element in which language appears may thus be interpreted as a 'historically determined language'.

The *incontrovertibility* of the *appearing* of the linguistic element in which thinking is de facto found is thus to be distinguished from the *problematic character* of the *interpretation* that posits that element as a 'historically determined language'. For it remains a problem (and not an appearing datum of experience) whether the linguistic element as part of which thinking is found should have the specific coordinates that interpretations ascribe to it (and to the other appearing determinations) as part of what is called a 'historical context'.

Thus, it is effectively the case that, as a matter of fact, thinking appears in its being linked with a word, but that the historicity of that word – and, therefore, its problematic and non-definitive character (which would overturn every alleged incontrovertibility of thinking) – is a consequence that originates from the application of an interpretation: an application that is, itself, problematic and non-definitive. The historicity of the word, as well as its problematic and non-definitive character, is therefore not a content that incontrovertibly appears. The problematic character of the word, and, therefore, of thinking is asserted on the foundation of an act – an interpretation – which is itself problematic.

Nevertheless, precisely insofar as something problematic is something possible, the controvertible and non-definitive character of thinking appears at this stage as a *possibility*: that is, as the possibility that the words through which thinking comes to life should be historically conditioned. (Furthermore, words are also seen to become independently of their being included in a 'historical context' by an interpretation; and the becoming of the word – in and through which thinking de facto appears – seems to overturn the alleged absoluteness of thinking.)

Are we then perhaps claiming that it is *possible* that there may exist no incontrovertible and definitive thought? In what follows, we are going to indicate why it is necessary that this second kind of question, too, should receive a *negative* answer. (In any case, the Platonic notion – shared by the entire Western tradition – of a thought that would appear outside of language contradicts what appears: i.e. it contradicts the *circumstance* in which the word constitutes the form and the element of thinking; even though, let us reiterate, it does not appear that this form or element consists in a 'historically determined' word, or a 'mother tongue', etc.)

3

Not even the philosophies of the 'linguistic turn' intend to deny that language is a sign, and that signs are references or relations: between the sign itself (i.e. the word) and that of which the sign is a sign – regardless of how this 'that of which' should be understood. Were a sign not relative to anything *other* than itself (which, according to those philosophies, is another sign – a sign, once again, but different from the first one), that sign would be a thing: that is, it would be a pure meaning (that pure meaning being an 'affection of the soul', a *prâgma*, or something still different). And if only pure meaning were to exist, there would be no language. Furthermore, meaning itself would exhibit precisely that character of purity and self-sufficiency that the philosophies of the 'linguistic turn' wish to refute. A sign is always a relation to something else: both in written or spoken language, and in the silent language through which the 'soul' dialogues with itself. Even if that of which a sign is a sign is in turn a sign, that of which a sign is a sign is the meaning of that sign.

And yet, meaning itself – *precisely in its being distinct from the sign (and in spite of this being distinct)* – is itself a sign. That is to say, it is, in turn, the meaning of a sign: but of a sign that differs from the sign from which that meaning is distinct. Precisely insofar as that meaning is distinct from that sign, it is, in turn, the meaning *of a word* (which is other than the sign from which that meaning is distinct) that belongs to a historically determined language; precisely insofar as meaning is distinct from the word, it appears, in turn, in and through a word.

If 'This is a lamp' is a series of written or spoken words, or a series of words that are part of an 'interior dialogue', the meaning of these words once again appears – precisely in its being distinct from those words – in and through a word (which, for the most part, but not necessarily, is part of one's mother tongue). The sign or the word is a sign, or a word, only insofar as it is in a relation with a meaning; this meaning itself, however, precisely in its being distinct from that sign or word, appears in and through a sign or a word that is part of a determined language (which, for the most part, is one's own mother tongue, but which could also be another historical or artificial language).

The meaning of 'This is a lamp' is this lamp, in its being one of the possible lamps; this lamp, however, in its being one of the possible lamps, and precisely in its being distinct from 'This is a lamp', is a meaning that appears *in and through* an expression (i.e. a sign or a word) of the English language: i.e. 'this lamp, in its being one of the possible lamps'.

This is the case even though the statement: 'This is a lamp' does not refer to that expression of the English language (that is, it is not a sign of this expression), but to this lamp – which, however, precisely in its being distinct from that expression, is in turn a meaning that is determined by an expression of the English language (or of some other language).

These considerations are analogous to the ones that the standpoint of idealism addresses to the realist theories of knowledge. According to the stance of realism, things stand apart from thought – their meaning and their determinacy being constituted independently of thought itself. The standpoint of idealism objects that things, thus separated, are nevertheless something thought, and, therefore, they are themselves thought representations. Thinking is already present in the things from which one would wish to keep it separate, *in the same way in which* the word is already present in the thing that would wish to present *its own* aspect – an aspect that differs from the one that the word confers to it. In the case at hand, however, it is thinking itself that, relative to the word, appears in the same way in which, according to the standpoint of idealism, things appear relative to thinking (thinking itself consisting precisely in the appearing thing, i.e. the thought thing). Thinking itself, in spite of its being distinct from the word, appears in the form of a word.

4

Through these last considerations, however, we have also remarked that there exists a multiplicity of ways of being a sign of this lamp (in its being one of the possible lamps), and that, therefore, as part of this *difference* of ways, there exists an *identity*. In order for this difference or multiplicity to exist, it is not necessary to speak different languages or use different expressions of the same language: it is enough to repeat the same sign (in the 'exterior' or in the 'interior' language). Repetition, as such, entails the self-differentiation of a sign.

We are claiming, however, that the different ways of being a sign of this being-a-lamp form a differentiation that refers to the identity constituted by this being-a-lamp. Language consists in a differentiation, in the domain of signs, of the multiplicity of identities that underlie the multiplicity of series respectively constituted by the different ways of being a sign of something identical. If one asserts that language consists in a pure differentiation of signs and meanings *without any persisting identity, one negates what one asserts: that is to say, one asserts an identity* – for, in asserting the existence of a set of differences, one also asserts their being identical as to their being, precisely, differences. (Every difference is, precisely, a being-a-difference, and every difference, in its being a difference, is identical to any other difference.) Asserting that, in language, there are no identities, and there are only differences, means asserting that what is identical as part of language is the very difference of signs and of that of which signs are signs.

This entails that, in language, the being-sign of every sign, too (i.e. its being a relation or reference to something other) is something identical; and so is the being-designated of everything that is designated (i.e. of the other to which the sign refers); as well as the self-being of every sign and of everything that is designated; as well as their not being, respectively, any other sign or designated meaning; as well as, therefore, the system of determinations implied by these identical determinations of those differences. A negation of identity coincides with its affirmation (and, therefore, with the affirmation of a structure of identities).

In order not to be compelled to affirm what one negates, it is therefore necessary to affirm that, as part of the multiplicity of ways of being a sign of something, there appears the identity of that something of which its signs are signs. This identity – implicitly acknowledged by every negation of identity – is what is referred to by the system of differences that constitute the language formed by that negation (which consists in a series of differences at least insofar as that negation is repeated). The identity that must necessarily be affirmed insofar as its negation is self-negating is not only the identity of those differences (their being identical *qua* differences), but it is also the identity of that which is referred to by those differences. If one rejects this second aspect of that identity, it is not even possible to speak of differences (or even of a single difference), for 'difference' is the identity that is referred to by the series of differences that indicate it (i.e. by the different ways of being a sign of 'difference').

As part of the (infinitely) many ways of being a sign of this being-a-lamp, there appears that identical thing that is this being-a-lamp. The identity we are discussing here is, precisely, the identity *of that to which* a series of signs *refers*; it is not the identity, in a sign form, of the signs that indicate it (be they 'exterior' or 'interior'). It is the identity of the meaning of those signs. If one affirmed the identity in the sign forms and negated the identity of the thing – thus negating the thing itself – the identity of the sign forms would itself come to coincide with the identity of the thing. When one speaks of something, one does not *eo ipso* speak of what is identical in the different ways of speaking of that something (i.e. in the sign form of its signs) – even though, precisely as it is happening now, the thing of which one speaks *can* be what is identical in the different ways of speaking of something. (In this latter instance, what is being spoken of – what is being referred to – is *this* sign identity and not, *eo ipso*, the sign identity that appears in the sign form of the signs that, in different ways, refer to that first sign identity.)

At the same time, stating that the different ways of being a sign of something indicate the identity in which that something consists does not mean that those sign differences *only* indicate something identical, but it means that that what they indicate is not only a difference, but also, and necessarily, a semantic identity. (The various expressions that, in different languages, 'have the same meaning' *also* have – as it is well known – different meanings: a difference being present not only in the sign, but also in the thing. This is also the case for the 'same' expression as it is uttered under different circumstances.)

5

Undoubtedly, the identity, *too*, constituted by the thing (for instance, this being-a-lamp) to which the various ways of speaking about it refer is a meaning that is determined by a certain way of speaking (i.e. it is and it appears as part of a certain way of speaking). The identity of these differences, too, is and appears as part of a difference. Even if one distinguishes what is internal (an identity) from what contains it and encloses it (a difference), the internal meaning de facto always is and appears as part of a certain way of speaking about it (i.e. as part of a sign difference.) If one wishes to think what, of a thing, lies beyond the linguistic expression that indicates it, this appears once again as part of another linguistic expression.

From all this, however, it does not follow that the identity of a set of differences does not exist and does not appear – for, as we have seen, this identity may not be negated. Rather, it follows that this identity is an identity of differences not insofar as it is a difference, but insofar as it is an identity that is and appears as part of a certain difference. This being-a-lamp, which is the identity to which the different ways of being a sign of it refer, is a meaning that appears as part of a (rather uncommon) expression of the English language ('this being-a-lamp'); however, it is an identity (of the differences that express it) not insofar as it is an expression of the English language (namely, not insofar as it is one of the differences that express it), but insofar as it is the meaning of that expression.

At the same time, identity, *qua* identity of differences, is not a pure identity separated from those differences, but it is an identity enclosed by a difference. Asserting that every difference encloses and contains the identity of the differences that enclose and contain that identity means asserting that one of the differences that enclose that identity (for instance, the difference consisting in the expression of the English language: 'this being-a-lamp') is adopted as the identity of those differences not insofar as it is a difference, but insofar as it encloses that identity. Those differences, in turn, are and appear only insofar as they are not – and do not appear as – pure differences that are separated from their identity, but insofar as they enclose that identity and appear in their enclosing it.

The fact that identity appears as part of a difference (leaving aside the problem as to whether this is a necessity or a constant fact) cannot entail a negation of the existence of identity, but, rather, constitutes a *circumstance* as part of which identity never appears outside of a difference. It is *in its* being thus enclosed – even though not *insofar as* it is thus enclosed – that identity is an identity of differences. (Furthermore, 'identity' consists of what is identical in all the *identities* addressed by language. All identities are identical in their being an identity.)

6

Identity may not be negated. As identities appear, however, they do not persist unchanged. It is not only words that change, but things as well. Since we started talking about it, this being-a-lamp has been replaced by infinitely many other ways of being this being-a-lamp; and this very infinite series has entered appearing, and it will supposedly leave it (in the same way in which infinitely many other infinite series have left appearing), should what we call 'the destruction of this lamp' come to appear. A thing, however, also changes insofar as every variation of its context determines a variation of its meaning (one of the elements of the context of a thing being the very sign of that thing, i.e. the word that indicates it). This, too, is an assertion that contemporary thinking may not be entitled to make, for it implies the existence of a necessary connection between a thing and its context, whereas contemporary thinking (if it is coherent to its own ground: namely, the faith in the existence of becoming) refutes every necessary connection. It is an assertion that not even the *epistéme* of the tradition of the West may be entitled to make, for no *epistéme* – that is, no necessary connection – is possible on the ground of the faith in the existence of becoming. (The necessary connection that links every being to every other being is the eternity of every being; a thing 'changes' in that its different aspects consist of a certain series of eternals that, one after the other, come to appear as part of appearing.)

Furthermore, a thing also changes insofar as the meaning in which it consists refers to infinitely many other meanings, and insofar as, through each of these referrals, the original meaning comes to be transformed. These referrals do not take place purely in the dimension of meaning: what is referred is a meaning that is enclosed by a word, as well as the word that encloses that meaning. The word that encloses a meaning refers to its own historical condition; it is a historical word. According to contemporary thinking, every word – and every thing – is historical. According to the philosophies of the 'linguistic turn', every thing is historical *because* every word is historical.

Given the way in which, at the beginning of the civilization of the West, the being (the being-a-thing) of a thing has been conceived of, the positing of the historicity of every thing and of every word is an *inevitable* consequence. The *epi*-stéme fails to *stand*.

The dimension of truth, however, which stands always already open – 'here', 'now' – *outside* of the 'history' and 'pre-history' of the West – and *outside* of the very occurrence of 'mortals' – manifests the impossibility of its own negation. Insofar as it may not be negated, this dimension coincides with what *stands*: de-*stiny* – the standing of truth (cf. *La struttura originaria*; *The Essence of Nihilism*; *Destino della necessità*). The destiny of truth is what may not be negated insofar as *its negation is self-negating*. The 'impossibility' of negating the destiny of truth coincides precisely with the self-negation of its negation (cf. 'Returning to Parmenides', par. 6, in *The Essence of Nihilism*). At the heart of the content of destiny there appears the eternity of every *being*: i.e. of every thing – including, therefore, those things that consist in the words and in the relations between words and things. The appearing of identity, too, according to the different ways of expressing it, is part of the content of destiny. (As we have seen, the negation of identity is, precisely, self-negating: i.e. it is an affirmation of identity itself.)

Here, however, we only wish to indicate that the destiny of truth appears in and through language; it appears in its being expressed by a word. This word, too, consists in a multiplicity of ways of being a sign of the destiny of truth. In this instance, too, the destiny of truth consists of the identity that is present in that multiplicity: the identity referred to by an infinite series of sign differences. *This identity, however, is the irrefutable.* Only this identity – which first of all constitutes the originary structure of destiny, namely, the standing of truth – is the irrefutable. Insofar as that identity is the irrefutable, it *abides* in its irrefutability through the infinite self-differentiation of the language that expresses it. The connection and the reference of the meaning of that identity to the infinitely many varying and historically conditioned meanings may not determine its refutability (even though that connection and that reference determine that specific 'self-contradicting' of the irrefutable discussed in Chapter VIII of *La struttura originaria* – the 'C-contradiction').

The identity in which the irrefutable destiny of truth consists, too – precisely in its being distinct from the sign differences that express it – appears as part of a difference: that is, as part of a certain historical language (which, in turn, insofar as it *reiterates* the irrefutable, consists of a series of differences). This, however, has nothing to do with the claim that the 'irrefutable', 'destiny', the 'self-negation of the negation of the irrefutable', etc. constitute a 'game' of a certain language – a game that is surrounded and confuted by other linguistic games. The English language is coordinated with other languages that are able to express the irrefutable. It is in and through these languages that the irrefutable appears as such. If any language refutes the irrefutable, that language negates its own negation of the irrefutable. (The self-negation of the negation of the irrefutable is concretely considered – as to its meaning and its necessity – in the writings recalled above.) If any language says something *other*, or the 'absolutely other', of the irrefutable, then that language may be refuted. What we are writing here, too, is part of a language that indicates the traits of the irrefutable. It is written in a certain language: this, however, does not mean that it is merely a linguistic game that may be replaced or transgressed.

7

A word may refer to a thing only if that thing appears – that is, only if the identity appears that is referred to by the different signs that indicate it. It is necessary that there should appear the semantic determination, though not separated by its difference, that consists in the meaning – for instance: *lamp, identity* – of the identity that is referred to by the different ways of indicating it. (The identity considered here is the identity of a certain meaning – that is, of a certain thing – and not identity posited *qua* identity; granted that this identical meaning may be the one of identity itself, precisely if one is speaking of identity.) If there appeared no identity, and things only appeared in their being differences – in such a way that the pure difference of things corresponded to the pure difference of words – there would not even appear the very difference of things: that is to say, there would not even appear a world (once again, the difference under consideration being the difference of meanings – i.e. of the different meanings – and not, *eo ipso*, of difference posited *qua* difference). Indeed, if *this thing and this other thing* appear (this appearing constituting the minimal structure of a world), this thing and this other thing are *identical* as to their each being the other of the other one; if there appeared no identity, however, this thing and this other thing would not be able to appear. Furthermore, if there appeared no identity (namely, what persists from a 'before' to an 'after'), there could not even appear a differentiation of things and signs (i.e. there could not appear the coming to pass of the eternal differences), for the appearing of that differentiation entails that the 'past' should continue to appear – identity being precisely what appears both when the 'present' has not yet 'passed' and when the 'present' has 'passed' (cf. *Destino della necessità*, Chap. VI; *La filosofia futura*, Part IX).

If the word is a reference to a thing (and if the irrefutable includes the authentic meaning of necessity), identity necessarily appears. It is however not necessary that a certain word should be the sign of a certain thing, nor that a thing should be the sign of another thing. That a thing should be a sign (i.e. that a thing should be the word of another thing), and that a certain sign should be the sign of a certain thing, is something *willed* (cf. *The Essence of Nihilism*, pp. 269–273; 289–292; *Law and Chance*, pp. 53–60; *Destino della necessità*, Chapter XII–XV; *La filosofia futura*, Part V). This is not an arbitrary will, through which humans relate to language in the way in which they relate to artificial languages. Humans *find themselves* being that will. Their finding themselves always already part of language coincides precisely with their finding themselves being that will.

The will, however, which assigns signs to things is part of the will that isolates the earth from the destiny of truth ('The Earth and the Essence of Man' in *The Essence of Nihilism*): namely, the will that, looking at itself, sees itself, in turn, as 'God', 'human', a 'people', a 'social institution', a 'scientific-technological apparatus'. Humans are not the subject of a will that may arbitrarily avail itself of language, but the will (i.e. the faith) that assigns signs to things is the same will that assigns to itself its being 'God', 'human', a 'people', a 'social institution', a 'scientific-technological apparatus'. Certainly, humans may not avail themselves of language: the will posits humans as well as language. (This assertion, too, constitutes a segment of the irrefutable – i.e. of the destiny of truth – which appears as part of language; language, however, also speaks of the will that posits it.) The distinction between an 'intentional' and an 'unintentional' attribution of a sign to a thing is *internal* to the will itself *qua* positing of language and of humans. Even when it is 'unintentional', the attribution of a sign to a thing does not take place with necessity; the will, in its originary meaning, consists precisely in the positing of what is not necessary.

Furthermore, the identity, referred to by the differences that express it, may in turn be a meaning that is *willed* as the determination of another meaning. In stating: 'This is a lamp', the meaning *lamp* (which is, or includes, the identity referred to by the different ways of expressing that being-a-lamp) determines the meaning that consists in the *this-ness* indicated by the word 'this'. However, *that* this this-ness (which consists in a series of empirical determinations: e.g. a form, a colour, a brightness, a resistance, etc.) should constitute a lamp is an interpretation: that is to say, it is the will for a meaning (a certain this-ness) to have an additional meaning relative to the one that it immediately appears to have (or that it appears to have in a relatively immediate way).

Not every meaning, however, which is posited as a determination of another meaning, consists in an interpreting will. As part of the dimension of the irrefutable, the fact that this series of empirical events should be a lamp constitutes a problem; but the fact that this collection should be a this-ness – or a being, or other than its other – does not constitute a problem, but a necessary connection.

The interpreting will and the will for something to be a sign of something else are part of the will that separates the earth from the irrefutability of destiny; on the ground of this will, the West conceives of

120 BEYOND LANGUAGE

the earth as a secure region, as part of which things issue from nothingness and return to it (thus bringing about the fundamental lack of security that characterizes humans). This is the thinking of nihilism: the extreme form of alienation; the essence of untruth. A *will* to assign words to things, however, is also present in the language that testifies to destiny. The will to speak of truth does not belong to truth itself. This is an additional problem that confronts the thinking that enquires into the meaning of the twilight of untruth.

8

The irrefutable is the originary (cf. *La struttura originiaria*). At the heart of the irrefutable, there appears the impossibility for beings not to be. Thinking that beings are not means thinking that beings are nothing. Therefore, thinking that beings, as part of becoming (time, history), issue from nothingness and return to it means thinking that beings are nothing. The fact that beings are not nothing – namely, the opposition of beings and nothingness – is a segment of the irrefutable in that the negation of that opposition is self-negating (cf. 'Returning to Parmenides', par. 6, in *The Essence of Nihilism*). The irrefutable is originary precisely insofar as it is impossible for that whose negation is self-negating to be posited on the grounds of something else. The originary has thus nothing to do with 'what appears for the first time' or with the 'instant' – which appear to constitute Husserl's notion of the originary (at least in J. Derrida's interpretation).

Beings – that for which it is impossible not to be – include in the first place those beings that appear; an appearing being consists in a relationship between a word and a thing, and, therefore, in an infinite repetition and differentiation of a thing in and through a word (as well as in and of itself, *qua* thing). Every thing consists of an infinite self-differentiation. (And every difference is eternal: the differentiation of a difference consisting in the eternal differences entering and leaving the circle of appearing.) Nor, therefore, is the originary a contraction of differences in an 'instant' or in a 'first time'; rather, it is the irrefutable appearing of differences and of their differentiations. Among the identities whose differences are those differences and their differentiations, however, there appears the structure of those identities whose negation is self-negating – the originary structure of the destiny of truth. That is to say, this structure consists in the appearing of the relationship between the (self-differentiating) identities of untruth and the (self-differentiating) identities of truth – the latter of which, as such (namely, since they are irrefutable in that their negation is self-negating), may not be overthrown or refuted by their own differentiation. It is thus the authentic meaning of this originary irrefutability that grounds that 'possibility of an infinite repetition of the originary' that, in Husserl's thinking, takes on the task of safeguarding the truth of the originary. The originary does not coincide with the destiny of truth insofar as, through an infinite repetition of its content, it is valid 'for everyone', but because *in spite of* that differentiation – which is (also, but not solely) due to an indefinite repetition of the content of the originary – the originary consists of the structure of identities whose negation is self-negating.

9

Already Plato and Aristotle – and Parmenides before them – think the identity that unifies the differences (i.e. the words) that express it. In stating that 'things' and the 'affections of the soul' are the same for everyone – contrary to writing and to spoken sounds – Aristotle precisely thinks that 'things' and the 'affections of the soul' are what is identical in the differences of words.

However, it should be remarked that the distinction between 'affections' and 'things' is internal to the very things – i.e. to the domain of beings – that are indicated by a word; all the same, it should be remarked that this distinction is internal to the word itself, for the thing de facto appears in and through a word. The reference from the word to the thing is halted at a thing that *at present* does not, in turn, appear as the word *of* another thing, but only as a thing – even though the latter *may*, in turn, appear as a thing that constitutes the word of another thing.

On the contrary, according to Greek thought, and to the entirety of the philosophical tradition, the thing is external to the word: that is to say, it is not, in turn, a word. Identity is external to the differences of its signs: it is not, in turn, a difference. This Greek standpoint is once again confirmed by the way in which Husserl, in the first of his *Logical Investigations* (§ 11), conceives of the relationship between the identity of meaning and the differences of language. Hamann, on the contrary, as Heidegger recalls, is arguably the first to think that the thing (as well as reason, in its comprehension of the thing) is always found in and through a word, and that every identity is always a difference: i.e. that 'reason is language, *lógos*'. Heidegger, and those who can be traced back to him, essentially remain within the perspective offered by Hamann.

If, however, the philosophical tradition separates the thing from the word – identity from difference – Hamann, Heidegger, and the entirety of contemporary thinking either fail to detect the presence of an identity across differences (Wittgenstein), or, if they do recognize it, they only recognize the identities (meanings) that have a historical character: i.e. the identities that may be challenged, modified, replaced, negated, overcome or destroyed. Contemporary philosophy destroys the immutable beings and definitive truths of tradition; these immutable beings and truths, however, are precisely identities (semantic structures) that claim to stand above a historical development *whose existence they nevertheless acknowledge*. The destruction of the immutable beings and definitive truths of tradition is an *inevitable* consequence of the Greek faith in the existence and self-evidence of becoming and in the existence and self-evidence of the development of history. The entirety of the civilization of the West unfolds as part of this faith.

The irrefutable, however – the destiny of truth and being – appears *outside* of that faith. Destiny appears outside of that faith as the originary semantic structure of the identities whose negation is self-negating. The destiny of truth and being, too, appears as part of language and as part of the historicity of language; destiny, however, *stands*, and is not overthrown by the becoming of the word: for, as part of destiny, the identity that appears in and through the differences of language is the irrefutable itself.

The irrefutable content – the irrefutable meaning – includes in the first place the eternity of every being. The eternity of every being includes the eternity of every word. Outside of the faith in the originary and definitive nothingness of all beings, the 'becoming' of the word consists in its entering and leaving, *qua* eternal, the eternal circle of appearing. If 'being that can be understood is language', language is being, and being (the totality of what is, the totality of beings) is eternal. This does not mean that there exists a dimension of being that is not intelligible: the intelligibility of being is the relation between being itself and the destiny of truth. The destiny of truth is the destiny of being. If the unintelligible confutes (negates) destiny, it refutes and supersedes itself (it is self-negating). If it is the 'absolutely other' of destiny (an absolute foreignness to destiny, an absolute impossibility to be expressed or to become intelligible), it is refuted and superseded by destiny. The destiny of being and truth asserts that every word – every thing – is eternal. Eternal are the words of untruth, and eternal are the words of truth. A necessary connection links the former with the latter. Truth binds itself to its own negation: it is the unity of itself and of the self-supersession of its negation.

As part of the Western faith in the existence of becoming, the word fails to be the word of a thing. It is inevitable that the word should realize that it is always the word of other words. The Western tradition *attempts* to posit the thing by positing an immutable being – which is 'the same for everyone' – above becoming (whose existence is thus acknowledged). If becoming exists, however, there may not exist any immutable beings. The principle according to which the word never lands at a thing is one of the most decisive ways in which the West destroys the immutable beings of its tradition. The word may succeed in being the word of a thing only if that thing is the destiny of truth and being – that is, only if the faith of the West comes to its twilight.

2 THE UNFOLDING OF LANGUAGE AND THE APPEARING OF DESTINY

1

In the philosophical tradition of the West, 'truth' primarily consists in the stable Meaning of the totality of beings. It is stable because it does not let itself be overthrown by the becoming of the world, but, rather, dominates it, makes it possible and sustains it. The domination of truth does not aim to be an event that takes place in time (i.e. as part of the becoming of the world): its domination is always already in place. This, however, means that truth has always already been the ultimate form of *power*. Truth is power – energy, act, force. Power acts upon the becoming of things: namely, on the sequence of events as part of which things (occurrences, thoughts, languages) stretch out of nothingness and return to it.

The incontrovertibility of truth coincides precisely with its stability: i.e. with its not letting itself be overthrown by the becoming of thought and of the world. In the philosophical tradition of the West, the incontrovertible is defined as that which may not be refuted; in the last instance, however, the impossibility of thinking the contrary of the incontrovertible is grounded in the impossibility for becoming to overthrow the stability of the incontrovertible.

The faith in the existence of becoming thus essentially belongs to the meaning of the incontrovertible. For, indeed, the possibility that becoming may overthrow the incontrovertible is ruled out precisely, and primarily, insofar as the existence of becoming is acknowledged. The negation that appears in that 'may not be negated' that pertains to the incontrovertible is essentially connected to the acknowledgment of the existence of becoming (as this has once and for all been conceived of in the 'history' of the West by Greek thought). Becoming does not succeed in negating the incontrovertible, and is thus always dominated by it. 'Truth' consists in the prevailing of the power of the incontrovertible over the power of becoming. Insofar as it prevails, truth is *epi-stéme*: namely, it is what *stands*, asserting itself *over* any negation that would attempt to overthrow it.

Certainly, the truth envisaged by Greek thought is also *alétheia*: unconcealment. However, what, as part of truth, is unconcealed is the stable and epistemic Meaning of the totality of beings. This Meaning is stable, on the one hand, because it is stably (i.e. incontrovertibly) unconcealed, and, on the other hand, because what is stably unconcealed is the relation between beings that become and the one un-becoming Being – the Immutable.

The Immutable (i.e. God), too, is not overthrown by becoming. Its not being overthrown, however, is not a simple hypothesis only if it constitutes an incontrovertible truth, and, thus, only insofar as the incontrovertible truth of the *epistéme* is the originary immutable within which the Immutables of Western metaphysics come to be erected one after the other. Precisely for this reason, the history of the *epistéme* comes to a close with classical idealism, with the knowledge that the authentic Immutable is the unity of the *epistéme* and of its immutable content (the 'Idea' being the content of the 'science of logic') – as a consequence of which it is therefore this unity that exerts its domination over becoming and that acknowledges the latter's very existence.

2

Truth acts upon becoming by dominating it – in the sense that it *prevents* it from prevailing: it *annihilates* the prevailing of becoming. The prevailing of becoming is always already annihilated; the meaning of the domination of truth, however, may not be separated from the annihilation of that prevailing. Precisely insofar as the truth of the *epistéme* acts upon becoming by dominating it, it does not simply attest that the prevailing of becoming is a nothingness, i.e. it is not an attestation of the nothingness of nothing, but it is a *turning* of the prevailing of becoming *into nothing*

– it is an (always already occurred) annihilation of a *positivity*. Truth does not posit the nothingness of something that is recognized as being nothing, but the nothingness of something that is recognized as a being – and, in fact, as a being that is originarily self-evident. Truth would not be a power that acts upon becoming by dominating it if it did not annihilate any part of becoming. If a form of power did not annihilate any part of what it acts upon, what is acted upon would be independent of that power, and, thus, that power would not be a power. A power that creates, too, must withhold within nothingness – and, therefore, annihilate in the domain of the created – all the possible worlds that it does not wish to create.

For, indeed, becoming – according to how, starting with the Greeks, it has been interpreted in the culture of the West – has no propensity for being dominated by truth. Becoming is a power that is antithetical to the power of truth, because the nothingness from which beings originate requires that beings themselves should constitute an *absolute* innovation: that is to say, an innovation that may not in any way be anticipated by the domination that truth exerts upon everything – including, therefore, what is still nothing. Truth is a power that annihilates becoming because becoming is a power that requires the annihilation of truth (a power that, ultimately, succeeds throughout the 'history' of the West in *obtaining that annihilation*, driving the truth of the *epistéme* to its twilight).

As long as the truth of the *epistéme* governs the 'history of the West', that truth annihilates becoming, for it prevents becoming from constituting that absolute innovation (free from the domination of truth) that pertains to what originates from nothingness. This annihilation of the prevailing power of becoming is the very anticipation of everything that arises. As part of this anticipation, the nothingness from which what arises originates is transformed into a being. The truth of the *epistéme* is an entification [*entificazione*] of nothingness (cf. *Law and Chance*, Part One; *Destino della necessità*, Chap. II; *La tendenza fondamentale del nostro tempo*, Chap. II, par. 9; *La filosofia futura*, Chap. V, par. 4).

According to the truth of the *epistéme*, the conviction that becoming succeeds in prevailing over truth – i.e. that it succeeds in being what, according to that truth, is a form of prevailing – constitutes the 'error'. Error is the conviction that what may not be is. According to the truth of the *epistéme*, however, what may not be is that becoming should succeed in overthrowing truth. According to the *epistéme*, in the same way in which truth is a negation of the prevailing of becoming (i.e. it is a negation of its own negation) – in the sense that truth has always already annihilated that prevailing – truth is a negation of the error, in the sense that truth is the annihilation of the error in time. Truth is the annihilation of the error *qua erring* – for the content of the error is always already annihilated by truth. Truth is a form of annihilation.

The *epistéme* certainly distinguishes negations *qua* 'logical' operations from negations *qua* real forms of annihilation; according to the *epistéme*, however, what lies at the foundation of the 'logical' operation of negation is a real annihilation. This real annihilation consists both of an (always already occurred) annihilation of the prevailing of becoming *and* of a temporal annihilation of the error *qua* erring: i.e. of the conviction that becoming prevails over and overthrows truth (these forms of prevailing and overthrowing, in turn, being conceived of as annihilations of truth). According to the truth of the *epistéme*, the purest of theoretical negations is a real annihilation of what is negated. The praxism of contemporary culture – as part of which the negation of the truth of the *epistéme* is, precisely, inseparable from the practical act of annihilating what claims to stand as an incontrovertible truth – belongs to the essence of the pure theoreticism of the *epistéme*.

3

In the 'history' of the West, however, the *epistéme* of truth is *destined* to its twilight. This 'destination' is something essentially more radical than any destruction of the truth of the *epistéme*, as carried out by philosophical thinking after Hegel. For, indeed, this destination is part of *destiny*: it is part of what always already *stands* (de-stiny), manifest, outside of the occurrence that isolates the earth from it – the occurrence as part of which the being-mortal of mortals occurs – and, thus, always already outside of the 'history' of the West. The 'history' of the West is the 'history' of nihilism; within it, humans testify to the isolation of the earth, and try to make the truth of the *epistéme* stable (cf. 'The Earth and the Essence of Man' in *The Essence of Nihilism*; *Destino della necessità*, Chap. XII–XIII).

The destiny of truth is not the *epistéme* of truth. It is not truth *qua* ultimate form of power that dominates becoming, acknowledging its existence and being thus destined to be overthrown by what it wishes to dominate. The destiny of truth is the incontrovertible; it is not a form of power, energy, act or force that acts upon becoming by dominating it. The incontrovertible, *qua* destiny of truth, is not a form of power, since it manifests the impossibility of the non-being of beings (i.e. the impossibility of their being-nothing before stretching out of nothingness, as well as the impossibility of their being something that has been and will return being nothing, and the impossibility of their being-nothing once they have returned being nothing.) The incontrovertible, *qua* destiny of truth, is not a form of annihilation, since it manifests the eternity of every being, thus manifesting the impossibility of the interpretation of becoming that governs the West. Precisely for this reason, the 'history' of the West is not a history in the sense in which the West thinks of history: namely, as a sequence of events in which beings issue from nothingness and return to it. The 'history' of the West consists in the progressive appearing of the eternals that constitute the extreme folly of the West – i.e. the conviction that beings are nothing.

The destiny of truth is, in its *essence*, the appearing of the totality of beings: namely, the totality of what (determinacies, meanings) is self-identical and other than its own other. The West fails to think the self-being of beings: it fails to think that, precisely insofar as beings are self-identical, they are other than their other, and, therefore, other than that other that is nothingness. Precisely insofar as beings are not nothingness, it is impossible that a being may not be. Every being is eternal.

The West fails to think the opposition between beings and nothingness. The *epistéme* of truth is 'destined' to its twilight because the destiny of truth consists in the *standing* of the opposition between beings and nothingness; it is as part of the appearing of this standing (and not as part of what the West thinks of the opposition between beings and nothingness) that the *epistéme* of truth appears as an entification of nothingness: that is, as that annihilation of becoming in which nothingness is identified with beings. The faith in the existence of becoming, which lies at the foundation of the entire 'history' of the West, consists in the conviction that beings are nothing; it is nihilism itself. In the tradition of the West, the truth of the *epistéme* adds to this conviction an entification of nothingness that annihilates the content of that faith, and that by that very faith is therefore destined to be annihilated.

The destiny of truth is the authentic and the incontrovertible – the authentic negation of its negation – but not in its being a power that prevails over the power of becoming by dominating it and annihilating its prevailing (as well as by acknowledging its existence). The negation that pertains to the destiny of truth (i.e. the negation of the negation of destiny) appears outside of the nihilistic meaning of negation (to which there belong both the negation exerted by becoming on the truth of the *epistéme* and the negation through which the truth of the *epistéme* dominates and prevails over becoming). As part of destiny, the positing of becoming thus appears as a faith and a will to power (i.e. as the originary form of the will to power of the West): as a faith that believes to be power.

As part of the destiny of truth, the positing of the existence of becoming appears as a negation of the destiny of truth itself; however, it does not appear as such a negation insofar as that existence is acknowledged as an incontrovertible self-evidence (that is, as the incontrovertible self-evidence that throughout the 'history' of the West drives the incontrovertibility of the *epistéme* to its twilight), but insofar as that existence appears as the content of a faith: that is to say, as the content of that being that consists in the conviction that (some or all) beings issue from nothingness and return to it.

The truth of destiny, *qua* negation of its negation, is not an annihilation of its own negation. The truth of destiny sees (that is to say: in the truth of destiny it appears) that the content of its negation is nothing. The truth of destiny sees nothingness as nothingness; it does not annihilate or posit as a nothingness something that it recognizes as a being. The truth of destiny is a negation of its negation precisely insofar as it sees the nothingness of the nothing constituted by the content of its negation. Destiny negates insofar as it is the appearing of the nothingness of the nothing of that content – which, as part of the negation of destiny, is instead posited as (i.e. it is believed or willed to be) a non-nothingness. This 'positing' (this erring) is negated by destiny precisely insofar as destiny sees that it is a form of faith or will: a faith in the non-nothingness of nothingness, a faith that, however, is not itself a nothingness, and that, *qua* being, appears in turn within destiny as that for which it is impossible not to be – i.e. it appears as eternal.

On the one hand, the truth of destiny does not annihilate its own negation because it sees the nothingness of the nothing constituted by the content of its negation, and it therefore does not posit the nothingness of something that is originarily recognized as a non-nothingness – this seeing consisting in a negation of the *content* of its negation. On the other hand, the truth of destiny does not annihilate its own negation because, insofar as it sees that, in that negation, the nothingness of that content is believed to be a non-nothingness, it sees the eternity of that faith, in such a way that the negation of the error *qua erring* is not an annihilation of this very erring.

As part of the truth of destiny, it thus also appears that the 'annihilation' of the prevailing of becoming, performed by the truth of the *epistéme*, as well as the 'annihilation' of the latter by becoming, is a nothingness that is *believed* in both instances to be a non-nothingness. (This is a faith that tends to remain *implicit* throughout the 'history' of the West, despite the fact that it is necessarily implied by the explicit meanings that becoming and the truth of the *epistéme* take on throughout that 'history'.) The truth of the *epistéme* and the interpretation of becoming given by the West are both negations of the truth of destiny; accordingly, the annihilation that they believe to accomplish – and, more generally, the becoming in the existence of which they believe – is a nothingness that they posit as a non-nothingness.

4

Destiny is a negation of its own negation, in that every negation of destiny (or of any of its segments) is self-negating (cf. 'Returning to Parmenides', par. 6, in *The Essence of Nihilism*.) The fact that this negation is self-negating does not appear as part of what that negation knows of itself, but as part of the gaze of destiny. Destiny's being a negation of its own negation belongs to the essence of destiny itself: destiny is what stands only insofar as it is that negation, and, therefore, only insofar as it includes its own self-negating negation (cf. *La struttura originaria*).

The negation that appears in that self-negation, however, is not the annihilation performed by the thinking of the West, and nor is it the non-annihilating negation that, as part of destiny, sees the being-nothing of the nothingness of the negated content *and* lets what is negated, *qua* erring, be in its eternal being. The negation that appears in that self-negation is a negation *as such*: i.e. it is what is identical in the annihilating and non-annihilating negations, and it belongs to what the negation of destiny sees of itself.

For, indeed, one thing is what the negation of destiny *is* in the gaze of destiny (destiny being the appearing of its being a negation of its own negation – this appearing being its gaze), another thing is what the negation of destiny *believes* to be (the 'being' of that negation – and of every being – being precisely what that negation shows to be in the gaze of destiny.) The negation of destiny first of all believes to be the *negation* of a determinate content (that is, it first of all believes to be the *affirmation* of another determinate content): it sees itself as a simple negation (or as a simple affirmation). It may or may not see that its negating is an annihilation; however, it may not see that what it affirms through its negating is a nothingness (since it believes it to be a being.) However, if it turns to itself, that negation cannot but see and know itself as a *negation*: as a simple negation – a negation *as such*. (This seeing, and knowing, is its appearing: an appearing that, despite showing itself in the gaze of destiny – i.e. despite being one of the contents that appear in that gaze – isolates itself from that gaze.)

Thus, as part of the self-negation of the negation of destiny (a self-negation whose concrete meaning is considered in the writings recalled at the beginning of this Paragraph), the negation that is self-negating is precisely a negation *as such* (i.e. not in its being an annihilating or non-annihilating negation). That is to say, it is what that negation, in turning to itself, necessarily sees of itself —which, in any case, appears in the gaze of destiny. It is in that gaze that there appears the necessity that the negation of destiny, in turning to itself, should see itself as a negation (as such), and that it should coincide with that self-negation, which, instead – in turning to itself – it cannot see.

This negation as such constitutes a segment of destiny. If one negates (or puts into question) that this negation as such has a meaning, this very *negation* of the meaning of that negation is self-negating (i.e. it negates its own meaning): that is to say, it is one of the self-negating negations of destiny. As part of destiny, it appears that the negation of destiny, in its being self-negating, is not self-annihilating. This self-negation is not a self-annihilation: the negation of destiny is that eternal being that fails to be meaningful as a negation of destiny without being self-negating. Eternal is the negation of destiny, and eternal is its being self-negating. ('The' negation of destiny is therefore the essence that is present in all the possible ways of negating destiny itself.)

That negation as such consists in what is identical in the non-annihilating negation through which destiny negates its own negation and in every other negation of destiny. The difference between destiny and the *epistéme*, as well as between destiny and every destruction of the *epistéme* carried out by contemporary thought, can be abyssal only insofar as there is something identical in what is altogether and utterly different. The 'standing' of destiny, 'destiny', 'beings', 'nothingness', 'relations', 'being', 'existence', 'affirmations', 'negations', 'appearing', the 'incontrovertibility', the *'élenchos'*, 'truth', 'becoming', the 'eternal', the 'structure', and the 'originary' all have, as part of destiny, a meaning whose difference with the one they exhibit throughout the 'history' of the West, and as part of the isolation of the earth from destiny, is abyssal; this difference, however, may be extreme only insofar as it consists of a differing of the identical. Those determinations appear both as part of destiny and as part of the earth that is isolated from destiny; it is however insofar as they appear as part of destiny that their negation is self-negating. Accordingly, their appearing as part of the isolated earth is an aspect of the way in which destiny appears as part of its own negation.

5

Destiny – what stands, the incontrovertible – is that whose negation is self-negating, and that which, for this reason, is an incontrovertible negation of its own negation. *That* whose negation is self-negating consists in the appearing of the totality of beings, which appear in their self-being and in their non-being other than themselves – as well as in their non-being that other of themselves that is nothingness: that is to say, in their being eternal. (Insofar as the self-negating negation of destiny is a being, it belongs to the totality of beings whose negation is self-negating. Insofar as it is a being, its being a being is irrefutable: its existence – namely, its being eternally existent – is irrefutable. The negation of destiny is not self-negating insofar as it is a being, but insofar as the meaning of that being consists precisely in a negation of destiny.)

Destiny, *qua* unity of itself (i.e. of the appearing of the totality of beings) and of the negation of its self-negating negation, is the unity of a multiplicity of determinations. It is a *structure*. It is, in fact, the *originary* structure, because it is the incontrovertible itself, which is not affirmed on the basis of anything else, but is self-affirming. The originary structure (cf. *La struttura originaria*) is the originary structure of destiny. Every determination of this structure is something whose negation is self-negating. This property, however, pertains to these determinations insofar as each of them gathers itself and all the other determinations in the unity of the originary structure; and that property pertains to this unity insofar as the latter is the unity of the determinations of the originary.

6

The originary structure appears. Destiny, *qua* appearing of the totality of beings, is the appearing of their originary structure – of their gathering together in that very structure. The language that speaks the originary structure, however, does not speak it once and for all. Like every language, it must endlessly reiterate what it says: it must run after it, grasp it again, retrieve it, repeat it. *Immer wieder.*

In Husserl's thought, however, this *immer wieder* consists of an endless rethinking and recreating of the ground or foundation itself; it is the eternal return of the ground – its endless self-annihilation and self-renewal. The ground is a gesture – a form of power, energy, force, act – which must indefinitely be repeated, and which, in fragmenting into the infinite multiplicity of gestures that posit its own elements, constitutes at the same time their infinite repetition.

The originary structure, however, is not a gesture, a force, an act, or a form of power: not only because it is the eternal being that consists of the originary structure of the destiny of the totality of beings, but also because it is a being that may not leave the circle of appearing: it is the never-setting background of everything that appears (cf. 'The Earth and the Essence of Man' in *The Essence of Nihilism*; 'Introduction' in *La struttura originaria*, par. 8).

And yet, language appears, and it appears as an endless reiteration of the originary structure of destiny. Language not only reiterates it, but it also speaks determinations of that structure that had not yet been spoken – and that, once spoken, are themselves endlessly reiterated. Nevertheless, the originary structure is *not* a fleeting spectacle, which founders here and there, slipping, vanishing at several points (or completely), letting itself be forgotten, and therefore needing to be continuously reassembled and brought back to light – a spectacle that, even when seemingly returning unchanged (i.e. even when seemingly enduring through a yet inevitable variation), lets the doubt persist as to whether what has been re-constituted is still that incontrovertible whose negation is self-negating. The originary structure does not let the doubt persist as to whether it succeeds in holding itself together as a whole and in being a standing whose negation is self-negating; that is to say, it does not let the doubt arise as to whether its claim to be the incontrovertible should once again come to be nullified, and whether the claim of the destiny of truth – of being something radically different from the truth of the *epistéme* – should once again be overthrown.

All of this now be indicated in more detail, taking up the question of the first chapter of *La struttura originaria*, titled: 'The Presentation of the Originary Structure'.

7

The self-being of appearing beings is that whose negation is self-negating. The negation of the being of appearing beings is self-negating, and so is the negation of their self-being. The self-being of appearing beings – i.e. of beings that appear as that whose negation is self-negating – constitutes the *essence* of the originary structure. 'The essence of the originary structure' means: 'the meaning (i.e. the semantic dimension) that has the property (i.e. that insofar as it is meaningful has the property) of being that whose negation is self-negating, and that thus appears'. *That* this property pertains to that essence has been concretely indicated elsewhere (cf. for instance: 'Returning to Parmenides', par. 6, in *The Essence of Nihilism*).

Here, let us begin to remark that if the language that speaks the essence of the originary structure *unfolds* (even if in an extremely irregular and unpredictable fashion), nevertheless, the appearing of this unfolding does not itself unfold – i.e. it does not become (not even according to the non-nihilistic meaning of becoming). The unfolding of language, like every other unfolding, only appears if there appears not only its beginning or its (provisional) conclusion, but if there appears the unfolding of that beginning into that conclusion – that is, only if there appear both (the eternal being constituted by) the beginning and (the eternal being constituted by) the conclusion. And if the content of appearing includes both the beginning and the (albeit provisional) conclusion of that unfolding, no unfolding may pertain to the content of that appearing.

The language that speaks the essence of the originary structure unfolds, but the appearing of this unfolding does not itself unfold, and the unfolding of the language that speaks that essence speaks what does not unfold. In fact, that essence, insofar as it coincides with the appearing of beings, includes every aspect of their unfolding: and, therefore, it also includes the unfolding of language. The unfolding of the language that speaks that essence (the continued reiteration of this speaking constituting a form of this unfolding) appears, and is incontrovertible, insofar as it appears as part of that essence.

What has just been said, too, consists in an unfolding of language (an unfolding as part of which it is stated that the appearing of the unfolding of this stating does not itself unfold), and the appearing of this unfolding, too, does not itself unfold – the appearing of this unfolding being, in its concrete meaning, an appearing that, as part of the essence of the originary structure, coincides with the appearing of every unfolding.

The unfolding of language 'includes' what does not unfold (namely, the essence of the originary structure); what does not unfold 'includes' the unfolding of language, as well as every other unfolding. In this second instance, however, this 'including' means being part of the content of appearing; in the first instance, on the contrary, that 'including' means something different: for, granted that there can be no language if there is no appearing of beings, language does not simply consist in the appearing of beings, and the meaning according to which language 'includes' what does not unfold differs from the meaning according to which appearing includes its own content.

The essence of the originary structure does not unfold. Every unfolding [*sviluppo*] consists of an advancing of the eternals into the circle of appearing, resulting in a progressive and increasing appearing. Every folding [*viluppo*] consists of an absence of those eternals. If the essence of the originary structure were to progressively appear, the segment of that structure that would thus begin to appear would not be something incontrovertible (the incontrovertible being not a part as such, but the totality of the originary – i.e. the part as connected to the totality); and the subsequent segments, in coming to join what is controvertible, would also fail to be something incontrovertible. If, for instance, beings were to begin to appear, but their self-being were not to do so, beings would appear as something that does not exclude its being other than itself (since that exclusion may appear only if the self-being of beings appears – and it may be asserted that a being *is* that exclusion only if that exclusion appears.) Appearing beings (including interpretations and languages) are incontrovertible – that is, their negation is self-negating – only if their self-being appears. This is the case even though language is an unfolding that leads or may lead into appearing the words (i.e. the linguistic sequences) that speak of the beings that appear, before leading those that speak of the self-being of beings.

In other words, the determinations of the originary structure may not arise as part of appearing, since, insofar as they are separated from one another (and if they arise – that is, if some of them appear without the

136 BEYOND LANGUAGE

others – they must be thus separated) they are controvertible: and, in fact, they are negations of the originary structure. And yet, they appear as part of an arising and an unfolding that is therefore not *their* unfolding, but the unfolding *of language*. If that unfolding were their own unfolding, the incontrovertible would not be able to exist; the incontrovertible, however, *qua* destiny of truth, does exist (for, indeed, the negation of the appearing of the self-being of beings is self-negating), and, therefore, it is necessary that the unfolding as part of which they appear should be the unfolding of language. The word is not the thing (even though words, too, are things, or beings), precisely because what is a thing is in the first place the essence of the originary structure of destiny. If appearing is a light, language does not bring the thing to light, but enters itself into that light – even though it is through language (i.e. through the form of the word) that the thing stands in light.

If the determinations of the essence of the originary are separated from their originary unity, they are other than what they are as part of that unity – that, is they contradict themselves. Precisely for this reason, however, it is impossible to attempt to posit the essence of the originary structure as a 'result' of a process in which the incontrovertible would come to its own fulfilment starting from the self-contradiction of its simplest determinations (as, for instance, 'pure being'), through an 'unrelenting course' (*in unaufhaltsamem . . . Gange*), as Hegel states in the 'Introduction' to the *Science of Logic*).

Language is an unfolding that speaks what does not itself unfold, and that continues to reiterate it to the extent that language may never speak once and for all – the conclusion of its speech being the very condition for having to repeat what it has just spoken. The impermanence of the language that speaks of the essence of the originary structure is not, however, the impermanence of that essence; the determinations of that essence must originarily appear in order for that essence to be the incontrovertible.

8

Which, however, are the boundaries of the essence of the originary structure? The language that, in unfolding, speaks of the originary speaks not only of the determinations of that essence, but also of determinations that, while not being part of that essence, are nevertheless necessarily implied by it. These determinations are thus implied because, without them, that essence would not be able to be the incontrovertible. The writings mentioned above constitute, for the most part, an unfolding of this form of the language that speaks of the originary structure.

At the same time, the language that speaks of those additional determinations of the originary structure shows the contradictions – or the 'aporias' – that arise as a result of the absence of those very determinations (cf. *La struttura originaria,* 'Introduction', par. 6.) The form shared by these contradictions consists in the following: on the one hand, the essence of the originary structure is the incontrovertible, and it appears as such – and therefore its determinations are themselves incontrovertible; on the other hand, due to the absence of those additional determinations, that essence is controvertible (and, in fact, it is contradicted by certain conceptual segments that, in turn, appear as being incontrovertible).

For instance, the self-being of beings is something incontrovertible (that is, its negation is self-negating); however, precisely insofar as beings are self-identical, this identity necessarily entails a difference between a being and itself: that is to say, the self-relation of a being, required for its self-identity, necessitates a difference between the terms of this relation (i.e. the difference that appears in A=A: the difference between the first A and the second one); accordingly, the identity of beings is not an identity (cf. ibid., 'Introduction', par. 2; Chap. III, pars. 10–14; Chap. VI, pars. 9–14; Chap. XIII, pars. 1–7).

Second example: the opposition between a being and nothingness is something incontrovertible; however, nothingness appears, and, insofar as it appears, it is a being (cf. ibid., Chap. IV).

Third example: the negation of the incontrovertible is self-negating (the *élenchos,* regarded as a determination of the truth of destiny and not as a determination of the truth of the *epistéme* – cf. 'Returning to Parmenides', par. 6, in *The Essence of Nihilism* – consisting precisely in the appearing of the self-negation of the negation of the incontrovertible); the argument that shows that this negation is self-negating, however, is something that differs from the incontrovertible itself, in such a way that the incontrovertible is incontrovertible on the basis of something other than the incontrovertible itself (cf. ibid.).

Fourth example: every being is eternal, and 'becoming' consists in the beginning and ceasing to appear of the eternals; and yet, appearing, too, is a being: therefore, every beginning and ceasing to appear is an issuing from nothingness, and returning to it, of that being that consists in the appearing of a being (cf. ibid., 'Postscript', par. 3; *Destino della necessità*, Chap. V).

The very argument developed from Paragraph 6 of this chapter onwards may be presented as an aporia of this kind: the essence of the originary structure is the incontrovertible; the unfolding of language, however, exhibits determinations that, while appearing in addition to the ones that constitute that essence (that is, while not being included in that essence), are nevertheless necessarily implied by it – in such a way that it is impossible that that essence should be the incontrovertible.

Or: if the incontrovertible is necessarily connected to determinations that differ from it, and that are progressively introduced by language – from which, however, they continually drift away and by which they must continually be chased back, re-captured, re-spoken – the *content* that claims to be the incontrovertible does not even succeed in constituting itself: for not only is it a content that is always open, but it also slides away from all sides, it endlessly increases and decreases, it must be continually re-assembled, re-constituted, re-gathered. What, then, are the boundaries of the essence of the originary structure?

It may however be asserted that an aporetic situation of this kind arises for each determination of that structure, provided that this determination is isolated from the other ones. It is precisely the unfolding of language that exhibits these aporias, as well as the determinations that, appearing in addition to the ones that form the essence of the originary, supersede the element responsible for the constitution of those aporias. The unfolding of language shows that these additional determinations are *originarily*, and necessarily, connected to the essence of the originary; accordingly, the aporias that appear in disregarding those determinations are superseded originarily, rather than in a moment that conceptually follows the originary one. And yet, their being originarily superseded only appears as part of the unfolding of language.

The unfolding of language thus progressively shows the additional determinations that supersede the aporias that, one after the other, come into appearing. There arises, however, a broader aporia, given by the fact that what is necessarily implied by the essence of the originary structure – namely, what is essential for that essence, which also includes the determination that supersedes this latter broader aporia – is, nevertheless, introduced by language at a moment that follows the originary one, in which that essence claims to stand as the incontrovertible.

Therefore, *how* is this broader aporia dissolved? Namely: *which* is the determination that supersedes this aporia?

9

Before answering this question (and answering this question entails showing what it means to answer a question that concerns the configuration of the originary), let us reiterate that all these aporias *do not* show that the negation of the essence of the originary is *not* self-negating: they do not show that this essence is not the incontrovertible, but, rather, they show that, *despite* its incontrovertibility, this essence is *contradicted* by certain conceptual segments, which, in turn, appear to be incontrovertible. That is to say, the aporia is such – i.e. it blocks the way – only if contradictions are conceived of as something that blocks the way. It is only insofar as a contradiction is negated that its appearing blocks the way to its negation: i.e. it precludes and negates that negation. An aporia is such only insofar as it presupposes the negation of its contradiction.

However, the essence of the originary structure – *qua* appearing of the self-being of beings and of their not-being their other – is precisely the negation of every contradiction. This means that it is impossible to supersede an aporia (i.e. to supersede a contradiction) by negating the essence of the originary structure (i.e. by negating that a contradiction is superseded), and it therefore means that it is *necessary* that the conceptual segment that contradicts that essence should itself contain a contradiction – a contradiction that moreover appears by presupposing the appearing of the incontrovertible.

This is a necessity, since the self-being of beings – namely, the negation of the contradiction contained in the essence of the originary – is that whose negation is self-negating, and asserting that that conceptual segment is incontrovertible is a negation of that essence. Showing that the conceptual segment that contradicts that essence is itself contradictory entails, at the same time, showing the determination whose absence gives rise to that aporia – a determination that appears in addition to the determinations that constitute the essence of the originary. This determination is therefore necessarily implied by the essence of the originary; it is essential to that essence.

However, how are this 'showing' and this 'absence' to be understood? How can something that comes to appear within the unfolding of

140 BEYOND LANGUAGE

language be essential to the essence of the originary? How can something that lacks what is essential to itself, and that is entrusted to the ebb and flow of language, constitute the essence of the incontrovertible?

10

Let us consider the first of the aporias presented in Paragraph 8: the self-identity of beings (A=A) is not an identity. This aporia appears if a being is isolated from its self-being: thus isolated, that being indicates, as part of its self-reference, something other than itself. In order to express the concrete meaning of identity in a formula, rather than simply A=A, it is necessary to write (A=A) = (A=A). (For the concrete meaning of this formula, see the sections of *La Struttura originaria* mentioned in Paragraph 6 of this chapter.)

The question considered here does not require a presentation of that concrete meaning (cf., in any case, the 'Note' at the end of this Paragraph.) Here, it is relevant to remark that this formula expresses that certain determination – let us call it d' – that, while appearing in addition to the determinations that constitute the essence of the originary, supersedes the aporia according to which the identity of a being is not an identity. That is to say, d' is that without which an identity is not an identity – and the self-being of a being is its being self-different.

This means that if the self-being of beings appears, but d' does not, what appears is not a self-being, but a being self-different; and this being self-different is not a segment of the incontrovertible: it is not something whose negation is self-negating, but constitutes, precisely, a negation of the incontrovertible.

This means, however, that the incontrovertible does not consist in the essence of the originary structure *qua* isolated from d' – that essence being isolated from d' if it appears but d' does not – but in the *synthesis* or unity of that essence and d'. The incontrovertible is the appearing of this synthesis. However, if the 'essence' of the originary structure coincides with the incontrovertible (that is, with the semantic unit that succeeds in being that whose negation is self-negating), the authentic essence of the originary does not precede d', but *includes* it: that is, d' does not arise as part of the appearing of the originary, but it originarily appears. If d' were to arise as part of appearing, the incontrovertible would not be able to be or to appear. The incontrovertible, however, *qua* destiny of truth, appears and is. This means that d' does not arise as part of the appearing of the originary, but originarily appears and originarily belongs to the authentic essence of the originary structure.

Let us indicate with $d', d'', \ldots d^n$ all the determinations of the same type as d': namely, all the determinations that are 'additional' relative to what we had kept referring to as the 'essence' of the originary structure, and that are necessarily implied by the latter (the determination discussed and investigated at the end of Paragraph 8 being also included in $d', d'', \ldots d^n$ – a determination that consists precisely in the meaning of the discussion that is now being unfolded). It is then necessary that the determinations $d', d'', \ldots d^n$ should be originarily included in the authentic essence of the originary structure, and that they should not constitute anything 'additional' relative to that essence. The incontrovertible is such only insofar as it originarily includes the determinations $d', d'', \ldots d^n$.

The incontrovertible originarily includes what, as part of the unfolding of language, is progressively and successively indicated, and continually lost and retrieved. What appears *qua* and in the originary structure always extends further than what is said by language as part of its unfolding. Originary appearing receives every unfolding and every arising, thus including the unfolding and the arising of language. Every unfolding – thus also including the unfolding of language – is itself included in the content of the incontrovertible. The determinations d', d'', $\ldots d^n$ arise – that is, they enter appearing (i.e. they enter the appearing of the originary) – *in and through the unfolding of language*; however, they arise precisely *insofar as they are indicated by words*: i.e. in their being thus indicated. Language does not simply consist of signs or words, but, rather, of the references of signs and words to meanings (the determinations $d', d'', \ldots d^n$ being the meanings in the case under discussion); accordingly, what arises in the circle of appearing, as part of the unfolding of the language that speaks of the originary, is not simply a sign or a word, but it is also their meaning. The meaning of the originary, however, does not arise *as such* – and, therefore, the determinations d', d'', $\ldots d^n$ do not arise as such – but in its being indicated by words and signs: the meaning of the originary arises in its being indicated (i.e. its being indicated arises.) The meaning *as such*, in which the determinations of the originary consist, does not arise as part of appearing, but is included in originary appearing itself (i.e. in that determination of the originary that consists in the very appearing of the originary).

Following their absence, the determinations of the originary appear as part of the unfolding of the language that speaks of the originary – precisely in the sense that, within the appearing of the originary, there arises the *synthesis* of a determinations and of its word, but not the determination as such. Prior to its arising, this synthesis is absent from the content of appearing, and those determinations are absent from this synthesis. Negating that this synthesis is absent from the content of appearing means negating the incontrovertible being that consists in the unfolding of language – i.e. the progressive coming forth of language into appearing. Negating that those determinations are absent from that synthesis (i.e. negating that they originarily appear in the dimension that receives the arising of language) means negating the existence of the incontrovertible: i.e. the existence of what may not be negated in that its negation is self-negating. At the same time, the synthesis of determinations and words – a synthesis that arises in appearing (and that consists in the will for something to be a sign and a word for something else) – is a being: that is, it is an eternal; and so is each of the determinations that are absent from that synthesis.

NOTE. The passage 142 b–143 of Plato's *Parmenides* shows that the hypothesis: 'The one is' necessarily implies that the one is not. In the *Sophist*, on the contrary, Plato had shown how it is possible to assert – *contra* Parmenides – that non-being is. 'Non-being' – as *different* from 'being', indicated by an 'is' – is a determination to which, precisely, an 'is' pertains. (A house, a tree, a star, a human are all determinations; of each of them one states: it 'is'.) Every determination is a unity. In the *Sophist*, Plato saves the world from Parmenides, for, indeed, the latter had ruled out that it should be possible to state of a determination: it 'is' (the world being, precisely, the totality of determinations.) The passage 142 b–143 of Plato's *Parmenides* thus puts back into question this result of the *Sophist*. Indeed, since every determination is a unity, the conclusion of the passage 142 b–143 of the *Parmenides* may be extended to every unity: i.e. the argument is able to include every unity.

The heart of this passage consists in the thesis that, in the assertion: 'The one is', both the one and its being (the 'is') – while differing from one another – include the other one within their respective self. The one-that-is is 'a whole', of which 'the one and being are parts'; however, it is impossible that each of these two parts should 'be lacking' (*apoleípesthon*) of the other one: that is, it is impossible that the one, *qua* part, should lack being (i.e. that it should not be a being), and that being, *qua* part, should be lacking of the one (i.e. that it should not be a unity.)

This thesis, however, gives rise to a *regressus in indefinitum*: 'So again, each of the two parts includes the one and being; and the smallest of parts, in turn, is composed of two parts; and thus, by the same argument, any part whatsoever always has these two parts, since the one always includes being and being always includes the one. Therefore, since every part always proves to be two, the one can never be'. This is the case both in the sense that neither of the two parts succeeds in being a unity, and in the sense that the 'whole' constituted by the being of the one (i.e. the 'one is') fails to constitute itself. The one – namely, the starting point of the thought: 'The one is' – is fragmented into an infinite multiplicity: that is to say, it does not constitute itself as a starting *point*, but it is multiplied into an infinity of points. The same is true of *being*: namely, of the end point of that thought. Not even being may successfully be posited as an end point. Thinking itself becomes impossible – and, in fact, thinking in its entirety, for the one may here indicate the unity constituted by any determination of the world. If the one is, the one is not. Plato, in his *Sophist* (251 ff.), rules out the possibility of the *absence of any koinonía* among determinations (being itself being a determination), as well as the existence of *a koinonía among all* determinations. The outcome of the passage 142 b–143 of the *Parmenides*, on the contrary, *confirms* the absence of any *koinonía* among determinations (that *koinonía* being the connection that links that starting point to that end point).

The aporia to which this passage of the *Parmenides* leads is caused by the same *isolation* that lies at the foundation of the nihilism of the West: the isolation of a determination from its being. Nihilism besets not only the content of Western thinking, but also its form. As to the content: every determination, since it is isolated from its being, turns into a nothingness (and it is precisely for this reason that it is possible to think that, as part of the becoming of the world, determinations issue from nothingness and return to it). As to the form: the subject, insofar as it is isolated from its predicate, may be linked to the predicate only through a *progressus in indefinitum*; that is to say, the subject remains forever separate from the predicate and is never linked to it (cf., also for what follows, *La struttura originaria*, 'Introduction', par. 2).

At the same time, every *progressus in indefinitum* represents a distorted image of truth. If thinking is a progress or movement, as part of which the subject comes to be identified with the predicate – and is therefore at first a simple subject, separate from the predicate – then, thinking is a contradictory identification of different determinations (the subject and the predicate). Thinking is not contradictory only if the subject, to which the predicate pertains, is not a pure subject, but is open to its predicate – i.e. it is the subject-of-the-predicate – and, in turn, only if the predicate is not a pure predicate, but the predicate-of-the-subject. The elements of the synthesis coincide with the synthesis itself. This is precisely what takes place in the passage 142b–143 of the *Parmenides*. The logic that in this passage leads to the aporia ('If the one is, the one is not') also indicates the way to overcome it. It is however unable to embark on that way, for, even if it catches a glimpse of the fact that the elements of the synthesis coincide with the synthesis itself, it continues to conceive of them as isolated – in such a way that the synthesis is multiplied and deferred *in indefinitum*: and it is thus negated. For, indeed, only if the subject is separated from the predicate is it possible to think that the subject-predicate synthesis, in which the subject consists, is different from the synthesis between the subject and the predicate (thus constituting a new synthesis, which is additional with respect to the originary one, and which constitutes the first step of the *regressus in indefinitum*). If the subject is not isolated from the predicate – i.e. if it is not isolated from its synthesis with the predicate – then the subject (as well as the predicate) does, indeed, coincide with that synthesis, but that synthesis is not a new one relative to the synthesis of subject and predicate, but it is the same originary synthesis of subject and predicate.

All of this means that thinking is not a progress or a movement (an act or a gesture) that connects the subject to its predicate – and that identifies the differents (S = P) in a contradictory way. Rather, thinking is the appearing of the identity of the identical – namely, of the identity between the subject of the predicate and the predicate of the subject: $S (= P) = P (= S)$, or $(S = P) = (P = S)$. Accordingly, the positing of the self-being of beings is not a simple $A = A$, but $A (= A) = A (= A)$ – or, as indicated, $(A = A) = (A = A)$. Outside of nihilism, it is not only the content of thinking that is different (for, indeed, there appears the eternity of all determinations), but also its form: every determination is united with its being – that is to say, it is eternal – and its being is the *self-being* of that determination.

11

Of the determinations d', d'', ... d^n, it must therefore be stated what has been stated of the determinations of the 'essence' of the originary structure: the former, as well as the latter, progressively appear as part of the unfolding of language (and they are continually lost, retrieved and reiterated by language), but they all originarily appear. What has thus been previously named the 'essence of the originary structure' is not, as we have already remarked, the authentic essence of the originary structure, but its *linguistic* essence: it is the *definition* that confines the originary structure of the destiny of truth within the finitude of language – that is, within the finite series of linguistic elements that constitute the definition of the originary.

Precisely insofar as it unfolds, every language, including the one that speaks of the originary, is always finite at each stage of its unfolding. At the same time, however, language does not constitute the ground of finitude as such – for, indeed, the originary structure of the destiny of truth constitutes the *finite* destiny of truth (cf. 'The Earth and the Essence of Man' in *The Essence of Nihilism*; *Destino della necessità*, Chap. XVI). Language is the ground of that form of finitude *within which* the incontrovertible fails to be incontrovertible because it *contradicts itself*. The linguistic essence of the originary structure contradicts itself – and yet, it is the incontrovertible.

That essence is not the incontrovertible by virtue of its explicit meaning, but by virtue of its *implicit* one: namely, by virtue of the totality of determinations of the originary structure that, while being originarily and necessarily implied by that explicit meaning, originarily appear already prior to their appearing as part of the unfolding of language (i.e. of the unfolding of the explicit meaning) – that is to say, already prior to their coming and going in and out of language. The 'implicit' element of the language that speaks of the originary is the *appearing* of the totality of the originary. This totality is the element that *underlies* the definition: i.e. the linguistic essence of the originary.

This essence, however, contradicts itself as to its *explicit* meaning: if the explicit meaning of the essence of the originary is isolated from the totality of the determinations of the originary itself, that meaning differs from what it intends to be. For instance, if the self-being of beings is isolated from the determination d' – namely, from the concrete meaning of self-being, which can be expressed through the formula $(A = A) = (A$

= A) – the meaning of that self-being coincides with that of being self-different. This contradiction (which does not simply consist in that being self-different, but in the contradiction given by the intention of being self-identical and the actuality of being self-different), is superseded, *within language*, as soon as language introduces the implicit determination *d'* – whose absence (from language) determines that self-contradiction of language. This 'introduction' consists of the arising, in the appearing of the originary, of the synthesis between that determination – which nevertheless originarily appears – and the language that expresses it.

12

The fact that meaning appears without the appearing of the word that indicates it can therefore be asserted – and, in fact, must be necessarily asserted – because, and only because, the incontrovertible exists. The truth of the *épistéme* is a failed attempt at positing the incontrovertible; it is therefore a failed attempt at positing meaning in its being independent of the word (cf. Chap. I and III of this Part Three). In relation to the failure of this attempt, the philosophies of the 'linguistic turn' indicate, if only remotely, the only direction along which thinking may then proceed: the one consisting in the inseparability of meaning and word.

The truth of destiny, however, is not the truth of the *épistéme*; the incontrovertibility of the *épistéme* is not the incontrovertibility of destiny. The incontrovertible, *qua* destiny, is; its very being necessarily implies that the originary determinations of the incontrovertible constitute the very dimension in which the language that speaks of them arises – and it therefore necessarily implies that this dimension already appears before the arising of that language. That the originary meaning should already appear prior to the language that speaks of it is, itself, a determination of that meaning.

13

The contradiction of the linguistic essence of the originary is superseded within the unfolding of the language that speaks of the originary. To this contradiction of language, which is superseded within language itself, there corresponds, as part of the originary that appears without language, the contradiction determined by the isolation – from the totality of the originary – of the determinations that constitute the meaning of that essence. The isolation of each determination from the totality of the originary determines a contradiction in the originary itself; as part of the originary, however, these contradictions are originarily superseded. That is to say, all the contradictions – which constitute the aporias that result from the absence, in language, of those determinations without which the originary would not be the incontrovertible – are originarily superseded.

The originary, however, does not consist in the superseding of the totality *simpliciter* of contradictions; that superseding pertains to the totality *simpliciter* of beings. If, as we have stated, the originary coincides with the appearing of the totality of beings (in their self-being and in their not-being their other), this does not mean that what appears beyond the originary is nothingness itself; rather, it means that, as part of the originary, beings appear in their being included in the totality of beings: which appears as a *formal*, abstract, and thus *self-contradictory* totality – a totality, however, that is self-contradictory *in a way that differs* from the one that prevents the incontrovertible from being incontrovertible (cf. *La struttura originaria*, 'Introduction', par. 8; 'The Path of Day' and 'The Earth and the Essence of Man' in *The Essence of Nihilism*). This a kind of contradiction (named 'C-contradiction' in *La struttura originaria*, Chap. VIII) which is not superseded through a negation of its content, but through the latter's concrete and total appearing. That is to say, the content of this contradiction is not negated as such, but insofar as it is a formal, abstract, and indeterminate content.

The difference between the totality *simpliciter* of beings and this formal totality, which includes the beings that appear as part of the originary, is itself part of the incontrovertible; here, let us simply remark that, since every being is eternal, the arising into appearing of specific beings entails that these beings should *be* (i.e. that they should be a non-nothingness: a self-being and a not-being their other) already prior to their appearing, and that they should also continue to be after their disappearing; that is to say, it entails that the totality *simpliciter* of beings should extend further than the dimension of appearing (which, in turn, extends further than the dimension of language).

If one asserted *of every being* what must be asserted of the beings constituted by the determinations d', d'', ... d^n – that is, if one were to assert that *every* being is something without which the incontrovertible would not be incontrovertible – it would follow that, in order to be incontrovertible, the incontrovertible would have to coincide with the appearing of the totality *simpliciter* of beings: that is, it would have to coincide with the infinite appearing of the infinite. However, if the incontrovertible were to coincide with the infinite and concrete appearing of the Whole, the arising of beings in the circle of appearing would be impossible. On the contrary, not only is this arising not impossible, but it is something incontrovertible.

The incontrovertible may not therefore consist of the infinite and concrete appearing of the Whole. It is therefore impossible that every being should be something without whose appearing the incontrovertible would not be incontrovertible (that is to say, it is impossible that that property of d', d'', ... d^n should pertain to every being – this property, however, pertaining to all the determinations that constitute the meaning of the linguistic essence of the originary). The (infinite) contradiction that pertains to the incontrovertible insofar as the latter only constitutes the appearing of the formal totality of beings is therefore contradictory *in a way that differs* from the one that prevents the incontrovertible from being incontrovertible.

This 'conclusion', too (which concerns the relation between mediation and immediacy in the originary; cf. *La struttura originaria*, Chap. VII), is part of the set d', d'', ... d^n: namely, it is a determination of the originary that originarily appears and whose synthesis with the word has arisen as part of the appearing of the originary.

And the assertion, too, of the inclusion of that 'conclusion' in that set is itself included in that set. That set also includes the ruling out of the possibility that a *progressus in indefinitum* should come to arise in this way. The ruling out of that possibility may be formulated in a way that is analogous to the one in which Paragraph 6 of the 'Introduction' to *La struttura originaria* rules out a *progressus in indefinitum* in the concept of the appearing of the appearing of a being. (This is the case even though the difference between the totality *simpliciter* of beings and the totality of what appears as part of the originary does not in itself rule out the possibility that the originary may consist of an infinite set of beings.)

In any case, in asserting that the *totality* of what is incontrovertibly asserted of the incontrovertible is included in the incontrovertible itself (let us call this assertion *a*), that totality must also *originarily* include the assertion *a*. Accordingly, in extending the argument through the inclusion of *a* in that totality (and then through the inclusion of that inclusion, and so on, *in indefinitum*), one simply *repeats* the originary inclusion of *a* in that totality, while instead believing to be positing a new content (and, then, an infinity of new contents). In order for this new inclusion not to be a repetition of that originary inclusion, it is necessary that a should not be originarily included in the totality of what is asserted of the incontrovertible; as a result, however, that totality would only seemingly be a totality. (Therefore, the assertion a is an element of the set d', d'', ... d^n.)

14

A negation of the originary is not only a direct negation of what the originary affirms, but it is also a negation of the existence or the appearing of the determinations of the originary. For instance, negating that the word 'beings' has any meaning acknowledges that the word 'meaning' is itself meaningful; a being, however, is precisely a meaning (not in the sense in which 'meanings' are placed in opposition to 'signifiers' or to 'bearers' of meaning, but in the sense that each of these determinacies is something meaningful). Therefore, that negation negates what it itself acknowledges: that is to say, it negates itself.

Moreover, if one asserts: 'The linguistic sequence "The self-being of beings is the incontrovertible" is meaningless', the meaning of this assertion is (intended to be) held firm: that is, one negates that this meaning should be identical to its negation, and one affirms – namely, one holds firmly and non-problematically, i.e. in a way that aims to be incontrovertible – that this meaning is self-identical. However, this affirmed self-being of the meaning of that assertion is precisely the self-being of the being that consist in the meaning of that assertion – and this is, precisely, a self-being that is held firm: i.e. that is regarded as that whose negation is meant to be incontrovertibly ruled out. As a result, that asserting affirms its own meaninglessness: that is to say, it negates itself.

Moreover, if one negates the existence of every meaning (or being), one affirms the existence of the meaning that consists in this very negation; that is to say, here, too, this negation negates itself. (If one replies that it is inevitable that this negation should negate itself – i.e. that it should affirm its own nothingness – precisely because there exists nothing, the inevitability of this conclusion continues to presuppose that form of existence that consists in the negation of every kind of existence; as a result, that negation negates that from which it, itself, originates – that is to say, it once again negates itself.)

Moreover, if one negates the existence of appearing, but acknowledges the existence and dimension of beings (for, otherwise, one would fall back into the previous case) – that is to say, if one negates appearing but affirms or posits beings – this positing of beings (which is distinguished from beings themselves) constitutes precisely their appearing. A being, which is, is what is posited or affirmed, and positing or affirming 'This being is' constitutes the appearing of what is posited. If one states: 'Only beings are, and not what is called 'appearing', 'affirming', 'positing' (that is, if one states that only the world exists, but not what is usually called 'consciousness' of the world), this 'Only beings (i.e. the world) are, but not ...' does not simply coincide with those beings: namely, it does not coincide with beings (i.e. the world) in their being left unsaid, but with beings in their being said – that is to say, with a saying, affirming or appearing of beings. As a result, that 'Only beings are, but not ...' is a negation of its own existence. ('Only x is' does not coincide with the x that is: the pure x that is does not assert: 'Only x is'.)

The infinitely many ways of negating the existence, appearing or meaning of certain (or all) determinations of the incontrovertible are, in any case, ways of (more or less directly) negating what the incontrovertible asserts: that is to say, they are forms of its self-negating negation. If it is, indeed, true that, according to neo-positivism, one thing is asserting: 'x (for instance, "God") does not exist', and another thing is stating 'x is meaningless', the negation of the meaningfulness of x is nevertheless one of the possible ways of negating the existence of what is regarded as meaningful by the one who affirms the existence of x. Precisely insofar as x is meaningless, its existence may not be affirmed.

Lastly, one must include among the negations of the incontrovertible the conviction that, for now or forever, what stand before humans throughout their lives are just contents of the world – things or earthly problems that have nothing to do with the originary structure of destiny. (As part of this conviction, one does not assert that these contents differ from that structure, but one simply speaks of them and lives them.) The originary structure of destiny, however, is the predicate of every being, and no being may appear if the being constituted by the originary structure of destiny does not itself appear (cf. 'The Earth and the Essence of Man', pars. 4 ff., in *The Essence of Nihilism*; *La struttura originaria*, 'Introduction', par. 8). Precisely for this reason, destiny constitutes the implicit element that underlies every language, and not only the language that speaks of destiny. That conviction therefore isolates the earth from destiny – and the earth, thus isolated, is nothing (cf. *La struttura originaria,* 'Introduction', par. 8). That conviction asserts that only the earth stands before humans as positively existing (i.e. only earthly things, problems and matters – but, therefore, also heavenly ones, insofar as the earth is always connected in some way to the heavens); that conviction thus affirms the nothingness of the earth; that is to say, it negates itself.

The aporias discussed in these pages are negations of the incontrovertible. Within these negations, the conceptual segment that negates the incontrovertible appears on the one hand as self-negating (for instance: in remarking that nothingness appears, and it is therefore something positive – i.e. a being – the negation of the opposition between beings and nothingness may negate that opposition only insofar as it opposes itself to nothingness; as a result, that negation negates that without which it, itself, would not be able to constitute itself – that is to say, that negation negates itself). On the other hand, however, that segment appears to be incontrovertible (in relation to the example above: since nothingness appears, its positivity appears to be incontrovertible). It is precisely in order to eliminate this appearance that it is necessary to introduce the determinations d', d'', ... d^n as additional determinations to the configuration of the originary relative to which those aporias appear; on the contrary, the introduction of these determinations is not required for the other forms of negations of the incontrovertible that, while being manifestly self-negating, do not appear to be incontrovertible.

15

If the authentic essence of the incontrovertible (*qua* originary structure of destiny) coincides with the totality of its determinations, the meaning of the linguistic essence of the incontrovertible is nevertheless that explicit meaning that is incontrovertible by virtue of the implicit one – the latter being the essential element that underlies the explicit meaning and that is necessarily and originarily linked to it. It is in this sense that it is possible to continue to speak of the essence of the originary structure, rather than simply of its linguistic essence. The essence of the originary structure is the explicit meaning of that structure insofar as it succeeds (by virtue of that implicit meaning) in standing as the incontrovertible. The 'explicitness' of a meaning is its being linked to words and signs: that is to say, its appearing as, and as part of, language itself (language itself continually varying even when repeating the 'same' content).

The appearing of the self-negation of the negation of the incontrovertible – namely, the appearing of the *élenchos, qua* determination of the destiny of truth – is therefore not a kind of logical mechanism that only works in relation to a certain finite set of determinations – not one more, not one less – which are supposed to constitute the explicit meaning of the linguistic essence of the originary structure. The *élenchos* involves the totality of the incontrovertible; that is to say, it underlies the totality of the originary and implicit meaning – this 'implicit' meaning coinciding with the originary in its appearing, but not in its appearing as, or as part of, language itself. On the contrary, the *élenchos*, too, *qua* finite linguistic segment (that is, *qua* specific and finite set of words) – or *qua* explicit meaning of that segment, isolated from the totality that underlies that explicit meaning – is self-contradictory (as we have remarked in the third aporia presented in Paragraph 8.)

16

The boundaries of the linguistic essence of the originary structure of destiny may therefore extend much further – but also much less further – than those indicated at the beginning of Paragraph 5 and Paragraph 7. It is possible to chart these boundaries simply by stating that the linguistic essence of the originary consists in the incontrovertibility of the self-being of beings. For, indeed, the negation of that self-being is a form of self-being: i.e. it is self-negating. By isolating this determination of that linguistic essence – that is, by isolating that self-being from the other determinations of the originary – one may believe that this determination does not differ from the way in which Aristotle presents the incontrovertible (i.e. the *bebaiotáte arché*) in the fourth book of the *Metaphysics*. However, through this isolation and this convergence with the Aristotelian principle, the self-being of beings – which is nonetheless that whose negation is self-negating – comes to contradict itself in multiple ways (i.e. it comes to be surrounded by a myriad of aporias): ranging from the one in which that self-being, *qua* simple A = A, is self-different, to the one in which, as a result of positing that worldly beings issue from nothingness and return to it, the self-being of beings entails at the same time the identity of beings and nothingness. (Within that isolation, the very meaning of incontrovertibility is self-contradictory, for the appearing of the self-negation of the negation of that self-being appears as being different from the very self-being of beings; accordingly,

LANGUAGE AND THE APPEARING OF DESTINY   **153**

if the incontrovertible – that which negates the self-negation of its own negation – coincides with that self-being, the argument that shows the self-negation of the negation of that self-being, in differing from that very self-being, is not an incontrovertible argument.)

On the contrary, even the difference between the simple self-being of beings (or even the simple determination: 'incontrovertible'), as linked to the totality of determinations of the originary, and the way in which Western thought has understood the self-being of beings (and the 'incontrovertible') is abyssal.

In any case, the boundaries of the linguistic essence of the incontrovertible may not be narrowed beyond certain limits. For instance, the meaning 'being' or the meaning 'appearing' may not be absent from that essence; nor may those boundaries be restricted by stating that the appearing of a particular content – for instance, the appearing of this red or the appearing of its self-identity – is *the* incontrovertible. That appearing is not *the* incontrovertible, but, precisely, one of its particular contents: that is to say, it is one of the contents of the appearing of the self-being of the totality of appearing beings; it is one of the contents of the linguistic essence of the incontrovertible. Asserting that it is one of these contents means asserting that that essence extends further than this particular content.

Asserting that the appearing of a specific being (e.g. this red) as well as of its self-being is the incontrovertible means therefore negating that the appearing of other beings (which, like that specific content, appear, and appear in their self-being) is something incontrovertible. That assertion is therefore a negation of the incontrovertible.

The linguistic essence of the incontrovertible is, indeed, something abstract, which, isolated from the other determinations of the incontrovertible, is self-contradictory; it is however something abstract that intends to say what the incontrovertible is – and this intention does not contradict itself (i.e. it is not nullified) if, *qua* non-isolated, it implicitly refers to that which underlies every assertion: the originary structure of the incontrovertible. On the contrary, asserting that the appearing of *a specific* being (for instance, this red) is incontrovertible does not intend to say what the incontrovertible is, but simply states one of its particular contents (for, as we have remarked, if it had that intention, this stating would constitute a negation of the incontrovertible. Concerning the relation between the positing of specific incontrovertible contents and the positing of the incontrovertible, cf. *La struttura originaria*, Chap. VII, pars. 13–19.)

17

La struttura originaria also shows (cf. ibid., Chap. X, par. 18, for the distinction between 'syntactic' and 'non-syntactic constants') the specific conditions that afford a resolution of the aporia, connected to the one considered above (Paragraph 13), and determined by the observation that certain particular contents of the incontrovertible (such as, for instance, the self-being of this red) are incontrovertible and, nevertheless, they enter and leave the circle of appearing – while we have remarked that no determination of the incontrovertible may arise or disappear.

That this lamp is lit is something incontrovertible (in the sense that what is incontrovertible is the existence of the being that consists in the interpretation that posits a specific series of events as the being-lit of a lamp.) The being-lit of this lamp, however, enters and leaves the circle of appearing. The being-lit of this lamp is incontrovertible (namely, it is a determination of the incontrovertible), but so is its entering and leaving the circle of appearing. The aporia consists in the (seeming) impossibility of firmly holding to both of these sides.

The being-lit of this lamp, the existence of this red, of this window, of these mountains, of these appearing clouds, and of the mood that accompanies them are certainly something incontrovertible. However, they are incontrovertible *in a way that differs* from that of the being of a being, from its appearing, self-being, not-being a nothingness, being part of the totality of beings, or from the self-negation of the negation of the incontrovertible. Those first determinations ('non-syntactic') are indeed something incontrovertible, but in that they are specifications, individuations, or concrete contents of the second ('syntactic') ones, which constitute the *formal* meaning – the 'syntax' or essence – of the originary structure and of the set of determinations d', d'', ... d^n. In stating that the determinations of the originary structure are that without the appearing of which the incontrovertible would not be incontrovertible, in the previous pages we have been referring to this latter kind of determinations: the syntactic determinations.

However, since the self-being of *every* being (that is, of every determination) is something incontrovertible, the specific content of every being, too (the grey shade of these clouds, the shade of this mood) is part of the content of the incontrovertible. That content is the Whole in its concreteness.

However, it is also incontrovertible that the Whole does not appear in its concreteness: precisely because specific determinations arise. Non-syntactic determinations arise, and so does the language that speaks of all determinations. Since the existence of the incontrovertible cannot be negated, this means that the non-appearing of the concrete Whole does not imply the non-existence of the incontrovertible, but, rather, implies that the originary structure of destiny constitutes the *originary contradiction* itself – in keeping with the meaning of contradiction ('C-contradiction', cf. *La struttura originaria*, Chap. VIII) recalled above in Paragraph 13, according to which this contradiction is superseded by concretely affirming or positing the originary structure, rather than by negating it. (This is an affirming or positing that is always already manifest as part of the infinite appearing of the Whole, but that, as part of the originary structure of destiny, constitutes an infinite task. It is in relation to the infinite appearing of the Whole – namely, in relation to the appearing of the concrete totality of destiny – that the originary structure of destiny is, precisely, *originary*.)

Thus, if the non-appearing of the concrete meaning of the self-being of beings – expressed by the formula $(A = A) = (A = A)$ – entails that this self-being is a being self-different, the non-appearing of this red (and, therefore, of its self-being) does not entail that the self-being of beings is a being self-different, but that the self-being of beings appears abstractly, formally and indeterminately. This formal appearing certainly constitutes a contradiction (precisely because the self-being of this red, too, is something incontrovertible), but a contradiction whose meaning differs from that according to which a determination of the incontrovertible (e.g. the self-being of beings) is negated by the non-appearing of a certain other determination of the incontrovertible – e.g. $(A = A) = (A = A)$.

At the same time, the *essence* of the originary structure – *qua* dimension that is distinct from the totality of determinations of the incontrovertible – is not a set that comprises only syntactic determinations (i.e. a set that does not include any non-syntactic determinations). The syntactic determinations of the originary structure themselves, *qua* isolated from the non-syntactic ones, constitute a negation of that structure. The 'what' of 'what is' – if separated from the concrete, specific and determinate contents of what is – is a nothingness (beings – the syntactic determination: 'beings' – consisting precisely in that 'what is'), and that 'what is' is equivalent to a 'nothingness that is'. Non-syntactic determinations thus enter and leave the circle of appearing, but their totality may not enter or leave that circle. Regardless of its configuration, the totality of non-syntactic determinations is a syntactic determination; *that* a certain set of non-syntactic determinations should appear – even if this set is continually varying as to its content – constitutes a syntactic determination.

The *essence* of the originary structure – as a dimension that is distinct from the totality of determinations of the incontrovertible – is, on the contrary, an abstract *synthesis* of syntactic and non-syntactic determinations. This synthesis is abstract because it does not include the totality of those two kinds of determinations. And this abstractness is not a negation of the incontrovertible since that totality constitutes the implicit element that underlies the abstract – namely, since the abstract (i.e. the meaning of the linguistic essence of the originary structure) is not isolated from the implicit element that underlies it.

18

The totality of determinations of the originary transcends the language that speaks of them, and this totality constitutes the implicit element that underlies this and every language. This assertion is itself a syntactic determination: language (namely, the synthesis of words and meanings), which is a part of that complex determination, therefore *also* appears in the *implicit* totality of the originary. That is to say, language also appears there where it does not appear – for the implicit totality of determinations of the originary constitutes precisely the dimension in which the language of the originary does not appear.

This latter assertion is not contradictory only if the way in which language appears in the implicit totality of the determinations of the originary differs from the way in which language appears as an arising being. (That the content of that assertion should appear as a contradiction, in a seemingly incontrovertible way, constitutes an additional aporia, which shares the same properties of the aporias presented in Paragraph 8.)

Even if one were unable to show the difference between these two ways in a determinate manner, the contradiction that appears here (like all the other aporias of the originary) is necessarily a merely apparent one, for the existence of the implicit determinations of the incontrovertible is incontrovertibly required by the very incontrovertibility of the incontrovertible. That contradiction must necessarily be an apparent one also because, in turn, the fact that language is transcended by the totality of the determinations of the incontrovertible is incontrovertibly one of those very determinations. It is impossible for the incontrovertible to contradict itself; the affirmation of this contradiction is one of the self-negating negations of the originary. (Moreover, the determinations of the originary structure are not comparable to the sets of axioms of hypothetico-deductive systems, in which axioms may always appear to be mutually incompatible at any point of the unfolding of an inference.) From this impossibility, there follows the *necessity* that the way in which language appears in the implicit totality of determinations of the originary should differ from the way in which language appears as an arising being. This is necessary – and that apparent contradiction is superseded – even if the determinate indication of this difference were to be absent (in such a way that, as a result of this absence, that apparent contradiction would indeterminately, and yet effectively, be superseded).

This argument may be more broadly formulated by stating that if everything that arises, including the very arising of what arises, were included in the implicit totality of the determinations of the incontrovertible – i.e. in the totality of what originarily appears, which receives everything that arises – this would negate the incontrovertibility of the arising of beings, according to what has already been remarked in Paragraph 13. At the same time, however, *that* this totality should receive the arising of beings is, itself, a determination of this totality; accordingly, the arising of beings, which is a part of this latter complex determination, is included in the implicit totality of the determinations of the incontrovertible – that is to say, it is included in that which does not arise. And this is a merely apparent contradiction, for the way in which that arising appears as part of the non-arising of that totality necessarily differs from the way in which that arising appears simply *qua* arising (i.e. not *qua* form of arising that is part of that non-arising.)

Language is precisely, and in a prominent way, one of the forms of the arising of beings: it is therefore necessary that the way in which language is one of the determinations of the implicit totality of the determinations of the incontrovertible should differ from the way in which the arising of language simply appears *qua* arising.

Since this second form of language constitutes a linguistic event that may be interpreted as a determinate 'historical' language (cf. Paragraph 2 of the previous chapter) – and since the possibility of this interpretation coincides with, or is included in, the way in which the arising of language simply appears *qua* arising – it follows that the way in which language is included in the implicit totality of the determinations of the originary (namely, the way in which the word is included in what appears prior to it) must be characterized by the absence of the possibility of that interpretation. That is to say, language is included in that totality *qua non-historical* language: i.e. *qua originary* language that, together with its meaning, appears in its being linked with 'historical' words as soon as language appears as part of the arising content. (Furthermore, that link is an eternal being that begins to appear together with the arising of those words – the eternal synthesis of meaning and the word, which begins to appear with the arising of language, being a synthesis between the historical word and the synthesis between the originary word and its meaning.)

Originary language is the condition without which the incontrovertibility of the arising of language – and, therefore, the inclusion of that arising in the totality of (syntactic) determinations of the originary – would not be possible. These two forms of language (its being, respectively, an arising or non-arising dimension) are both specific to language *qua* image of the isolated earth (cf. *Destino della necessità*, Chap. XIV, par. 1) – that is to say, they are both specific to language in its being part of the originary form of the will to power: namely, the isolation of the earth. Destiny leaves a trace in the language of the isolated earth – the language that speaks of the originary structure of destiny being itself a language of the isolated earth – and this trace is left in both of those forms: that is to say, it is also left in what we have been referring to as 'originary language'. Through its still undeciphered trace, the language of destiny speaks deeper than the originary language of the isolated earth.

19

As part of the totality of the syntactic determinations of the incontrovertible, no determination arises into appearing and no determination disappears: for, otherwise, that totality would not be incontrovertible. However, not even the totality of the determinations of the incontrovertible may arise or disappear: if it were to enter or leave appearing, that appearing would not be the appearing that is included in the incontrovertible (precisely insofar as it is assumed that it receives and therefore precedes the incontrovertible, persisting after the latter's disappearing); that appearing would thus be a form of untruth, and, *qua* untruth, it would not be able to constitute the appearing *of* the incontrovertible. There can be no truth in truth's entering and leaving the domain of untruth. Nor can there be any truth in the annihilation of the appearing of the originary structure of the incontrovertible. That structure is the never-setting.

The *linguistic* essence of the originary structure, on the contrary, begins to appear and then disappears. The totality of the explicit determinations of the originary – *qua* explicit or posited determinations – appears and then disappears. Nevertheless, the appearing and disappearing of the totality of these determinations may be part of the domain of truth only insofar as the truth of the originary already appears in the silence of historical languages; and that appearing and disappearing may be something explicit – i.e. it may be included in a (historical) language – only insofar as that originary truth appears within a larger linguistic configuration of the originary truth: i.e. one that is larger than that appearing and disappearing explicit totality. Therefore, the linguistic essence that arises and disappears is always a past relative to the *present* and *actual* linguistic configuration of that essence.

In that configuration, the language that speaks of the originary says everything: it says the sayable determinations of the originary, as well as the existence of the unsaid totality of the determinations of the incontrovertible (which is not said by any historical language). The word also speaks of silence, and of the unsayable – if the unsayable is the Whole, the infinity of destiny that always already abides outside of the contradiction of language: this contradiction being the (eternal) contradiction of the will to name things and to elevate the things that are said above those that are not (regarding the former as stable and the latter as transient).

The language that speaks of the originary speaks the unsaid and the unsayable – not in the sense that the unsaid and the unsayable are thus made identical to what is said, but in the sense that the very being-unsaid of the unsaid and the very unsayability of the unsayable come to be said by language.

In an analogous way, *that* beings are, and *that* they are eternal, even when they are not part of the circle of appearing, is something that appears: it appears that, were it not the case that beings are even when they do not appear, beings would be nothing; *that* the very non-appearing

160 BEYOND LANGUAGE

of beings appears means that – when beings are not part of the circle of appearing – they do not *simpliciter* appear, but they appear as something that does not appear. At the same time, what does not appear may not be so alien to appearing as to prevent its non-appearing from appearing – in the same way in which the unsayable may not be so alien to speech as to prevent its unsayability from being spoken.

20

In the first chapter of *La struttura originaria* (par. 10), the distinction between 'synthesis' and 'analysis' of the originary corresponds to the distinction between the appearing of the totality of determinations of the originary and the unfolding of language – which in that chapter is referred to as 'discursivity' (cf. ibid., par. 12), while the term 'language' is used to refer to the empirical forms of language.

That chapter posits the 'unity' of synthesis and analysis (cfr. ibid. pars. 9–15): namely, the *impossibility of separating* the originary structure from the language that speaks of it (i.e. from 'that essential unfolding or historicity that may not be disregarded once the content [of the originary] should have all come to be manifested', and that must therefore continually be 'retraced'. Ibid., par. 15.)

At present, the meaning of the originary appears in language – in those linguistic forms that may be interpreted as the historical forms of language. That is to say, the meaning of the originary appears as part of the very unfolding of language. It is by appearing *within* language that the originary manifests its very transcendence of language (even if, as indicated above, in the sense that the originary includes that 'originary language'). It is as part of a circumstance in which the word is inevitable that there appears the necessity for the thing (i.e. for destiny) to transcend and enclose the word itself.

The word is inevitable as part of a certain 'circumstance': this is the circumstance as part of which the isolation unseats the earth, and separates it from destiny. As part of the circumstance in which the earth is unseated, the originary, which nonetheless contrasts the isolated earth, is inseparable from language. The previous chapter and the next one address the meaning of this inseparability. This circumstance does not yet appear as such in *La struttura originaria*, which however indicates the inseparability of the originary and language that constitutes a part of that circumstance. Not even in that circumstance, however, is the originary surmounted and nullified by the becoming and historicity of language

It may be stated that a circumstance is a 'fact' (cf. Paragraph 13 of the next chapter and Paragraph 5 of the previous one). Stating that the inseparability of language and the originary takes place as part of a 'circumstance', or a 'fact', does not mean that what cannot be separated is in fact separated, but that the eternal being that consists of the unity of the originary (i.e. of the originary structure of destiny) and of language admits beside itself, within being, the eternal being that consists of the originary in its having left language behind. This is the eternal being of destiny, *qua* infinite Totality, which has always already surpassed every contradiction – thus including the contradiction of language – and that always already abides above the isolation of the earth, and encloses it.

3 LANGUAGE AND DESTINY

1

'Onto-theology': this expression of Heidegger's indicates the relation that, as part of traditional thought, links the reflection on beings *qua* beings to the positing of an ultimate Being. It is an appropriate expression, in that traditional ontology does not formally coincide with theology itself, and yet it develops and culminates into the latter. Beings *qua* beings are not the ultimate Being, for lesser beings, too, are beings; and yet, according to traditional thought, a reflection on beings *qua* beings requires beings to be arranged in a hierarchical order – one in which God dominates the world and brings it into being. God is the ultimate Being in that it is the eternal Being that immutably and unfailingly includes the totality of the perfections of beings – regardless of whether this totality should have the configuration of a 'thinking of thinking', of an 'eminent' being, or of the dialectical circle of the Idea: above, the Immutable; below, the ever-changing.

'Onto-theology' means that the experience of the ever-changing beings requires the existence of an immutable Being. The 'experience' of the ever-changing grasps the originarily manifest dimension of beings *qua* beings. As part of this 'experience', beings appear as stretching out of their own nothingness and returning to it. This 'experience' constitutes the fundamental faith of the West. On the basis of this faith, however, Western thought has come to a refutation of every Immutable being. The 'experience' of the ever-changing requires the non-existence of the Immutable. Johann Georg Hamann's principle – according to which: 'Reason is language, *lógos*', i.e. reason is not independent of language – lies at the heart of the philosophies of the 'linguistic turn'. The 'linguistic turn' constitutes one of the (most relevant, widespread and timely) ways in which contemporary philosophy comes to a radical refutation of the Immutable – and, at the same time, determines the meaning of the ever-changing.

For, indeed, throughout the entirety of Western thought, changing beings are always conceived of as something that oscillates between being and nothingness; this oscillation, however, comes to be displaced in different ways: what oscillates is first regarded as a reality that is independent of human thought, it is then identified with thought itself, and, lastly, it is identified with language. At first, the tradition of the West acknowledges the impossibility of separating being from thought; later, the impossibility of separating thought from language. At first, being is linked to the becoming of thought; later, thought is linked to the becoming of language. In asserting that 'being that can be understood is language', language is regarded as the authentic being that becomes, and every immutable being is regarded as inconceivable.

While remaining within the fundamental faith of the West, these conclusions are inevitable (even though contemporary thinking is rarely aware of the inevitability that pertains to it insofar as it develops – together with modern science and technics – from this fundamental faith of the West). That is to say, onto-theology – insofar as it believes to be able to posit beings and the thinking of beings in their independence of the becoming of language, and insofar as it erects an immutable Being above becoming – is inevitably destined to its own twilight.

2

Aristotle, taking up an issue already developed by Plato – as we have remarked (cf. Part III, 'On Identity and Difference', par. 1) – presents a sequence in which written letters are 'symbols' (*súmbola*) of spoken sounds, which, in turn, are 'signs' (*semeîa*) of the 'affections of the soul', which, lastly, are 'images' (*homoiómata*) of 'things' (*prágmata*) (*De Interpretatione*, 16a 3–8.) 'Things', contrary to written letters and spoken sounds, are 'the same for all'. The 'affections of the soul', too, are the same for everyone, but this can be the case only if there exist 'things' – of which those affections are images – that are the same for everyone. 'Things', however, may be the same for everyone only if they are immutable: that is, only if, even when they change, they change in the same way for everyone – in such a way that this sameness in their mode of change is what is immutable through their change. What is the same for everyone immutably persists through the coming and going of humans and things.

What is immutable through the change of things, however, is grounded, in the last instance, in a 'Thing': that is, in an immutable and heavenly Being. The sequence that leads from the written letters to the spoken sounds, and then to the affections of the soul and to the things, culminates in an immutable Being that is, pre-eminently, the same for everyone. The Immutable is the ultimate reference point of language. In the last instance, language always speaks of God.

If this remark remains implicit in the text of the *De Interpretatione*, it had been made completely explicit by Plato in his *Seventh Letter* (341a ff.), where the sequence that leads from words to things culminates in a being that may be neither produced nor destroyed. 'It is not subject to any of this [namely, it is not subject to any production or destruction]' (*oudèn páschei toúton*, 342c). This being is 'other' than everything in which 'there is nothing fixed with sufficient firmness' (*medèn hikanôs bebaíos eînai bébaion*, 343b.) The intentional sequence that leads epistemic (*epistéme*, 342b) knowledge from words to things culminates in an absolutely stable Being. As part of this sequence, this Being is what is 'knowable' and 'true' (*gnostón te kaì alethés estin*, 342b). In the last instance, language always speaks of the Eternal.

3

In his *Tractatus Logico-Philosophicus*, Wittgenstein still holds that, in the last instance, language refers to the Eternal – or, more precisely, to a multiplicity of eternal objects. In his *Philosophical Investigations*, in presenting this thesis of the *Tractatus*, and in distancing himself from it, Wittgenstein remarks (n. 58) that the word 'indestructible' expresses 'still more strongly' what is indicated by the word 'eternal' [*zeitlos*]. What is eternal is what is indestructible: 'What cannot be destroyed; what remains the same in all changes' (ibid., n. 59). What is indestructible are the *simple* 'elements' or 'objects' of reality.

The *Tractatus* defends precisely the thesis that 'a name ought really to signify a simple' (ibid., n. 39); it defends this thesis on the basis of the principle that 'a word has no meaning if nothing corresponds to it' (ibid., n. 40.) For, indeed, if a word refers to nothing – if it is a word of nothing

– it is meaningless; words, however, continue to be meaningful even when that to which they refer has been destroyed, and 'no longer exists' (ibid., n. 39, n. 55). It is therefore necessary that what may be destroyed should consist of indestructible elements, by virtue of which words continue to be meaningful even when their reference has been destroyed:

'What the names of language signify must be indestructible; for it must be possible to describe the state of affairs in which everything destructible is destroyed. And this description will contain words; and what corresponds to these cannot in that case be destroyed, for otherwise the words would have no meaning' (ibid., n. 55). 'Everything that we call 'being' and 'non-being' consists in the obtaining and non-obtaining of connections between elements' (ibid., n. 50). These connections are the ever-changing and destructible beings; the elements are the eternal beings that, in the last instance, language must address.

The development of Wittgenstein's thought leads precisely from a standpoint according to which beings and the thought of beings (the 'idea' that 'we already had in mind', ibid., n. 59) are independent of language to a standpoint according to which they depend on language. In Wittgenstein's perspective, the determination of this dependence is concurrently an acknowledgement of the fact that there exists nothing eternal or immutable. (On the one hand, he argues that there is no reason why a description of the world – the persistence of the meaning of which leads to the positing of those simple and eternal objects – should succeed in avoiding its own destruction. That is to say, the persistence of the meaning of words that refer to what is no longer present is itself provisional: ibid., n. 55. Thus, at most, it should be asserted that there must exist simple objects *until* a certain description of the world is destroyed. On the other hand, if no destruction – regarded as a separation of the connections between elements – may be ascribed to simple objects, the simple can however be destroyed in the sense that it may 'vanish': 'But don't we say 'The red is vanishing'?', ibid., n. 57.)

4

Words speak of something. However complex the relation between the word and the thing may be, language consists of this relation – i.e. of this reference or referral – of the word to the thing. This relation obtains both if the word takes the form of writing, gestures or spoken sounds, and if the word takes the form of that 'inner conversation', discussed by Plato, 'which the soul entertains silently with itself' (*Sophist*, 263 e; this conversation is something more profound than a series of imagined or represented words: i.e. it is something more profound than what Husserl, in the first of his *Logical Investigations*, refers to as 'expressions of solitary life' isolated from their 'function of communication', or as 'imagined representations' of spoken sounds and written letters). If one refutes the notion that language consists of a reference of a word to a thing, and one only retains the word – if one asserts that only the word appears – the word itself becomes a thing: i.e. a pure meaning – that very pure meaning (separated from a word) whose appearing is deemed impossible by the philosophies of the 'linguistic turn'. If only the word existed, and not what the word speaks of, language would not exist.

The 'relation between thing and word', Heidegger writes, 'is not a connection between the thing that is on one side and the word that is on the other ['Here the word, there the meaning', Wittgenstein writes, 'The money, and the cow one can buy with it.' *Philosophical Investigations*, n. 120]. The word itself is the relation which in each instance retains the thing within itself' (*On the Way to Language*, p. 135). Thinking that language does not consist of a relation between separate terms, and that the word itself constitutes a relation between itself and the thing, is a way of understanding language as a relation between the word and the thing. This relation is affirmed even in claiming, together with Wittgenstein, that 'the meaning of a word is its use in language' (ibid. n. 43). If, according to Wittgenstein, the 'relation between name and thing named' (ibid. n. 37) may not be univocally defined, it nevertheless exists.

However, regardless of all this, the distinction or relation between the word and that of which the word speaks *appears*; and what appears is irrefutable, in that appearing constitutes a segment of the destiny of truth – i.e. of the dimension that is always already open outside of the fundamental faith of the West and beyond the very occurrence of 'mortals' (cf. 'The Earth and the Essence of Man' in *The Essence of Nihilism*; *Destino della necessità*, Chap. XII). That of which the word speaks – the 'thing' – is the meaning of the word: that is to say, language is meaningful; meaning appears in its being said by the word.

However, it also appears that meaning, precisely in its being distinct from the word, consists in turn of a word (cf. Part III, 'On Identity and Difference', par. 3). The word says: 'The night comes'; the meaning of these words is the coming night. The coming night, however, is a meaning that appears, precisely, as *the coming night* – that is, as an expression or a set of words of the English language: 'The coming night.'

In saying: 'The night comes', the word certainly does not indicate an expression of the English language, but the darkness that obscures the shapes and the colours, in which the stars shine and sounds fade away: the word indicates a thing – the thing that consists in the coming night, and that also includes many other things (that darkness, those stars, this silence). And yet, the coming night – precisely in its being distinct from the word that indicates it – is a meaning that, in turn, appears *in the form* of a word: *through* or *as part* of a word. Things appear – meaning appears; the *form* of the thing, however, is a word. The word is the way in which meaning is meaningful; meaning does not appear separately from the way in which it is meaningful.

The form of the coming night can either be 'The night comes' (in its being uttered or imagined) or 'The coming night'. The form of the thing in which the coming night consists may also be given by words that are not part of the English language. In order to indicate the coming of the night, Latin says: *Nox adest*; and to the one who speaks in this way, the coming night is *nox appetens*; and *nox appetens*, too, as a thing, appears in and through a form constituted by the word of a determinate language.

5

Meaning appears; the word appears as the form of meaning. Granted that the word appears as the form of meaning, however, the *necessity* does *not* appear that the word should be the form of meaning. Authentic necessity coincides with the *standing* of the destiny of truth. The forms of 'necessity' considered by the philosophical tradition of the West are the immutable beings that contemporary thinking inevitably leads to their twilight. Every necessary connection is an immutable being; every immutable being is a necessary connection. In Western thought, the *epistéme*, *qua* knowledge of these necessary connections, constitutes the ground upon which all the immutables of the tradition of onto-theology come to be erected.

Precisely for this reason, when contemporary thinking posits the 'relation between the thing and the word', and refutes the idea that this should be 'a connection between the thing that is on one side and the word that is on the other' ('here the word, there the meaning'), it may not regard this relation as a necessary connection. If it does so, it falls back

168 BEYOND LANGUAGE

into the very onto-theological realm that it aims to destruct. Meaning appears in and through the word; it appears together with the word: the conceptual structure of contemporary thinking, however, must lead to the affirmation of a pure factuality of the connection between the word and the thing. The regular concurrence of the word and the thing is thus a de facto unity of separated terms (as a result of which the thing, even if united with the word, is 'on one side', and the word is 'on the other'). It is effectively the case that, based on the faith in the existence of becoming, beings are united as to their co-belonging in becoming itself (cf. Part III, 'On Identity and Difference', par. 2); at the same time, however, becoming is the very process in which beings come to be separated: becoming may therefore not only drive a being into nothingness and let its word persist, but it may also drive this word (every word) into nothingness and let that being, or even its appearing, persist.

The impossibility that beings *qua* beings may not be appears at the heart of the destiny of truth – that is, the eternity of every being appears. Eternal is not what hovers above the transient; beings are not split between Immutable beings and becoming ones; there is no hierarchy in the forms of being a being; every being is eternal. The difference between the destiny of truth and every form of onto-theology, as well as every destruction of onto-theology carried out as part of the fundamental faith of the West, is abyssal. Since every being is eternal, so is every relation, thus including the relation between the word and the thing as this appears as part of appearing. The relation between the word and the thing is thus necessary. However, it is necessary for a *transcendental* reason: i.e. insofar as it is an eternal being – insofar as it is contradictory to negate that this (or any other) being is eternal. It is not necessary in the sense that there appears the *specific* contradiction that would be produced in asserting that the word and the thing are separable and that the thing may appear without the word. That specific contradiction does not appear (nor may it be ruled out that it could appear). The eternal being that consists in the relation between the word and the thing has entered the circle of appearing; it is possible, however, that there should also exist the eternal being consisting in the thing without the word (not in the thing *qua* this thing united with this word – this unity, too, being an eternal – but *qua* meaning that bears a specific similarity to the thing *qua* this thing; cf. *Destino della necessità*, Chap. VI); and it is possible that this latter eternal being, too, should come to enter the circle of appearing. (It is possible: that is, it is not presently contradictory to affirm it.)

LANGUAGE AND DESTINY **169**

Let us repeat the objection (cf. Part III, 'On Identity and Difference', par. 2): how is it possible to speak of the destiny of truth, if one concedes that the word is the form of the thing, and that, therefore, meaning always appears in and through a word? De-*stiny* is the *standing* that the onto-theological *epistéme* has in vain attempted to be. Destiny is the meaning that stands. The words, however, in and through which meaning appears, are historical words: that is, they are essentially unstable. For, indeed, historical words indefinitely refer to other historical words that influence and modify their meaning, divesting them of any stability. If the meaning in which the destiny of truth consists appears in language, and as a historical language, it seems that the destiny of truth, too, may only consist of a will to stand – one that, sooner or later, will be overthrown by the very language that it, itself, speaks. Even though the relation between the thing and the word is only factual, and not necessary, the language that speaks of the destiny of truth appears as part of this factuality. The meaning in which de-stiny consists cannot constitute itself in a circumstance as part of which meaning appears in and through – and is influenced by – the instability of the word. As part of that circumstance, meaning is an 'occurrence', 'event' or pure arising (without a whence or a whither) – a *Geschick*: of which it is relevant to recall the consonance with *Geschichte* and *geschehen*, for it has nothing to share with the standing of de-stiny. The meaning of de-stiny turns its back on the meaning of *Geschick*.

6

Before presenting, in a more detailed form, the response to this objection indicated in the previous chapter (cf. par. 3 ff.), let us repeat that the existence of a determinate historical language – and, therefore, the very existence of a multiplicity of languages – is not an unquestionable reality, but it is something *willed*. (That is to say, it is something whose existence is willed – i.e. in the existence of which one has faith – without knowing that one wills it; in fact, this existence is for the most part willed while believing that what is willed is something that is witnessed or attested: something that it is already there, independently of any human will.) The existence of 'history' itself, *qua* diachronic system, is something willed. The will that isolates the earth (namely, the will that isolates the eternals that enter and leave the circle of appearing) from the destiny of truth (cf.

'The Earth and the Essence of Man', in *The Essence of Nihilism*; *Destino della necessità*, Chap. XII) is the very will that wills that something should be the word of something else – and that words should come together in those systems that we call 'historically determined languages'. Certainly, language is not born out of a particular act of human will – for it is the will itself that posits what we call a 'human': it is the will itself that, referring to itself, believes to be (i.e. wills to be), in turn, 'God', a 'human', a 'people', an 'institution', the 'scientific-technological Apparatus'. Language does not depend on the will of humans, for it is the will itself that wills both humans and language – as well as the historically determined forms of language. 'Humans' find themselves being this will; as 'mortals', they always already find themselves being part of it. (It is as part of this will that 'humans' posit themselves as 'mortals'.)

According to Heidegger, *being* is not 'a primary and absolutely irreducible meaning', for 'as it is fixed in its general syntactic and lexicological forms within the Western linguistics area and philosophy [...] it is still rooted in a system of languages and an historically determined "significance"' (J. Derrida, *Of Grammatology*, Baltimore: Johns Hopkins University Press, 1997). Heidegger, however, and all those who can be traced back to him, appears to forget that this being 'fixed' and 'rooted' of 'being' (but not only of 'being') in the linguistic system of the Western region of the world consists of a set of hypotheses of the sciences of language. That the set of events usually regarded as what we have inherited of ancient Greek should constitute a unitary linguistic system – in which all words indefinitely interact with each other and with the words of other linguistic systems of the same region – is a set of hypotheses of the sciences of language. In the same way, that a certain set of events should be commonly considered as what we have inherited of ancient Greek also constitutes an interpretative hypothesis. It is not sufficient for a word to appear together with other ones in a book, a codex or a scroll in order to assert that these words form an objective linguistic system. The 'objectivity' of a system consists in a will – in which one always finds oneself – for a certain set of events to constitute an objective system. Upon observing that this will is, precisely, a will, that objective system appears as a hypothesis, a possibility or a project (and, therefore, as something that may be altered or refuted).

That the meaning of *being* (and of the other fundamental and non-fundamental words of the West) should plunge, drift and be lost in the linguistic systems of the Western region of the world is thus something willed – and, as part of its being willed, it is something transformed into a form of self-evidence. It is willed by that very will that wills that certain things should be the word of certain other things, that certain words should come together as part of certain linguistic systems, that certain events should form a 'history' and others a 'nature' – and that the earth should be the only content of appearing.

Meaning thus appears as part of a certain determinate language; the relations, however, between the elements of that language (namely, the relations that make the set of these elements a system), as well as the relations between that language and other 'historical' languages – and the very fact that this language is a 'historical language', or a 'mother tongue' – are all not objective and indubitable realities: they are not incontrovertibly self-evident. They are, on the contrary, something willed: something that is posited by an interpreting will, something that is the content of a faith – of the same faith that isolates the earth from the destiny of truth.

It is on the basis of this faith that, within the linguistic form assumed (as a matter of fact) by meaning, there appears that which prevents meaning from constituting itself *qua* de-stiny – the instability of the linguistic form of meaning consisting precisely of those relations as part of which every word of a linguistic system (that is, of the system that structures that linguistic form) refers to other words of that system and to words of adjacent systems (which, in turn, are adjacent to other systems).

That is to say that, when contemporary philosophy asserts that 'being' cannot be a primary and absolutely irreducible meaning, because it is 'rooted' in a system of languages and in a 'historically determined significance', contemporary philosophy forgets that it, itself, consists of a destruction of the immutables, and becomes instead a vindication of that immutable being that is the necessary connection between a meaning (for instance, 'being') and the system of historical languages in which that meaning is 'rooted'. Contemporary philosophy thus conceives of this rootedness as a necessary connection (that is, it disregards its hypothetical character): and it is, once again, a form of onto-theological *epistéme*.

In the eye of contemporary thought, however, if this rootedness is no longer regarded as a necessary connection, the indefinite reference of each word to other words can then only be a possibility: that is to say, the indefinite historical determination of the meaning of every word is only a possibility. Words are found alongside other words: however profoundly and persistently may each word summon other words, those other words

172 BEYOND LANGUAGE

are all free to not attend the call and to not intervene. In order to not fall back, once again, into a form of onto-theological *epistéme*, contemporary thought must assert of words, too, what Wittgenstein asserts of things in the *Tractatus*: 'Each thing can be the case or not the case while everything else remains the same' (1.21). The meaning of every word is independent of the meaning of any other word (this fact, however, being precisely what Wittgenstein himself – contradictorily – wishes to avoid). Each word is immersed in the sea of historical languages, but does not soak water (that soaking constituting a causal and therefore necessary connection). The intensity with which words conjure, and respond to, one another corresponds to the intensity of the will that invokes them. The will forcefully invokes them: if one turns one's back on the will, and only looks at what has been invoked, one sees the strength with which the words hold themselves together and speaks of the way in which each word is 'rooted' in a host of invoked words. That is to say, one transforms something willed into an indisputable objectivity.

That the historical determination of the word should constitute a necessary connection, however, remains an open problem for the destiny of truth. If this problem were to be authentically solved, it would be solved on the ground of the destiny of truth itself; and if the solution to this problem were to consist in a positing of the necessary character of the historical determination of the word, that necessity would not be able to be understood in the same way as that instability of the word, which, in speaking of destiny, renders its stability impossible. If the relations between words are necessary connections – according to the authentic necessity that pertains to the destiny of truth – no word is unstable.

7

The word is the form of the thing (par. 4). This appears. On the contrary, the necessity that links that form to the thing does not appear (and nor does the necessity that links the form of the word to other words). 'The night comes': insofar as this word comes to be uttered, the sound of the voice is an event (an eternal being) that appears together with those other events (with those other eternal beings) that consist in the human body and soul. In this sense, it may be said that humans speak. (The synthesis in which human speech consists, too, is an eternal being, and, in this sense – but only in this sense – it is necessary.)

'The night comes', however, speaks of the coming night. The coming night is not an uttered word: it is a meaning. And yet, that meaning appears in the form of a word: 'The coming night' is a silent word (so silent that the tradition of philosophy has been able to regard it as a pure meaning), but it is nevertheless a word. Regardless of the extent to which thought may focus only on meaning, and keep it separate from a (more or less) sensory word, meaning always appears in and through a silent word. It may be replaced by other silent words (*nox appetens*, etc.); that silent word itself is ever-changing even when it seems to remain the same; meaning, however, as a matter of fact, always appears in and through a word. As a matter of fact, a silent word remains the form of meaning.

This coming night is a meaning – the opening of a signification – and so is *this coming night, qua* meaning that persists even well into the night, and after the night ends and the light of day comes. Wittgenstein refers only to this second meaning as 'meaning', while calling the first one a 'name-bearer' (*Philosophical Investigations*, n. 40). Wittgenstein would state that when the night (this night) disappears, its meaning persists. This is the case, however, only if one keeps to the common use of the word 'meaning'. The distinction between 'name-bearer' and 'meaning', however, is internal to meaning itself; it indicates two modes of meaning: i.e. of not being a nothingness. A meaning is a being – a thing. The word, too, *qua* form of the thing, is a thing.

Insofar as the word is the form of the thing, it may be said that the thing speaks. It is not a human being who speaks of this coming night, but this coming night itself. Strictly speaking, however, neither humans nor things speak: it is the interpreting will that makes them speak. If the thing and the word are not linked by a specific necessary connection (aside from the transcendental connection that links them *qua* eternal beings, and even though the word always de facto appears as the form of the thing), it is an interpreting will that holds them together in a specific connection – and it is an interpreting will that wills that the speaker should be a human, when the word is spoken, or a thing, when the word is silent.

It is therefore a will that connects the word to that thing (i.e. that meaning) that consists in the destiny of truth. The will to speak of truth is not part of truth itself; the testimony of truth is not part of truth. And humans are certainly not able to free themselves from the will – by which, on the contrary, they are themselves willed.

8

The thing does not cease to exist as a result of having a word as its form. It *cannot* cease to exist because it is the *identity* referred to by the different ways of speaking about it. The different and infinite ways in which the word refers to this coming night speak of this coming night. This does not mean that no difference in the thing corresponds to a difference in the word (and that, in fact, a difference in the word is not itself a difference in the thing itself), but that, in spite of this correspondence, the difference in the word – or in the thing – *may not* go as far as erasing that identity.

Identity is the self-being of beings – i.e. their being themselves and not their other. Identity, however, regarded as to this fundamental meaning, is not something different from the *persistence* of a being. The persistence of a being is its very identity – but not that identity as it is as such, but as an identity that, while persisting in appearing, is in relation to what does not persist: i.e. what enters and leaves appearing. (The different ways of speaking of a thing consist precisely in the arising and coming to pass of those things that consist in the words of that thing – for the different and infinite ways of speaking of a thing are not all spoken together, but as part of a sequence: a sequence that is such in relation to the persistence of an identity.)

The different ways in which the word may indicate this coming night are the different ways in which the word may be the form of the thing that consists of this coming night – the thing being the identity to which the word refers. If one refutes the existence of this identity, the different ways in which the word is a word of this coming night are mutually incommensurable, and each of them speaks of something of which the others do not speak. If one rejects the existence of that identity, i.e. if one denies that this coming night is the identical meaning that underlies a set of differences of the word, one must have before one's eye – in the very act of negating it, and precisely in order to be able to negate it – precisely this very identical meaning. In order to be able to negate something, this something must be understood: it must appear. If one denies that this coming night is an identical meaning – a meaning that is able to unify the differences that express it – this very meaning stands before one's eye as the very identity that one is attempting to negate. If what is negated has *a* meaning, the negation of the *unity* of this meaning presupposes what it aims to negate. It is precisely for this reason that a repetition of the

LANGUAGE AND DESTINY **175**

negation of an identity negates *the same* identity: for, otherwise, the repetition of that negation would always negate different meanings.

This is to be asserted of every thing that appears in and through the form of a word. It is thus also to be asserted of that thing that is language itself: if one denies that language has a unitary meaning that underlies its different forms (Wittgenstein), this unitary meaning of language must necessarily manifestly appear: it is necessary that what is negated should be understood. What, of a thing, can be negated may not be part of what allows one to negate that thing: if one denies that the differences of the word refer to an identity of the thing, one negates precisely that identity – i.e. one negates the identical meaning that must necessarily appear in order for that negation to exist.

Taking into consideration the whole scope of the issue, the necessary existence of identity also appears in the following, additional, way (as already noted, cf. Part III, 'On Identity and Difference, par. 4): *if one negates identity* – that is, if one asserts that language is a pure differentiation of the word, as a result of which there only exist differences, and no identities – *one also affirms identity itself*, for those differences are identical as to their being, precisely, differences. Every difference, insofar as it is a difference, is identical to any other difference.

On the one hand, it is indeed the case that the identity that is necessarily affirmed as part of the negation of identity is an identity *of* those differences, and not the identity *to which* they refer. On the other hand, however, the identity *of* those differences suffices to refute the thesis that language (and the world) consists of pure difference without any identity. At the same time, if the identity *to which* those differences refer did not exist, neither would the identity *of* those differences. For, indeed, each difference is identical to every other difference as to its being a different way of speaking of something; however, if there existed no identity *to which* those differences refer, those very differences would not constitute a different way of speaking *of something* – precisely because that something (the fact that what they speak of is something) is precisely the identity *to which* those differences refer. If language speaks of something, this very being-something (this very being a being) is the identity *to which* the differences of language refer – for, otherwise, language would not be speaking of anything.

Therefore, it may be stated: if one denies the existence of the identity *to which* a set of differences refer in their speaking of something, one affirms that very identity, because that identity is precisely the thing of which it is acknowledged that those differences speak. (Differences are therefore identical not only insofar as each of them is a difference, but also insofar as each of them is a way of speaking of something. And the structure of their identity does not end here, for each difference is identical to the other ones in its being 'an each': in its being self-identical and different from the other ones.)

Furthermore, the appearing of identity is that without which the very arising of differences (and, therefore, the arising of the differences of the word) would not be able to appear. The arising of the night may appear only if the day – namely, that relative to which the night arises – does not disappear, but persists in appearing. If the day ceased to appear when the night arises – or if what of the day appeared were to be *altogether* different from the day itself, in such a way that it would not even be possible to state that something *of the day* still appears – the night would not arise in relation to anything. If that relative to which the night arises did not appear, the very arising of the night would not appear. Precisely because it is necessary, when the arising of the night appears, that there should appear that relative to which the night arises, it is necessary for the day to appear before the appearing of the night – and for the day to continue to appear (that is, to *persist*) when the night appears. That is to say, it is necessary that the day that appears beforehand should be *the same* that appears afterwards: namely, it is necessary that an *identity* should underlie the *difference* (which is itself undeniable and necessary) between the day as it appears before and the day as it appears after. This identity is the self-being that, after having appeared 'before', persists in the appearing of the 'after'. (Or: an eternal identity persists across the arising of the eternal differences.) The appearing of this identity is precisely the ground of the appearing of that 'after' in its being an 'after' (cf. Emanuele Severino, *Studi di filosofia della prassi*, Milan: Adelphi, 1984, Second Study, Chap. II, as well as Addenda n. 31, 32; *Destino della necessità*, Chap. V–VI; *La filosofia futura*, Part Nine). Therefore, a negation of identity, which is at the same time an acknowledgment of the arising of a set of differences, is an affirmation of the identity that makes the appearing of those very differences possible.

Wittgenstein rejects the notion that an identity could underlie the differences of language, because 'the meaning of a word is its use in language' – i.e. the rule of that use – and the use of words is diversified, in the sense that there exist infinite ways of using them. Nevertheless, the *use* (i.e. the meaning) of a word constitutes a form of stability. Wittgenstein speaks of a 'stable use' (*Philosophical Investigations*, n. 198), but this is a pleonastic expression. A use consists in 'following a rule', and following a rule is not 'something that it would be possible for only *one* person, only *once* in a lifetime, to do' (ibid., n. 199). Following a rule constitutes a form of stability – namely, an identity that underlies a set of differences of the word (i.e. the re-occurrences of a word). A use (namely, a meaning) may change, and a stability or an identity may disappear; nevertheless, the stability of the use of a word refutes the negation of the identity of meaning.

9

The word appears, as a matter of fact, as the form of the thing. A differentiation of this form appears: the coming night may be indicated by different words (which are different either because they are different words of the same language or because the 'same' word – 'The night comes' – is different each time it is repeated). The coming night (the thing or the meaning) is the identity indicated by these differences.

However, the identity, *too*, referred to by those differences, appears in and through a difference. That is, the identity, too, constituted by the coming night appears in and through a word – namely, in and through a form constituted by a word. An identity may not be reduced to any of its differences: it stretches out of them; and yet, this very stretching out appears in and through a difference. An identity stretches out because the negation of an identity is, at the same time, its affirmation; presently, however – as a matter of fact – this stretching out is not the expression of a pure meaning, i.e. one separated from a word.

Identity may not be negated (for the will to negate it coincides with its affirmation); therefore, the fact that every identity appears in and through a difference means that an identity is not identical insofar as it is enclosed by a difference. Insofar as an identity is enclosed by a difference, that identity is a difference. The identity in which the coming night consists is the identity to which a set of differences of the word refer – but not insofar as that identity is enclosed by an expression of the English language (i.e. 'the coming night'). That identity is the identity that it is even if it is enclosed by *nox appetens* or by the other 'equivalent' expression of other languages (or of the English language itself); moreover, since we started talking about the coming night, the 'same' expression 'the coming night' has in fact differentiated itself. Identity is identical in its being enclosed by any difference whichever [*una qualsiasi delle differenze*] that indicates it.

In turn, however, a difference of the word is not itself a pure difference: it encloses the identity of a set of differences – this identity being identical in that it is found within those differences. The coming night is the identity to which the different words that indicate the coming night refer; this identity, however, appears as part of an expression of the English language ('the coming night'). In the language that we are speaking, that expression is the *bearer* of the identity referred to by all the words (or expressions) that, together with that one, differently indicate the coming night. Identity is always (presently) borne by a difference; the bearer itself, however, is unable to altogether obscure or silence what it bears.

For, indeed, not only is it necessary that this identity (the identical content to which a set of differences of the word refer) should exist, but – as we have seen – it is necessary that it should *appear*. The night *changes* through every new shade of darkness or last light, and through every feeling, imagining and speaking with which humans accompany the coming to pass of the night; and yet, while changing, it is the *same* night that arises. While infinitely *changing*, and while changing through each new shade (each new shade being an eternal), the night *persists*: the *identity* that consists in the coming night persists. Only if this identity appears may its very change do so. What persists is that identity in its underlying that change. In the circle of appearing, only what persists may change. If there appeared no identity, no change would be able to appear *qua* change *of that identity*. In other words, the coming of the night is not a punctual event: its coming and taking place entails a before and an after, in both of which the night is. (This lamp, too, and this room, this piece of paper, this tree – and infinitely many other things that appear – come, step forth, and persist: that is, they become; but not according to the meaning that the West ascribes to becoming and to appearing.) The night, in its being present before as well as after, is what is identical in a certain part of the totality of that before and in a certain part of the totality of that after. If that identity did not appear, there would be no memory of the before (a memory being precisely the persisting of a before in an after). Accordingly, that very after would not appear as an after, and the coming and stepping forth of the night would not be able to appear. If the negation of the appearing of an identity holds onto the appearing of the variation of that identity, then – let us repeat – since the appearing of this variation entails the appearing of that identity, that negation holds firm (i.e. affirms) what it negates.

LANGUAGE AND DESTINY   **179**

The identity to which the differences of the word refer necessarily is and appears. And yet, we are claiming that this identity appears in its being enclosed by a difference of the word – even though this enveloping does not conceal or suppress that identity. Identity is not separated from difference; it is however distinct from it. Asserting that that identity necessarily appears is equivalent to stating that it necessarily appears in its being thus distinct. Once again, however, the identity of the coming night – as distinct from the differences of the word – appears in its being enclosed by a difference of the word: that is, by a word (or expression) of the English language or of another language. In what does this identity consist, then, given that it is necessary that it should appear in its being distinct from that difference, and in its stretching out from the latter?

Certainly, whatever may be *said* of this stretching out implies that this very stretching out is thus *said*, and it does not stretch out of that saying. Nor, however, is that identity something which, stretching out of that saying, would be found *beside* it – as something that, in trying to remain unsaid, would thus inevitably come to be said. Identity is not the unsayable: in fact, it is precisely what is said. It is not distinguished from the differences of speech insofar as it is unsayable, but insofar as it differs from those differences.

Identity differs from those differences because it may be any difference whichever [*una differenza qualsiasi*] (in a certain set of differences), which, *in its being any* difference *whichever* – i.e. not in its being that specific difference that it is – is what is identical in what is referred to by all the differences of that set. Identity is not identical insofar as it is enclosed by a difference (that is, insofar as it submits itself to the form of a word, i.e. to a specific form), but insofar as it is any difference whichever. This indifference of difference (or: this indifference with respect to difference) constitutes identity's being enclosed by a difference without being concealed or silenced by it.

Precisely insofar as difference, *qua* any difference whichever, is the identity *of* what is referred to by all the differences of a certain set, asserting that difference, *qua* any difference whichever, is an identity means asserting that this identity is *in relation* to that totality of differences. The appearing of identity is the appearing of this relation.

The word speaks of an infinite multiplicity of identities; each identity may infinitely differentiate itself in and through the words that express it. The coming night is one of these infinitely many identities. What is referred to by what we are speaking about here is another identity, which is extremely more complex, in that it gathers in itself the totality of all identities and of their differentiations in and through the word. The identity referred to by what we are speaking about here is the destiny of truth. Destiny appears in its being enclosed by 'historical' words (that is, by the infinite differentiation of words that are interpreted as being historical); destiny, however, is the identity referred to by the various languages that may speak of it: for the language that here speaks of destiny is any language whichever, which, in its being any language whichever – and, therefore, not in its being that specific language that it is – constitutes what is identical in what is referred to by all the languages that may speak of the destiny of truth.

10

In the 'Introduction' to his *Treatise Concerning the Principles of Human Knowledge* (par. 12), Berkley writes that 'an idea, which considered in itself is particular, becomes general, by being made to represent or stand for all other particular ideas of the same sort'. In his *Essay Concerning Human Understanding*, Locke had maintained the possibility (albeit fraught with many 'difficulties') of forming general ideas, such as the idea of a triangle, in which this triangle 'must be neither oblique nor rectangle, neither equilateral, equicrural, nor scalenon; but all and none of these at once' (Book IV, Chap. VII, par. 9). As part of a confrontation with Locke, Berkley writes: 'It is I know a point much insisted on, that all knowledge and demonstration are about universal notions, to which I fully agree: but then it doth not appear to me that those notions are formed by *abstraction* in the manner premised; *universality*, so far as I can comprehend, not consisting in the absolute, positive nature or conception of anything, but in the relation it bears to the particulars signified or represented by it: by virtue whereof it is that things, names, or notions, being in their own nature *particular*, are rendered *universal*. Thus, when I demonstrate any proposition concerning triangles, it is to be supposed that I have in view the universal idea of a triangle; which ought not to be understood as if I could frame an idea of a triangle which was neither equilateral nor scalenon nor equicrural. But only that the particular triangle I consider, whether of this or that sort it matters not, doth equally stand for and represent all rectilinear triangles whatsoever, and is in that sense *universal*' (ibid., par. 15).

Berkley observes that Locke's 'general idea' is in itself contradictory. In his *Logical Investigations*, Husserl essentially confirms Berkley's observation ('Investigation II', Chap. II, § 11). According to Kant, 'it is not images [i.e. "particular forms"] of objects, but schemata that ground our pure sensible concepts' (*Critique of Pure Reason*, 'The Analytic of Principles', Chap. I). A schema is a 'method', a 'rule' or a 'general procedure of the imagination for providing a concept with its [own] image'. An image, insofar as it is a particular form, is never adequate to the universality of the concept. 'No image of a triangle would ever be adequate to the concept of it. For it would not attain the generality [i.e. universality] of the concept, which makes this valid for all triangles, right or acute, etc., but would always be limited to one part of this sphere'. The schema of the triangle, on the other hand – which 'can never exist anywhere except in thought' – constitutes the 'rule' through which the imagination produces the figure of a triangle 'without being restricted to any single particular shape that experience offers me or any possible image that I can exhibit *in concreto*'. One may say that a schema is a particular insofar as it is taken to represent all the particulars of its kind. The 'rule' and the 'method' of a schema consist precisely in this 'insofar as'.

Despite their profound contextual differences, Berkley, Kant and Husserl – together with many others – may all be traced to an Aristotelian anti-Platonism, according to which universals do not exist in themselves, as separated from particulars.

Here, however, we wish to remark that in the circle of appearing, too (insofar as it is a segment of the structure of the destiny of truth), universals, in their being separated from particulars, appear once again in the form of a particular. The contradiction of the universal triangle (noted by Berkley) – i.e. of a triangle that must at the same time be all particular triangles and none of them – refers to a universal regarded as an image appearing next to other images: that is, it refers to a universal that is once again posited as a particular, and, thus, as something that may not include contradictory determinations. The meaning: 'The identity that is present in a set of differences – i.e. of mutually contradictory determinations' is however not a contradictory meaning, since it does not state, for instance, that *a certain* triangle is at the same time isosceles, scalene, etc., but that being-a-triangle – triangle-ness itself – is in a synthesis with different ways of being a triangle. The identity that is present in a set of differences, however, is a difference that, in its being *any* difference *whichever* – and not in its being the specific difference that it is – constitutes what is identical in the totality of differences of a certain kind. (Triangle-ness always appears as a certain triangle – that is, as a difference; this difference, however, appears as that triangle-ness, rather than simply as a certain triangle, insofar as that difference is any difference whichever of being-a-triangle.) Identity is the indifference of any difference whichever to being the identity of differences.

It is this indifference that Berkley addresses in stating that a particular idea is 'made to represent or stand for all other particular ideas of the same sort' – this 'making something' 'represent' or 'stand for' being precisely the 'rule' in which Kant's 'schema' consists. Husserl, in turn, acknowledges the 'justifiable sense' of the doctrine of 'general representation' (*Logical Investigation*, 'Investigation II', Chap. IV, § 27) in relation to that 'making something represent': a justifiable sense insofar as that which represents (i.e. that which is in-the-place-of) does not simply indicate a collection of particulars (as is the case for nominalists), but refers to what is identical among them – by virtue of which they are 'of the same sort'. When Husserl speaks of the justifiable sense of the doctrine of representation he is essentially thinking of nothing but the Aristotelian universal.

Our discussion, however, has come to a higher – if analogous – level than the one at which the authentic meaning of universality is found.

A universal is a particular that, in its being *any* particular *whichever* (and therefore not in its being that particular that it is) not only indicates, but also *is* the identity that is present in all the particulars of a certain set. This set is a multiplicity of differences that are underlain by an identity; identity is the relation that links any difference whichever to all the differences of that set. The identity *of* a set of differences is precisely any difference whichever's being in relation to the totality of differences.

Insofar as a difference is a unity (*unum*) that is in relation to (*versus*) other unities (*alia*) of the same set, that difference is *unum versus alia*: i.e. 'universal'. These *alia*, however, are not certain others, but the *totality* (*hólon*) of the elements of a certain set; and the being in relation with (*katá*) this totality, in which a universal consists, is *kathólou*; according to Aristotle, a universal is *tò kathólou*. If a difference, in its being any difference whichever, is separated from its being a *unum versus alia*, and is isolated in its unity, that difference is not a universal – and, therefore, it is not an identity: it is a simple difference. A universal is not simply a semantic element, but a semantic-apophantic one – i.e. a predication: the one in which an identity is the predicate of a set of differences.

The differences *of the word* refer to the identity in which the thing consists; this thing may itself be a universal or a particular. Relative to the differences of the word, a particular thing, too – for instance, the coming night – is an identity: namely, it is what is identical in what is referred to by a set of differences of the word. As already remarked, however, this identity, too, appears in its being enclosed by a difference of the word: i.e. this identity, too, is a universal. This night is a universal relative to the infinitely many ways (i.e. differences) through which the word indicates the coming night; this is the case because the difference (i.e. the English expression 'the coming night'), which encloses the identity in which the coming night consists, is the identity of all the differences through which the word indicates the coming night insofar as it is *any* difference *whichever* (and not insofar as it is that specific difference that it is). (The relationship between difference, *qua* any difference whichever, and the non-historical 'originary language' discussed in Paragraph 18 of the previous chapter remains here an open problem.)

11

The word speaks of the thing: that is, of the identity referred to by the differences of the word that speaks of the thing. The word, too, is a thing; and so is every difference of the word, as well as every difference that pertains to a thing insofar as this thing *persists* while differentiating itself. A thing is a meaning: that is, a being. The word, *qua* language, speaks of the totality of beings: i.e. of the totality of identities. A 'thing', a 'word', a 'being', a 'meaning', an 'identity', a 'difference', an 'affirmation', a 'negation', as well as 'becoming', 'appearing', 'being', 'nothingness', a 'unity', a 'multiplicity', a 'relation', etc. are also identities referred to, respectively, by the differences of the words that express them. The 'destiny of truth', too, is the identity to which the languages that may speak of it refer (for not every language may speak of the destiny of truth). Destiny is the identity as part of which there incontrovertibly appears the totality of identities and the very relation between identity and difference. What is addressed by the present remarks is a segment of the structure of destiny. At the heart of destiny, there appears the eternity of beings *qua* beings – including therefore, and primarily, the eternity of those beings that appear. The eternity of an appearing being is the eternity of an identity that is enclosed by a word – i.e. it is the eternity of the word *qua* form of the thing.

The isolation of the earth from destiny (cf. 'The Earth and the Essence of Man' in *The Essence of Nihilism*; *Destino della necessità*, Chap. XII) is the isolation of the identities that enter and leave the segment of destiny constituted by the circle of appearing. The identities of the earth also appear in the domain of untruth; the identities of the earth appear and disappear both in the domain of truth and in that of untruth. As the day comes, and the night is forgotten, the night that, in coming, had entered the circle of appearing, leaves it. (The night, however, leaves the circle of appearing after having persisted through the arrival of the day; the night persists as the before relative to which the day may appear as an after. When the night is forgotten, the day continues to appear, but no longer as something that has arisen after the night.) As part of the untruth of the West, these appearing and disappearing are interpreted as an issuing from nothingness and a returning to it.

In both the domain of truth and in that of untruth, identities persist until they disappear. As part of the domain of untruth, however, every identity of the earth may be negated. It is possible that the coming night may be an erroneous word; and, in any case, it is a word that is exposed to a refutation. Precisely because, in the circle of appearing, the thing is always (de facto) enclosed by a word, every thing, outside of the destiny of truth, is a word that may be refuted. (However, untruth, too – and every refutable word – is eternal.) This word may also be refuted insofar as it seems to refer to infinitely many other words, which modify and alter its meaning. In the domain of untruth, the identities of the earth are meanings and words that founder and that are born transient (the night comes and goes away), also because the word, *qua* form of identity, refers to and is lost in infinitely many other words. The philosophies of the 'linguistic turn' are aware of this (while, nevertheless, remaining within the domain of untruth). Identity is lost in its infinite self-differentiation – every word is historical.

What is historical, however, is precisely each word that speaks outside of the destiny of truth. *The destiny of truth is the identity whose negation is self-negating.* Destiny *stands*: precisely in that its negation is self-negating. This is the crucial segment of destiny. It is crucial as a concrete meaning (cf. 'Returning to Parmenides' in *The Essence of Nihilism*, par. 6; '*Élenchos*' in *La tendenza fondamentale del nostro tempo*) and not as the indeterminate and abstract indication that appears here. An aspect – itself indeterminately indicated – of the self-negation of the negation of the destiny of truth has appeared above, as it was shown that a negation of the existence of identity coincides with an affirmation of that existence, in such a way that this negation is self-negating. Outside of the fundamental faith of the West, authentic necessity is the negation of that self-negation. The standing of destiny consists in the immateriality of its negation. Moreover, the identity of destiny neither enters nor leaves the circle of appearing (which is itself a segment of destiny).

Nevertheless, the identity of destiny, too (i.e. the identity constituted by the structure of the destiny of truth) appears in turn in the form of a word. In this instance, too, identity is identical relative to the differences of this word. In the domain of untruth, the interpreting will does not appear as such: i.e. as the origin of untruth (the isolation of the earth from destiny being precisely the originary interpretation). The interpreting will refers the words that speak of destiny to infinitely many other words (i.e. to infinitely many other eternals.) In this instance, however, this stream of words does not sway or consume the waterfront of identity: it does not sway it or consume it because, in positing itself as a negation of that identity, it sways and consumes itself.

The interpreting will wills that certain things should be the words of other things, that they should constitute human activities and express the inner dimension of humans, and that they should allow every human individual to communicate with other individuals. In the same way in which the thing is not the word, but it is willed as such, so the word *is* not an interpretation, but it is *willed* as such (it is interpreted as an interpretation.) Its being an interpretation – i.e. its being a theoretical structure – consists in its referring to a system of words, as well as to the systems surrounding these words. The problematic dimension of this referral and of this interpreting does not however undermine the irrefutable, for to overthrow the irrefutable means to negate it, and therefore to be a self-negating negation.

The destiny of truth – and, therefore, the self-negation of its negation, too – appears in and through language. The interpreting will posits that the language in which destiny appears belongs to the linguistic region of the West. Destiny may appear in and through these languages – and in and through other ones (but not in and through all languages). Is destiny therefore something that is 'only' part of language – or even only part of certain languages but not of other ones? Is destiny therefore only a linguistic game? If a game is something that one may not take part in – something that is based on arbitrary or adjustable rules, and something that allows infinitely many other games beyond itself, in which something different takes place – then, the destiny of truth is *the* non-game: it is the *only* thing that is not a game. Destiny is the irrefutable. But does not this irrefutability take place within language? Certainly. And the other languages? If they are commensurable with the language that testifies to destiny, the irrefutable may also appear in and through them. As part of these languages, too, destiny may be negated in different ways: if a language negates destiny, however, that language negates itself. The languages that are incommensurable with the language that testifies to destiny – the languages that speak of the 'absolutely other' – speak of something that, *qua* other than destiny, is itself a negation of destiny, and that, *qua* absolutely other than the irrefutable, may itself be refuted.

But 'as part of reality', outside of the language (or languages) in which the irrefutable appears, may something appear or occur, which altogether differs from what – in language – appears as the irrefutable?

The destiny of truth is the destiny of *being* (and, therefore, of every 'reality' and of every 'occurrence'). Precisely insofar as destiny is the irrefutable, the irrefutable is the destiny of being, because any dimension ('reality', 'being'), within which an occurrence would refute that irrefutable destiny, is impossible. The irrefutable is the destiny of everything that is not a nothingness. Only nothingness escapes destiny – in that nothing escapes destiny. Destiny is in the word, but as its irrefutable content.

12

The interpreting will, and the way in which the earth appears as part of it, appear in the circle of the appearing of destiny. This coming night, this town, the history of the peoples, the West and the East all belong to the earth in its appearing as part of the interpreting will (cf. *Destino della necessità*, Chap. XV). The interpreting will not only wills that something (sensory events, or their images in the soul) should be the word ('The night comes') that indicates the coming night – that is, the interpreting will not only wills that something should be a difference of the word that indicates a certain identity – but it also wills that the identity in which the coming night consists should be the meaning of other things: i.e. the meaning that gathers in itself a series of other meanings, conferring a unity on them (e.g. that darkness, the stars in the sky, the fading away of forms and colours, the mood that accompanies all this, etc.)

The fact that the identity in which the coming night consists should be a meaning that also determines those other meanings is an interpretation (i.e. the fact that a certain series of events should form the coming night is an interpretation): it is something willed – and, therefore, an open problem. This is the case for all the things that are part of the earth that appears in and through the interpreting will. It is an open problem that 'The night comes' should indicate the coming night. (What is not an open problem, however, is the existence of a will that wills for a certain audible or visible event to constitute the words 'The night comes', and for these words to indicate the coming night.) It is an open problem that the identity in which the coming night consists should be the meaning that determines and unifies those other meanings (i.e. those other identities) that consist in that darkness, those stars in the sky, those forms and colours of the night. Traditional thought, according to which the coming night (and every thing of the earth) is a 'real' individuation of an essence, does not realize that the individuation of an essence (i.e. of a certain kind of meaning) is an interpretation.

At the same time, the thing of which the word is the form may in turn appear as a word that is the form of another thing. *The coming night*, too, in its being indicated by a word, is, precisely, a meaning that is enclosed by a word (i.e. by an expression of a historical language); it is a meaning that is indicated by the word that encloses it. The form speaks of what it encloses; it indicates this content. 'The coming night', however, does not indicate the darkness, the stars in the sky, the fading forms and the fading colours, or the mood that accompanies the arising of the night. 'The coming night' (this word) indicates the coming night: namely, a meaning that – certainly – once again appears in its being enclosed by a word that is similar to the one that indicates it, but a meaning that differs from those other meanings (the darkness, the stars in the sky, the mood, etc.) of which, according to the will of the interpreting will, 'the coming night' constitutes the unitary meaning (these other meanings themselves appearing in their being enclosed by the words that indicate them).

Thus, if, and since, the coming night appears, it is necessary that the thing in which it consists should, *in the last instance*, appear as a thing, and not as a thing enclosed by a word. If the referral from the word to the thing were to be infinite, the thing would never be reached: that is to say, the thing would not appear, and neither would the word. (The referral, too, that refers a word to other different words – a referral that is to be distinguished from the referral of a word to a meaning which in turn appears in its being enclosed by a word – is halted by a word that, despite being able to refer to other words, as a matter of fact does not do so.) In the circle of appearing, the thing, in its being distinct from the word, always appears (as a matter of fact) as being once again enclosed by a word: in the last instance, however, it is necessary that it should not appear *as* being thus enclosed, but *as* a thing – as the coming night.

In an analogous way, the interpreting will may will that each of those other meanings – i.e. each of the other things consisting in the darkness, the lights of the stars, the fading forms and colours, etc., which are willed as having a certain meaning (i.e. the coming night) as their unifying meaning – should, in turn, constitute the unifying meaning of a set of simpler meanings, and so forth. However, the referral of these interpretations, too, must be halted at a set of meanings that – while potentially be willed as unifying meanings – are, as a matter of fact, held firm, and only appear *qua* unified meanings. In the circle of appearing, for each unifying and unified meaning, a word refers to a thing. *As a matter of fact*, this referral is halted at a thing: in the sense that it is necessary that, in the last instance, things – while appearing in their being enclosed by a word – should *not* appear *as* being enclosed by a word.

The destiny of truth encompasses the interpreting will; the interpreting will, however, wills that the word should also speak of the destiny of truth. Insofar as destiny is distinct from the word, and despite its being thus distinct, destiny, too, once again appears in its being enclosed by a word: i.e. in its being indicated by the word that is its form. Destiny is a structure as part of which it may not occur that a meaning should be willed as a meaning that unifies other meanings: the structure of destiny is the irrefutable insofar as it is structured according to necessity, rather than according to an interpreting will. And yet, the interpreting will wills that the word should also speak of the structure of destiny. In this instance, too – given that destiny is a meaning (i.e. the meaning that is the destiny of all other meanings) that, as a matter of fact, always appears in its being enclosed by a word (also by virtue of its very being distinct from the latter) – it is however necessary that, in the last instance, and in that segment of destiny constituted by the circle of appearing, destiny should *not* appear *as* being enclosed by a word, but as a thing and a meaning. Destiny is precisely the dimension in which there also appears its own having to appear in the last instance, in the reference of the word to the thing, as a thing and a meaning.

13

Meaning, however, is not simply what must appear in the last instance, in the sense that we have just indicated. Meaning surpasses the word. Precisely for this reason, we have continued to assert that, in the circle of appearing, meaning always appears, *as a matter of fact*, in its being enclosed by a word. Let us simply present a schematic remark concerning this most prominent issue.

Every being is eternal. *Therefore* (cf. *The Essence of Nihilism*, Second Part; *Destino della necessità*, Chap. XVI), every contradiction (i.e. every instance of *contradicting oneself*, which is itself eternal, and which is distinguished from its own content – i.e. from the contradictoriness of a being, which is itself nothing) is eternally *superseded*. The superseding of the totality of contradictions is neither a possibility nor an impossibility: it must have necessarily always already – eternally – taken place. The originary structure of destiny, as the *finite* appearing of the Whole, is a contradiction (cf. *La struttura originaria*, Chap. VIII). It is a contradiction that is eternally superseded in the infinite appearing of the Whole, wherein the segments of the originary structure of destiny are superseded in that they are *concretely* posited. They are not superseded as such – i.e. as to their content – but as to their being abstractly manifest.

The isolation of the earth from the destiny of truth is instead the origin of the totality of the contradictions that are eliminated through a negation of their content. The will to speak – the will that wills that something should be the word of something else, the will to assign a word to a thing – is part of the will that isolates the earth. The will to speak of the destiny of truth, too, is therefore part of the will that isolates the earth from the destiny of truth.

Every will to speak, too, is thus contradictory – and the superseding of this contradiction, too, is eternal. The will that isolates the earth from destiny is eternally superseded, and so is the will that wills that something should be the word of a thing and of destiny. The superseding of the contradiction that originates from the will that isolates the earth and invokes the word is the eternal and infinite appearing of a pure meaning that – in its eternity – always already surpasses the word. Contradictions, too – as well as, therefore, the word – are eternal; but they are eternal in their being surpassed. (Pain is a form of contradiction, and so is everything that is willed by the will – thus including humans themselves.)

The isolating will may assign a word to meaning precisely insofar as meaning originarily surpasses the word. In order to assign a word to meaning – i.e. in order to will that meaning should appear in and through a word – the isolating will must be able to see that meaning. Is the will that encloses meaning in the word only part of the isolation of the earth, or is it also part of the destiny of truth *qua* finite appearing of the Whole?

Insofar as destiny constitutes the finite appearing of the Whole, destiny is that whose appearing is necessarily required by the appearing of the isolated earth; destiny thus stands here manifest even if language ignores it (cf. 'The Earth and the Essence of Man' in *The Essence of Nihilism*). That is to say, meaning does not surpass the word only insofar as it is the meaning constituted by the superseding of the totality of contradictions – the superseding that always already appears as part of the infinite appearing of the Whole, i.e. as part of the infinite form of the destiny of truth; meaning also surpasses the word insofar as it consists of destiny *qua* finite appearing of the Whole. Insofar as it is not testified to by language, it is the latter's 'unconscious'. Insofar as it is the infinite appearing of the Whole, it does not appear in the circle of appearing that is part of destiny *qua* finite appearing of the Whole. And yet, the infinite, *qua* superseding of the contradiction of the finite, is what the finite in truth is. The infinite is the most profound region of that 'unconscious'. It surpasses the finite form of destiny. It surpasses the word, and it may never be surpassed by it. And contrary to the finite form of destiny – which surpasses the word, but which is also reached by it – the infinite form of destiny, as the pure light of meaning, eternally leaves the word behind.

NOTES

Being Beyond Language

1 Benso, Silvia. *Viva Voce: Conversations with Italian Philosophers.* Suny Press, 2017.

2 Esposito, Roberto. *Living Thought: The Origins and Actuality of Italian Philosophy.* Stanford University Press, 2012.

3 Agamben, Giorgio, *Homo Sacer: Sovereign Power and Bare Life.* Stanford University Press, 1998.

4 On January 20th, 2022, a Symposium was held: *The Other Side of Italian Thought: Emanuele Severino,* organized by Giulio Goggi, Federico Perelda, Damiano Sacco, Ines Testoni, in cooperation with FISSPA Department (University of Padua, Italy), the Istituto Italiano di Cultura in Berlin and the Italienzentrum of the Freie Universität Berlin.

5 Severino, Emanuele, *Legge e Caso* (1979; *Law and Chance*). London: Bloomsbury, 2023.

6 Hegel, Georg Wilhelm Friedrich. *Science of logic* (1812–16). London, New York, Routledge, 2014.

7 Severino, Emanuele, *Istituzioni di Filosofia* (*Institutions of Philosophy*). Brescia, Morcelliana, 2010. This text was published in the form of a set of lectures in 1968 at the Catholic University of the Sacred Heart in Milan and is one of the last moments of the philosopher's teaching at this university as he was subjected to an inquisition process by the former Holy Office that considered his thought irreconcilable with the Catholic doctrine.

8 Severino, Emanuele, *Filosofia Moderna* (*Modern Philosophy*). Milano, BUR, 1996.

9 Carnap, 'Überwindung der Metaphysik durch Logische Analyse der Sprache', *Erkenntnis*, 2, 1932, pp. 219–41.

10 Hegel, Georg Wilhelm Friedrich, *Grundlinien der Philosophie des Rechts* (1820–21; Elements of the Philosophy of Right). Cambridge University Press, 1991.

11 Carnap, Rudolf, *Der Logische Aufbau der Welt* (1928; The Logical Structure of the World) and *Pseudoproblems in Philosophy*. Open Court Publishing, 2003. Translated by German into Italian by Severino Emanuele, *La Costruzione Logica del Mondo. Pseudo-problemi Nella Filosofia*, Torino: Utet, 1997

12 Wittgenstein, Ludwig, *Tractatus Logico-Philosophicus* (1921, 1922). London, New York, Routledge, 2013.

13 Ogden, Charles Kay and Ivor Armstrong Richards, *The Meaning of Meaning: A Study of the Influence of Thought and of the Science of Symbolism*. (1923).

14 De Saussure, Ferdinand. *Cours de Linguistique Générale* (1916; Course in General Linguistics). Columbia University Press, 2011.

15 Frege, Gottlob (1892). ,Über Sinn und Bedeutung', in *Zeitschrift für Philosophie und Philosophische Kritik*, 100: 25–50; ('Sense and reference', *The Philosophical Review*, 57.3 (1948): 209–230.

16 See: McKerrow, K. Kelly, and Joan E. McKerrow. 'Naturalistic misunderstanding of the Heisenberg uncertainty principle.' *Educational Researcher* 20.1 (1991): 17–20.

17 Priest, Graham. 'Paraconsistency and dialetheism' in *The Many Valued and Nonmonotonic Turn in Logic* 8 (2007): 129–204.

18 See: Neurath, Otto, and Otto Neurath. *Radical Physicalism and the 'Real World'*. Springer Netherlands, 1983.

19 Testoni, Ines, *Beyond Alienation: Severino's Removal of Pathological Contradiction.* 'Eternity & Contradiction,' *Journal of Fundamental Ontology* 4.7 (2022): 45–60.

20 Severino, Emanuele, *La Struttura Originaria, Brescia, La Scuola*, 1958/2014; revised edition, Milano, Adelphi, 1981.

21 Severino, Emanuele, *Essenza del Nichilismo* (1982; *The Essence of Nihilism*), Edited by Carrera A. and Testoni I. London, New York, 2015.

22 Severino, Emanuele, *The Essence of Nihilism*, cit., pp. 67–68.

23 For more details, cf. Goggi, Giulio, «"Golden Implication". The Primary Foundations of the Eternity of Being». Eternity & Contradiction, Journal of Fundamental Ontology 1.1 (2019): 43–56.

Beyond Translation

1 D. Sacco, 'The Translation of Destiny, and the Destiny of Translation' in Emanuele Severino, *Law and Chance* (London: Bloomsbury, 2023). For an introduction to the main elements of Severino's theoretical apparatus, see also: D. Sacco, 'Emanuele Severino: A Testimony of the Language that Testifies to Destiny', in *Journal of Italian Philosophy*, Vol. 6, 2023.

2 The meaning of nothingness that appears in this way is the *positive* meaning of nothingness, namely one of the two 'moments' of the self-contradictory meaning – the other one, the *nihil absolutum*, being instead 'something' that neither is nor appears. The self-contradiction of the meaning of nothingness is given precisely by the appearing (positive moment) of what may not in any way appear (the negative moment). See Emanuele Severino, *Intorno al senso* *del nulla* (Milan: Adelphi, 2013) and Chapter IV of *La struttura originaria* (Milan: Adelphi, 1981). A partial translation of the latter has appeared in Emanuele Severino, 'The Aporia of Nothingness', *Eternity & Contradiction*, Vol. 3 (4), 11–38.

3   The same considerations apply when considering the case of the 'same' expression or difference as uttered under different circumstances.

4   A thorough discussion of this issue, however, well exceeds these schematic remarks, for these are to be taken with the following proviso: that this is 'the genuine nature of essential thinking: that, in its mediation, it sublates mediation itself' (*Encyclopaedia Logic*, § 50). Namely, the concrete (God) is a result only on condition that the abstract mediation (the world) is something in and for itself null and void (*an und für sich Nichtiges*), thus turning that result into a concrete immediacy: 'And while this elevation is a *passage* and *mediation*, it is also the *sublating* of the *passage* and the *mediation*, since that through which God could seem to be mediated, i. e., the world, is, on the contrary, shown up as what is null and void. It is only the *nullity* of the being of the world that is the bond of the elevation; so that what does mediate vanishes, and in this mediation, the mediation itself is sublated' (ibid.).

Part One, Chapter 3

1   Translator's note: Latin in the text [*species, speciei*]. '*Species*' in italics signals Severino's Latin throughout this chapter.

Part Two, Chapter 1

1   Translator's Note: 'A coming into being, not having been before, and, therefore, a perishing having been before'.

2   Translator's note: The comment in square brackets is Severino's.

BIBLIOGRAPHICAL NOTE

'Violence and Salvation' has been written for the meeting with Emmanuel Levinas, devoted to the theme 'Only a God Can Save Us Now', organized by the *Centro Studi e Ricerca sull'Identità Culturale Europea* (Bergamo, December 12, 1988.)

A version of 'Anxiety and Will to Power' has already appeared in *Le paure del mondo industriale* (Bari: Laterza, 1990).

'Scientific Specialisation and Nothingness' is the text of the lecture held at the 51st *Congresso della Società Italiana di Cardiologia* on December 12th, 1990 in Rome.

'Nietzsche and Gentile' is the text of the lecture held at the University of Tübingen on November 28th, 1987 as part of the conference 'Nietzsche e l'Italia', organized by the *Istituto Italiano di Cultura* of Stuttgart and by the *Europa Zentrum* of Tübingen. The lecture has been published in *Nietzsche und Italien*, (Tübingen: Stauffenburg, 1990).

'Problematicism and Actual Idealism' has appeared in *Il pensiero di Ugo Spirito* (Rome: Istituto della Enciclopedia Italiana, 1988–1990).

'Socrates, Silenus, and Virtue' appears for the first time here, and revises in a unitary form different short writings that have appeared on different occasions.

An abridged version of 'On Identity and Difference' has appeared in *Filosofia '90* (Bari: Laterza, 1991).

The second and third chapter of Part Three ('The Unfolding of Language and the Appearing of Destiny' and 'Language and Destiny') appear for the first time here.

Previously published works appear here with the changes and additions required by their integration into a unitary text.

INDEX

Absolute 81, 84, 88
Aeschylus 99
alienation 58, 61, 121
annihilation
    and death 95
    form of 19–25
    joy of 58
    and negation 131–132
    and nothingness 130
    of a positivity 127
    saving from 28–32, 34–36
    of things 9–10, 26, 30
    of truth 127–128
anti-intellectualism 80, 82, 88
antinomy 73–74, 76
anxiety
    and destruction 19
    and nothingness 99
    and Technics 35
    in the West 22
Apology (Plato) 91–95, 97, 99–100
aporias 138–141, 144–145, 155, 157
Apparatus
    overstepping borders/boundaries
        20–21
    scientific-technological 30–34, 171
    theological-epistemic 24–25, 27,
        29, 31, 36
Aristotle 10–11, 44, 59, 65, 68,
        100–101, 105–107, 122, 153,
        164–165, 183

becoming
    Aristotelian theory of 10–11
    of becoming 68
    being/non-being 64, 76–77, 81
    existence of 86–88, 125–126

    and faith 14, 26, 28, 59–60
    Greek meaning of 54–55, 83
    of language 66
    nature of 82
    non-refutation of 80
    and nothingness 109
    other than itself 8–10, 18
    self-evidence of 84, 87
    of thought 64, 75–76
    and truth 126–127
    will to power 130
    world of 46–47, 61
    see also dialectics
'being-lit of this lamp' 155
being/beings
    appearing 136, 161
    and becoming 54–55, 64, 70, 81,
        86, 124
    eternal 190
    existence of 151
    immutable 79
    knowable and true 165
    meaning of 21–22, 47, 171–172
    negation of 68
    and non-being 77, 129, 133, 166
    and nothingness 69, 99, 121, 129,
        138–139, 152–153
    qua beings 163, 169, 184
    and self-being 135, 138, 140,
        148–150, 153–156, 175
Bergson, Henri 95
Berkley, George 181–183
Burke, Edmund 96

causality principle 48
Christianity 13, 23–24, 84, 95, 100–101
cold bodies 11

conclusiveness 80, 84
consciousness 63, 81, 83

De Interpretatione (Aristotle) 105,
    107, 165
death 35, 80, 92–99
decisions 39, 41–42, 49
Derrida, Jacques 121, 171
Destino della necessità (Severino) 15,
    139, 146, 169, 185
destiny 117, 123–124, 130–133, 147,
    156, 159, 162, 172, 186–187
destruction
    avoidance of 25
    form of annihilation 19, 21
determinations 143–149, 152, 155–161
dialectics
    and becoming 63–64
    Hegelian 73–75
    of life 81, 83
    metaphysical 84
    problematic 84
    see also becoming
diánoia 107–108
    see also soul
difference 8–9, 113–114, 121, 177,
    180–184
'Dionysian' 57, 67–68, 99–100
domination 26–27

earth 21, 25, 38–41, 120–121, 128,
    133–134, 151–152, 159–161,
    170, 185–187, 190
Eleatics 68, 70
Epictetus 95
epistéme
    and becoming 117
    and death 92–98
    and destiny 132, 170
    meaning of 22–25
    as a measure 4
    onto-theological 173
    and science 101–102
    and truth 34, 85–86, 126–131, 134,
        138, 147
    twilight of 5, 7

Epistle to the Romans 100
*Essay Concerning Human
    Understanding* (Locke) 181
essence 81, 129, 139, 156, 187
The Essence of Nihilism (Severino) 15,
    120, 131, 134–135, 138–139,
    146, 148, 151, 185
eternal 18, 96, 117–118, 123–124, 129,
    132, 136–139, 165, 169, 174,
    190
Euthydemus 98
evil 100
existentialism 95

faith/faiths 13–15, 18, 26, 59–61,
    70–71, 130, 172
fetishism 61
fides quae creditur 13

Gentile, Giovanni 55, 62–63, 66,
    68–70, 73–74, 76–77, 80
Geschick 170
God
    absolute power of 23–25
    an immutable being 13
    anxiety induced by 28–29
    of Christian theology 84
    creational will of 13
    'God is dead' statement 57
    and humans 84
    immutable 126
    and language 165
    and nothingness 19
    and salvation 12, 17
    and the soul 32–33
    and Technics 20, 32
    true world of 62
    the ultimate Being 163
    violation of 4
gods 61–62, 101
Greeks/Greece
    and annihilation 68
    and becoming 54, 64, 75, 78, 83,
        123, 127
    inheritance of 171
    and issuing from/returning to 76

200   INDEX

and nothingness 47, 50, 79
and reality 77
and thought 22–24, 30–31, 35, 44,
 70–71
and truth 126

Hadot, Pierre 95–96
Hamann, Johann 122–123, 163
happiness 3–4, 34–35
hate 17
Hegel, Georg Wilhelm 44, 53, 58–61,
 63–66, 68, 73–74, 76, 78, 80,
 106, 137
Heidegger, Martin 50, 99, 106–108,
 110, 122–123, 163, 171
history 11, 64, 70, 77, 117
homoiómata 105
humans
 and actions 38–43
 and contents of the world 151
 and evil 100
 and existence doubt 84
 'human' is dead statement 57
 and language 108, 120
 liberation from death 30, 34
 and nothingness 19–20, 24–25, 47,
  92–94
 and science 101
 and the soul 32–33, 105
 and speech 173
 and things 174
 transformation of 49
 and will 119–120, 171
Humboldt, Wilhelm von 107
Husserl, Edmund 121–122, 134, 167,
 182–183

idealism 62, 66, 74, 76–78, 80–85,
 88–89, 113
identity 16, 115–116, 118–119,
 175–181, 183, 186–188
Il giogo (Severino) 92
images 55–56, 58, 105, 107, 164, 182,
 187
indeterminacy principle (Heisenberg)
 48

indifference of difference 180
infinite 14–16, 191
intellectualism 63, 65–66, 69–70, 74,
 78–84, 88, 102
intolerance 17
irrefutability 118, 120–122, 187

Judeo-Christian tradition 3, 13, 17

Kant, Immanuel 3–4, 182–183
kathólou 183
Kierkegaard, Søren 94–95
koinonía 144

La struttura originaria (Severino) 15,
 134–135, 138–139, 141,
 148–151, 155–156, 161–162
language
 and being 123
 contradiction of 160, 162
 and destiny 186
 determinate historical 170
 and the eternal 165
 and humans 120
 and identity 106–114, 118, 176
 and originary structure 134, 141,
  146, 158–159
 sciences of 171–172
 and thought 164
 and truth 170
 unfolding of 135–139, 161
 unitary meaning 176
 a word to a thing 167
Leibniz, Gottfried 63
life
 annihilation of 30–31
 bearable for humans 56–58
 fabric of 24–29
 mode of 39–40
 and nothingness 67
 nullification of 74
'linguistic turn' 163–164
Locke, John 181–182
Logical Investigations (Husserl) 167, 182
lógos 70, 107–108
love 12, 17–18, 25

Marx, Karl 61, 74
meaning 150, 169, 174, 178, 187–190
metaphysical dialecticity 84
Metaphysics (Aristotle) 153

nature, and human beings 6
negation of negation 118, 121–123,
    131–135, 138, 140–143, 150,
    152–155, 185–186
Nietzsche, Friedrich 55–70, 91, 95
'The night comes' ('The coming
    night') 167–168, 174–175
nihilism 121, 129–130, 144
non-being 11, 64, 75–77, 129, 133,
    143
    see also being/beings
non-contradiction principle
    (Aristotle) 59, 65
nothingness
    absolute negativity of 50
    and becoming 78–79, 109–110,
        126–127
    and being 69, 121, 129, 138–139,
        152, 156–157, 163–164
    and destiny 5, 10, 14–16, 187
    and happiness 35–36
    and Hegel 68
    and history 64
    and humans 92–94
    issuing from/returning to 10, 28,
        31, 54, 76, 87
    meaning of 45–47
    of nothing 69, 130, 153
    and the originary 148
    and self-evidence 78
    sheltering from 20–21, 23, 25, 27
    the thinking of 49
nuclear conflicts 21
nullification 73–74

Of Grammatology (Derrida) 171
*On Truth and Lie in a Non moral
    Sense* (Nietzsche) 55, 58
'Onto-theology' (Heidegger) 163
originary
    contradiction 156

and destiny 156, 159
and determinations 157–160
error 66
essence of 140, 146–148, 152
form of self-evidence 55, 60, 62,
    75, 84
form of Western rationality 43
and the irrefutable 122
and language 107, 161–162
meaning of 142–143
and necessity 9
negation of 150
and nothingness 87
and salvation 24
structure 118, 133–140, 151,
    153
and truth 122
and the will 26, 28, 35–36, 120
Ovid 100

Parmenides 68–69, 77–78, 117, 122,
    143–145
Paul the Apostle 100, 102
Phaedo (Plato) 92, 95–96, 99
phenomenology 58
Philosophical Investigations
    (Wittgenstein) 165, 167
Plato 4, 44, 54, 66, 76, 91–92, 96–97,
    105–108, 122, 143–144,
    164–165, 167
post-industrial society 31
power
    and anxiety 35–36
    and God 17
    and truth 125, 127, 129
    will to 23, 25, 27, 130
predictions 20, 22, 25, 29–30
problematic dialecticity 84
problematicism 73, 76, 80–81, 83–85,
    88
Protagoras (Plato) 4, 100–101

reality 62, 73, 75, 77–78
reason 60, 163
revelation 13
Rochefoucauld, François de La 96

202 INDEX

salvation 12, 17, 19, 24, 26
scepticism 53, 85, 88, 97
science
    essence comprehension 50
    and goods 98
    meaning of 101–102
    specialization of 37, 43, 46–49
Science of Logic (Hegel) 137
scientia 14
scientia qua scitur 14
self-annihilation 28, 132, 134
self-evidence 13–14, 28, 70, 75, 78, 80,
    84, 87
self-knowledge 81–82
self-positing 82
Seventh Letter (Plato) 105, 107, 165
Severino, Emanuele 92
signs 112–115
Silenus 91–95, 97, 99–100
Socrates 91–102
Sophist (Plato) 107, 143–144
soul 32, 105, 108–109, 112
species 37–38, 44
spirit 68, 88
Spirito, Ugo 73–74, 76, 80–85, 88–89

Technics
    age of 25–27
    civilization of 31–34, 54, 70
    dominion of 41
    and modern science 3, 19–20, 29
    and the soul 32
    and truth 35
*Teoria generale dello spirito come atto
    puro* (Gentile) 74, 107
things
    and 'affections of the soul' 122,
        164–165
    becoming 9–10, 14–15
    and humans 174
    and words 118–123, 167, 169, 173,
        175, 184–185, 187–189
thinking/thought
    and Aristotle 101
    and becoming 29, 77
    and beings 121

and Christianity 100
contemporary 55, 55–56, 106, 117
and Gentile 69
and Heidegger 99
historical 109–111
and idealism 113
and Marx 61
mode of 93–94
and Nietzsche 59–60
philosophical 44, 53, 96
present and actual 62–68, 75–76, 79
and the West 7, 9, 19, 47, 49–50,
    108
when contradictory 145
'this being-a-lamp' 112–116, 119–120,
    155
this-ness 120
tolerance/intolerance 12, 17
Tractatus Logico-Philosophicus
    (Wittgenstein) 165, 173
transformation 20–21, 44–45
*Treatise Concerning the Principles of
    Human Knowledge* (Berkley)
    181
triangles 181–183
true world 61
truth/truths
    and anxiety 29
    and becoming 128–129
    and death 96–97
    definitive 123–124
    and destiny 117–121, 130, 134,
        141–142, 146–147, 153,
        169–170, 173–174, 184–188,
        190
    existence of 35–36, 88
    and humans 34
    identities of 122
    in itself 61, 65
    and Nietzsche 55–60, 62
    and nothingness 50, 127
    philosophical contemplation of
        22–24
    and power 125–127
    and untruth 160
Twilight of the Idols (Nietzsche) 57

Übermensch (Nietzsche) 57–58, 92
unhappiness 25
universals 183–184
untruth 121–122, 160, 185
    see also truth

Verstand (Hegel) 59–61, 63
violence
    and faith 18
    infinite 17
    most extreme form of 14
    obtaining what it wills 6–7, 12
Vita come ricerca 73
voluntarism 102

West, the
    and anxiety 19–20, 22–27
    and becoming 55, 59, 61, 70–71,
        123–124, 127
    and being 164
    and destiny 186
    destruction of the immutables 75
    dominant thinking of 50
    and the earth 120–121
    and eternals 129
    fundamental faith of 4, 6–7,
        89, 167
    and humans 31, 33
    issuing from/returning to 76
    meaning of 34–35
    nihilism of 144

and nothingness 17, 35, 47
philosophical-theological
    tradition of 88, 168, 171
and salvation 12
and scepticism 85
and technics 54
and thinking 9, 131
and truth 125
Whole, the
    and beings 149, 155–156
    comprehension of 88–89
    essence of 29
    and humans 39–44, 46–47
    infinite appearing of 190–191
    meaning of 69, 79, 86–87
    and nothingness 69, 79
    and truth 22, 96
    and the unsayable 160
will
    and annihilation 6
    and being 172
    existence of 102
    and humans 119–120
    and the impossible 7, 14
    interpreting 120–121, 186–187
    obtaining the impossible 18
    to power 17, 26
Wittgenstein, Ludwig 123, 165–167,
    173–174, 176–178

Zarathustra 61–62

Printed in the USA
CPSIA information can be obtained
at www.ICGtesting.com
LVHW011235070624
782597LV00003B/95